The Curious Naturalist

The Curious Naturalist

National Geographic Society

The Curious Naturalist

Published by
The National Geographic Society

Gilbert M. Grosvenor
President &
Chairman of the Board

Michela A. English
Senior Vice President

Robert L. Breeden
Executive Adviser to
the President for Publications
& Educational Media

Prepared by
The Book Division

William R. Gray
Director

Margery G. Dunn
Senior Editor

Charles O. Hyman
National Geographic
Book Service

Staff for this book

Jennifer G. Ackerman
Editor

Linda B. Meyerriecks
Greta Arnold
Illustrations Editors

Paulette L. Claus
Research Editor

David M. Seager
Art Director

Charlotte Golin
Designer

David W. Wooddell
Art Coordinator

Mary B. Dickinson
Writer-Editor

Leslie Allen
Catherine Herbert Howell
Alison Kahn
Joyce B. Marshall
Maria Mudd
Cynthia Russ Ramsay
Shelley L. Sperry
Caption Writers

Ratri Banerjee
Cathryn P. Buchanan
James B. Enzinna
Timothy H. Ewing
Sallie M. Greenwood
Joyce B. Marshall
Carolyn L. Mudd
Maria Mudd
Lise M. Sajewski
Shelley L. Sperry
Anne E. Withers
Editorial Researchers

Ellen Gross
Rebecca Lescaze
Margaret Sedeen
Lynn A. Yorke
Contributors

Bryan K. Knedler
Indexer

Elizabeth G. Jevons
Sandra F. Lotterman
Teresita Cóquia Sison
Marilyn J. Williams
Editorial Assistants

Artemis S. Lampathakis
Laurie A. Smith
Illustrations Assistants

Richard S. Wain
Production Project Manager

Lewis R. Bassford
Heather Guwang
Production

George V. White, *Director*
John T. Dunn, *Associate Director*
and R. Gary Colbert
Manufacturing &
Quality Management

Pages 2-3: Sandhill cranes
along the Rio Grande
in New Mexico.

First edition 111,000 copies
288 pages, 291 photographs,
32 watercolor paintings.

Contents

By John Hay

Introduction

When I was first called a naturalist, I was very pleased, not by the notion that I had been given a professional status, but because I was glad to be included in that company. In school I had heard great things said about such famous naturalists as Charles Darwin, Alexander von Humboldt, and Carolus Linnaeus. I had read *Walden* and was pleased, too, by Henry David Thoreau's affirmation that joy is the condition of life.

As the years went by, I found a certain resistance in adult society to my often inchoate enthusiasms. Nature, it seemed, was acceptable only if it did not get in your way. That this great world of life should be outside human experience was a puzzle to me. If we were not part of it, how could we speak for it?

When I was very young, in the early 1920s, there were some 100 million people in this country as compared with the present population of 250 million. The great open spaces had been fenced in by barbed wire long before. Whole forests had been destroyed and rivers filled with factory wastes; farmers were beginning to be dispossessed of their land. But there was still open country from one coast to the other, and one could smell the continental winds, which still reign supreme over the land. Even in the city of New York, with its millions of people, I remember springtime on our street of brownstone houses as a wonderful advent from the wide world beyond. The sweet, warm air and the yellow light flowed through newly opened windows and made all things open and free.

I did not really know what was meant by "wilderness," unless it was the night and the unknown, lying out over the city and in the forests. In a dark corridor of New York's American Museum of Natural History, there was an exhibit of timber wolves chasing deer across the moonlit snow, which I went back to a number of times. It fascinated and haunted me. I could hardly be dragged away from it.

At the age of nine or ten, I was sent to a school in the country, and there I joined up with a few other boys for a bird-watching class. It was conducted by the local minister, who led us out into the fields and the woods behind the church. We were given a little field guide, not much more than a pamphlet, but it served for a beginner. So I learned that grackles have light eyes and starlings dark ones, and I discovered the sources of the bubbling calls and musical whistles I heard in the meadow.

The naturalist wanders with an inquiring eye, pauses, ponders, notes the bloom of a prairie pasqueflower (opposite). It is a tradition that goes back to Aristotle and earlier: observing and identifying earth's myriad life-forms, and discovering the connections that bind them. For those with such interests, said British naturalist Miriam Rothschild, "life can never be long enough."

Naturalists may get their start in a specialized field, such as geology or forestry, or through an unstudied fascination with the world around them. Explorer and writer John Muir (top) translated his passion for the wilderness into preserving land in the American West. His many books and eloquent pleas resulted in the creation of forest preserves and national parks. Naturalist Aldo Leopold (above), a forester, wildlife manager, and teacher, set forth the idea of a "land ethic." In his classic *A Sand County Almanac* of 1949, he urged his readers to regard the land not as a "commodity belonging to us," but as a "community to which we belong."

The countryside was the place to experience the natural world and the realities of the seasons. There, many people cultivated an interest in the bluebirds that came to the orchard, counted the migrating shorebirds, or identified the wildflowers. Even budding naturalists, however, had been brought up in a society that had a strong distaste for disorder and the wild. One must hold the lid down to keep the demons from getting out. Wilderness had been put at a safe distance and should be kept in its place. (Now, of course, we have our own, manufactured demons to hold down.)

"Wilderness" did not describe a desert in the Old World sense, but a whole continent of unparalleled abundance. It had millions of bison, uncounted numbers of passenger pigeons, multitudes of species of all kinds, and hundreds of thousands of square miles of forest. Over several centuries, the immigrants poured in, settling the land from coast to coast, burning, cutting, and shooting on the way, often abandoning what they leveled to those who came behind them. In terms of human as well as earth history, this conquest took a relatively short time. It turned us into a restless nation, whose chief characteristic has been a migratory nature, a general mobility on wheels and in the air. We keep abandoning what we come to. We crowd in, displace nature wherever we go, and sometimes retreat again like the tides.

Perhaps we are slowing down. We are beginning to look around and wonder what became of the original America, and we are trying to identify its life in the habitats around us, so that it will not be lost to us. We never know what we do not make an effort to see. The "environment," as we call it, any environment, will never be much use to us if we are unable to recognize what it contains. It will only be an empty term.

In recent years, open country has been drastically reduced, especially on the two coasts. This has increased the need for education in the values of the land on many levels and in many ways. The more we lose the essential details, the very substance of the land, the more ignorant we become.

From the beginning, naturalists in America have relied on a tradition of broad education, from the humanities to modern science. William Bartram, who published his *Travels* in 1791, was a botanist and an artist. He wrote of his journeys through a southern wilderness whose beauty and riches staggered his imagination, making extensive notes and drawings of the flora and fauna he met on his way.

John Muir, born in Scotland in 1838 and an immigrant to this country as a boy, never faltered in his love for wild nature, "the great fresh unblighted, unredeemed wilderness." He was an intrepid mountaineer and as close to the great heights, the storms and trees, of his beloved Sierra as any naturalist has ever been. Although he was a student of geology, he was not so much a scientist as a leader in the defense of wilderness. He had a lifelong, religious commitment to nature.

Aldo Leopold, a professional in forestry and wildlife management,

Finely rendered portraits reflect the traditions of the naturalist-artist. American ornithologist John James Audubon painted the now extinct passenger pigeons (top) when they were so abundant "the light of noonday was obscured." Audubon, whose masterful *Birds of America* appeared in the mid-1800s, was influenced by English naturalist Mark Catesby, who painted colonial America's wildlife (above) nearly a century earlier.

PAGES 10-13: Quaking aspens offer habitat for elk and moose. Deer and spider share the riches of a meadow. An understanding of life's complex web comes in part from exploring the earth by ecosystem, be it woodland, meadow, desert, or rocky shore.

was the author of *A Sand County Almanac.* This book, famous for its discussion of a "land ethic," was published a year after his death in 1948. "A land ethic," he wrote, "changes the role of *Homo sapiens* from conqueror of the land-community to plain member and citizen of it. It implies respect for his fellow-members, and also respect for the community as such." He pointed out that land is a fountain of energy running through soil, plants, and animals, and that we, too, are a part of it.

Rachel Carson, trained in biology, did a great deal after World War II for public understanding and appreciation of the marine life along our shores and beyond them in *The Edge of the Sea* and *The Sea Around Us.* She wrote with care about this rich environment and all its intricate life relationships, portraying it in such detail as to encourage a great many readers to look at it with fresh eyes. Her *Silent Spring,* published in 1962, was the first book to speak with great eloquence and authority about the terrible effects that chemical pesticides were having on the natural environment.

Joseph Wood Krutch, who died in 1970, originally taught dramatic literature at Columbia University and became a full-time naturalist after his retirement, when he moved to Arizona in 1952. There he spent the rest of his life studying the plants and animals around him, such as the spadefoot toad, the giant saguaro cactus, the yucca moth, and the kangaroo rat called *Dipodomys,* which, in arid regions, gets the water it needs from dry seeds. As an educator and philosopher, he thought deeply about the whole design of nature, and he was a keen observer and student of desert life and its adaptations. He thought of the animals as his neighbors, with whom he could converse when he met them face-to-face.

The Curious Naturalist describes itself as a beginner's guide to the natural world, but it ought to be emphasized that its contributors are also beginners, in the best sense of the word. They do not lead or direct so much as explore the possibilities of the habitat they are writing about. While they are experienced in sorting out the elements of a landscape and in describing them in a cogent and accurate way, they also introduce us to what they themselves are only beginning to find out. That is the essence of discovery. The naturalist can lead you in and suggest some useful tools for interpreting what you are looking at, but it takes more than a hand lens, a notebook, and a pair of binoculars to put yourself into what you see. The aim of this book is to encourage the practicing amateur to stop, look, and listen. You can consult a field guide or a textbook to find out whether your facts are right or wrong, but it is just as important to enlarge your personal space, to unite your mind and your senses with what you see. Behind the landscape are more directions than we are aware of.

"Naturalists," says writer Ann Zwinger, "are born wanderers." Recognition comes through wandering, with a keen eye to what you discover on your way. It is through this wandering that we can begin to open our eyes to worlds that were never made by us, but which form the basis for our existence.

The Tools of a Naturalist

Though the naturalist requires no special equipment, a few tools can enhance exploration in the field and at home. A pocket-size magnifying lens—either x8 or x10—is useful for examining such details as an insect wing. A light microscope with magnifications of x10 to x500 can reveal otherwise invisible life-forms in a drop of water from sea or pond. Telescopes and binoculars enable you to view birds and other animals up close and in detail. A pair of 7 x 35 binoculars with coated lenses and central focusing is a good choice for first-time buyers, but try several kinds to see what suits you best.

Once you've observed "a white bird with a long bill" or "some kind of oak," it's time to consult a field guide—an indispensable tool not only for identifying specific plants and animals, but also for learning about their behavior, range, and habitat. Field guides may cover broad subject areas—North American birds, for instance—or narrow ones, such as mammals of the Rocky Mountains. Before selecting a guide, peruse the introduction, index, and a few entries to see if it matches your interests and depth of knowledge.

It's a good idea to make a detailed record of your observations. Jot down your impressions in a sturdy notebook. Note the date, location, and weather. Try illustrating the journal with simple sketches in pencil, pen-and-ink, or watercolor.

To capture your subjects on film, use a 35-millimeter single-lens reflex camera with interchangeable lenses.

By Ted Levin

Local Wilderness

From my seat on a Florida-bound jet, I see New York's Long Island stretch below me: the sweet salt air; the greenbelts, long and thin, hemmed by malls and office buildings that pass quickly into endless rows of houses; Long Island Sound and the Atlantic, with their attendant islands, deepwater harbors, and bays that together total more than 2,000 miles of shoreline. I am haunted by this image of Long Island, by the greenbelts and barrier islands, by the landscape of my youth. Its features are as familiar to me as old friends.

My parents moved into a virgin neighborhood on the island in 1952. We had a corner lot, a quarter-acre site, with a nondescript, Levittown-like house. A nearby three-story white farmhouse, shoehorned between the rows of tract houses, and the deep, rich soil were my only links with the neighborhood's agrarian past. I picked strawberries in the beds behind the farmhouse, dug earthworms and fat, white beetle grubs from under a blue slate path that led to our clothesline, and watched my father attack the pretty dandelions and dainty-flowered crabgrass that sprouted in his deep-green lawn. Since our neighborhood lacked native vegetation, it became a melting pot for immigrant trees. We sponsored Japanese barberries, Norway maples, Chinese mulberries and weeping willows, London plane trees, and Canada yews.

In an older, woody section of town, my parents' friends, the Shapiros, lived in the last house on a dead-end street. They had moved there in the late 1930s, when Nassau County supported a more even mix of farmers, fishermen, and commuters. Their woods, a vestige of the maritime forest, supported black oak, red maple, shagbark and bitternut hickories, American holly, black cherry, and beech on the richer soil; while patches of tall, shaggy pitch pine and scrub oak grew on the drier, sandier soil. Color came to the woods in October: yellows and muted reds mostly, but here and there a splash of electric red where an old tupelo or sweet gum broke into the canopy. Until the end of World War II—when farms were dismembered—white-tailed deer visited the Shapiros. Every October they came to their backyard for acorns and hickory nuts.

By the mid-1960s, theirs was not the last house on the road. Rising taxes and economic pressures had forced landowners to subdivide. The maritime woods were splintered into house lots, then grew ranch-style homes. Dotted with big trees, the new subdivision still

Mixtures of trees, shrubs, flowers, and grass, suburban gardens such as this one form part of a greenbelt that supports a diversity of wildlife. Insects feed on nectar from the many flowering plants. Birds nest in the shrubbery, and robins and blackbirds find close-cut lawns an ideal hunting ground for worms. Birds and mammals also benefit from the wide variety of garden-grown nuts and fruits.

A white-tailed deer rears up to graze an apple tree. Spreading suburbs have shrunk the deer herds' woodland habitat and created a favorable, predator-free environment. The adaptable deer now thrive on cultivated crops and plants—to the distress of many farmers and gardeners.

The gray squirrel, another forest resident well adapted to the city, is bolder there than in the country and less choosy about nut species. In fact, its urban diet may range from pizza to candy pried from a vending machine.

Charles Darwin noted that bumblebees, such as this one climbing on a teasel, favor urban nesting sites, where cats keep down the mice that eat the bees' grubs and honey.

had something to recommend it. Whenever I jogged through the neighborhood, I stared at the tops of the towering trees, at the weft of branches and their attendant gray squirrels—a ubiquitous expression of wild Long Island—and imagined the weaving of sea and land, of native plant and animal communities, of an island without pernicious suburban sprawl.

From the air, Long Island looks like a long, narrow fish, perhaps a mackerel, swimming southwest. This is not an original thought. Walt Whitman wrote it first, and in my fourth-grade local history studies, the point was driven home that the island is fish-shaped, 118 miles long, and between 12 and 23 miles wide. On a map this fishiness is quite apparent, but from 10,000 feet, seeing it is a personal triumph, a scaled-down version of seeing earth from outer space.

Rising from the sea along the north and south shores, two terminal moraines—long, low ranges of hills formed of unconsolidated boulders, gravel, sand, and clay, which mark the end runs of Pleistocene glaciers—provide Long Island with its only topographical relief. The moraines are the island's physical framework. Twenty thousand years of erosion and deposition have filled in the south shore, adding a wide, sandy outwash plain.

I grew up on that outwash plain, thirty miles from the Manhattan line, four miles from the Atlantic Ocean. I grew up down there, four miles from a transcontinental highway for migratory birds. One sunny late September day, I saw more than 10,000 flickers and 5,000 hawks pass my sand dune perch, and on another day I estimated 100,000 tree swallows in a single boiling flock. Each fall, too, broad fronts of monarch butterflies fluttered above the outer beaches en route to Mexico.

I grew up down there, four miles from where fish schools measured by the acre travel unseen beneath the gray chop. My fishing friends set their calendars to those runs—striped bass by April 15, bluefish two weeks later—as I set mine to bird migrations. I learned to expect squadrons of hyperactive terns by May 15, dark, wavy lines of autumn cormorants, summer egrets, and winter owls.

I grew up down there, four miles from fertile salt marshes where horseshoe crabs (whose ancestors crept through warm trilobite seas 500 million years ago) come ashore to lay their eggs, and diamondback terrapins dig May nests in the open sand. I could smell the marsh on the way to Jones Beach, a thick manurelike smell, spiked with a jigger of salt and a twist of methane.

I grew up down there, four miles from all of that, and not once did I visit the beach on a school-sponsored field trip. The closest I got was in the second grade, when Mrs. Roweworth took us to the Park Avenue pet shop to buy guppies for the classroom fishbowl. If she had continued another half mile south, we would have reached the Great South Bay.

I press my face to the window and look down. Jones Beach and Fire Island—skinny barrier islands—run below me, wild and fragile. From the air the island beaches shine—long, thin, luminous streaks

bounded by the gray of the ocean and the gray of the bay. At the edge of Jones Inlet, a monstrous jetty interrupts the longshore current and its westward flow of sand. A parking field and a concession stand, which serve thousands of bathers every sunny summer afternoon, invade the dunes and swales east of the jetty. In the open sand behind the field, a busy ocean highway loops through a nesting colony of 1,100 pairs of common terns and 50 pairs of black skimmers. Several years ago, close to 50 percent of the 1,400 fledgling terns took their first flight head-on into traffic and were killed.

I saw my first snowy owl down there, a female, perched like a deity on the crest of a windswept dune, her back to the jetty and Jones Inlet, her face hard into a northeaster. The big white bird stayed put on the west end of Jones Beach for more than a month, feasting on voles and shrews and cottontails, and I regularly hitched to the beach to visit her.

Big mammals were harder to find. Of those that once roamed Long Island—black bears, wolves, mountain lions, bobcats, elk, moose, and bison—only deer made it past the middle of the 19th century. Today deer are thriving in many northeastern suburbs. In fact, on Fire Island they may be doing too well.

An oasis in a sea of suburban sprawl, Fire Island is a composite of a national seashore, a state park, a county park, a United States Coast Guard reservation, and several very private, very exclusive beach communities. Although connected to Long Island by two bridges, Fire Island has few roads, and most of its territory is accessible only by ferryboat or ambitious legs.

Since barrier islands offer marginal deer habitat, deer rarely visited Fire Island. It is thought that a few deer—perhaps driven by mainland development—swam the Great South Bay in the 1950s or crossed over on winter ice, and stayed.

Years ago I had watched deer, wild and cautious, move through the Smith Point dunes in the wilderness area on the island's eastern end, but until the fall of 1988, when I counted 11 fearless does and fawns under the gnarled Japanese black pines along the Robert Moses Causeway, I had never seen a deer on the western end of Fire Island—the end closest to the city. Clearly, something had changed.

Protected from hunting since 1964, the deer population had steadily increased over the past 15 years, splitting into two herds with a combined population of between 400 and 600. One herd

American goldfinches and house finches enjoy a generous meal at a multiple finch-feeder. Backyard birdbaths and nest boxes, too, attract house finches and house wrens, and even the occasional bluebird. Feeders of all kinds, from bags of suet to peanuts strung on a wire—along with berries from such bushes as holly and pyracantha—help nonmigratory birds survive harsh winters.

FOLLOWING PAGES: Flowers such as these in a mixed border lure diverse nectar feeders. Blue and yellow flowers—some marked with ultraviolet "nectar guides"—attract bees and other insects. Few except butterflies can discern the color red. Nightflying moths are drawn by the heavy scent of white tobacco flowers.

Its bilobed shape and glowing color gave this perennial its common name, bleeding heart. Unlike the open-faced design of flowers such as roses, the bleeding heart's petals have joined to form saclike lobes. Wild and cultivated varieties grow freely in many parts of North America. A woodland relative, whose elongated white flowers resemble upside-down pantaloons, is known as Dutchman's-breeches.

remained in the wild part of the island; the other, in and around the beach communities. Fire Island has only seven or so square miles of deer habitat. This limited area may shelter 70 or more deer per square mile. State biologists believe that Fire Island's carrying capacity—the number of deer that can be adequately supported by its habitat—is only 12 to 16 per square mile.

For a decade the biologists encouraged the National Park Service to sanction a limited hunt on the national seashore to reduce the number of deer before they reduced their browse, destroyed their habitat, and starved to death. For a decade the situation lay in bureaucratic limbo as the two herds grew.

By the summer of 1988, the biologists noted that deer had eaten almost all the herbaceous ground cover in the wilderness area and in the Sunken Forest, a relict maritime forest. Atlantic white cedar and American holly had stopped regenerating. Every red cedar I saw in the open dunes along the western end of Fire Island wore a browse line, uniform and high, as though gardeners had pruned back the branches. Landowners in the beach communities complained bitterly about damaged ornamental shrubs. Several deer carcasses, autopsied by biologists, showed rumens containing pitch pine, a resinous last-resort food, the nutritional equivalent of cardboard.

That year the National Park Service granted a short, controlled archery and shotgun season, which eliminated 60 deer. By taking blood samples from the hunter-killed deer, Park Service biologists found evidence that 75 percent of the animals had been exposed to the spirochete *Borrelia burgdorferi*, a corkscrew-shaped bacterium that causes Lyme disease. Deer ticks are vectors for the spirochete, of which white-footed mice are a reservoir. Although most wildlife is unaffected by Lyme disease, people not treated soon after infection may develop an insidious arthritis-like disorder.

On Long Island, where thousands of people are bitten by infected ticks each summer—many in their own backyards—Lyme disease is epidemic. (It has also appeared in 42 other states.) Fighting it means fighting ticks, finding a weak link in their life cycle. For several years, Park Service biologists scattered cotton balls soaked in permethrin—a biodegradable pesticide approved by the Environmental Protection Agency—around the island. White-footed mice took the cotton to line their nests and killed larval ticks in the process. Although temporarily effective, the procedure proved expensive and was discontinued. Eliminating the deer population may be the last resort for controlling the spread of Lyme disease on the national seashore—and there is no guarantee that even this step would work.

I see coastal New Jersey below me. The barrier islands of Long Beach and Island Beach are impaled by jetties. From the air, the beaches have a saw-toothed look. On the north side of each jetty they are wide and sloping; on the south side, steep and narrow, the result of uneven erosion. In trying to protect the investments of a privileged few, we are disrupting the longshore current with jetties. It is a precarious and expensive proposition that requires constant

Collecting, Pressing & Mounting Plants

Observing plants in their natural setting is a rewarding pastime, but sooner or later every serious botanist needs to take a closer look. Careful study of plants requires collecting specimens, preserving them, and arranging them systematically in a herbarium.

Some basic rules for collecting: Obey all laws regarding plant life. Choose plants only from among thriving communities; *never* take one that is the only specimen of its kind in a given area.

Select a plant in good condition. Handle it sparingly and place it in a self-closing plastic bag to keep it fresh. Give each plant a different number. Write the number on a slip of paper and put it in the bag. Also record the number in a notebook, along with details about the plant's location and growing conditions. Find at least two samples of a plant; individuals within a species vary.

To make a press for preserving your plants, you will need clean newsprint, blotting paper, corrugated cardboard, and materials for the frame: two pieces of hardwood lattice measuring 12 x 18 inches long (or two pieces of quarter-inch plywood of the same dimensions), and two straps 5 feet long.

Arrange each plant inside a folded piece of newsprint, maintaining the natural position of the leaves and other parts. Write the plant's number on the front of the newsprint and then place the

folder between two pieces of blotting paper. Put cardboard (with the channels running horizontally) on either side of the blotters. This will ventilate the specimens.

Prepare other plants similarly, until you have a stack of packets no more than 18 inches high. Place the frame on either side of the stack and secure the straps. Put the press in a cool, dry place.

Plants shrink as they dry, so tighten the straps from time to time.

The plants should dry within a week or so. Then you can mount them. Carefully remove a plant and apply a thin line of glue to its back. Position it on a clean sheet of heavy white paper. Copy the plant's number and collecting data onto a label and attach it to the lower right-hand corner of the paper. Organize your specimens by species, locale, or other system in a folder or notebook, and you have a fine herbarium.

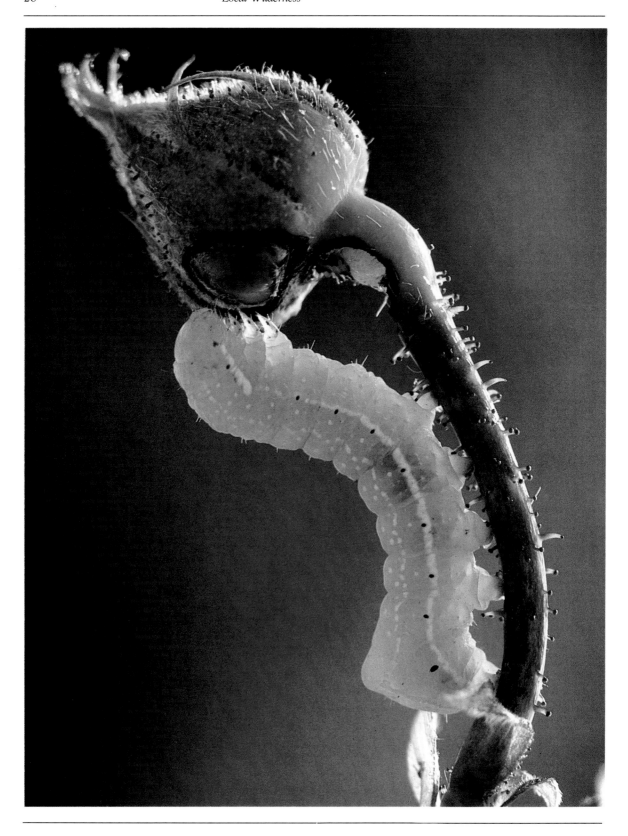

Garden plants are good places to find and study insects. Many moths, butterflies, and other insects lay their eggs on leaves, where the emerging larvae find a ready food supply for large appetites. Like other caterpillars, this hawkmoth larva on a rosebud can eat several times its weight in leaves each day. Such larvae usually have a hornlike tail, giving them the name "hornworm." One hornworm species feeds on tomato leaves.

Aphids cluster on plants from roses to apple trees, sucking sap from stems and leaves. Eggs laid in fall hatch into female aphids in spring. These females produce live young of their own gender (upper) by parthenogenesis—without fertilization. Later generations produce males and egg-laying females, which mate and repeat the cycle. Aphids secrete honeydew, relished by ants. Some ants tend herds of aphids like cows (lower), stroking or "milking" them to encourage the flow of honeydew.

dredging and filling at a high cost, a cost shared by taxpayers. In the end the beaches, hollow-cheeked and haggard, will die anyway.

Looking inland, I see the Pine Barrens, the still wild core of otherwise congested New Jersey. They are brown with oaks and green with cedars, laced with shimmering rivers that reach the coast of Great Bay. There tens of thousands of greater snow geese rest en route from their breeding grounds in northwestern Greenland and eastern Canada to their wintering grounds on the coasts of the mid-Atlantic states.

Last winter at Edwin B. Forsythe National Wildlife Refuge (formerly known as Brigantine)—a birding paradise on Great Bay, within a short drive of some 20 million people—a biologist told me that in late October, waves of white geese arrive like squadrons of jet-liners out of the northern sky. Wings set in a sweeping arc, webbed feet lowered, they begin their descent into the refuge four or five miles up the coast. And then, he said, "it rains snow geese all day."

South of Great Bay lies Atlantic City, where buildings sprout from the sand like mushrooms. Down there somewhere Mickey Mantle and Yogi Berra shake hands with casino guests.

I see the Delaware River, progressively widening south of Philadelphia into Delaware Bay, where it is then pinched by Cape May's long, thin neck. Only an hour and a half by car from Philadelphia and three hours from Washington, D. C., Cape May is the hawk migration capital of North America. The day after I saw those 5,000 hawks over Fire Island, more than 21,000 passed over Cape May.

Eventually, central Florida's planned communities come into view—future suburbs—where roads and driveways lie across wet hinterlands like so many cement candelabras. This new wave of Sunbelt suburbanization mirrors the wave that swept across the Northeast and Midwest in the 1950s.

From St. Petersburg, on Florida's west coast, I drive north to Brooksville, where my parents retired in 1983. Florida's new suburbs (my wife, Linny, calls them the "elderburbs"), carved out of wild and tangled cypress swamps and sandy oak and pine hammocks north of Tampa, are peopled with retirees from the industrial Midwest and Northeast. Here, raw, howling nature—fat black bears, alligators, limb-thick water moccasins—meets America's leading advocates for weed-free lawns. This pristine section of the Gulf Coast is a windfall for developers, but it is not the natural habitat for urban senior citizens, who are doomed to pass their final years chasing palmetto bugs across their patios.

Down here, constantly on guard against the little forces of nature, my mother tries to maintain a hermetically sealed home. Embracing the theory of spontaneous regeneration, she believes that loose particles of food transmogrify into hideous insects—ants, roaches, and, worst of all, palmetto bugs. There is no convincing her otherwise.

She is not alone in her aversion to things that crawl. Her neighbor, a freckled woman in her mid-60s, once chased a pair of recalcitrant green treefrogs around her living room and into a closet, where she gassed them with Raid. The woman proves as thin-skinned as the frogs: She grows irritated at my suggestion that she has perpetrated a crime against amphibians, that she has staged a cold-blooded execution. Frogs, I say, are much better alive than dead: They dine on insects and don't share their warts. My remarks fall on deaf ears.

The swift clearing, leveling, and draining of this Florida land, the carving of canals and the straightening of rivers, have left a wake of displaced wildlife. In Brooksville, Route 19, the busiest four-lane road on the Gulf Coast north of Tampa, bisects one of Florida's best—and one of its last—black bear ranges. Although bright yellow signs post the critical bear zone, few drivers heed them and slow down. Animals that have wandered the wooded coast for thousands of years are now being forced into compromising habitats, where they run afoul of both traffic and elderburbs.

Last year, after a round of golf, my father returned home to find a terrified black bear between the beauty salon and the entrance to Heather Walk. The bear hugged the trunk of a longleaf pine less than a hundred yards from Route 19 until a game warden shot it with a tranquilizing dart and took it to nearby Chassahowitzka National Wildlife Refuge, an occasional drop-off spot for untoward wildlife.

The bear was not—is not—alone. I see bobcat and gray fox tracks in the almond-colored sand behind Heather Walk, alligators in the weedy ponds between the villas, and otter in the clear (for the moment) Weeki Wache Spring. As the new suburbs spread into Florida

Reading Soil

Soil is not the homogeneous substance the word "dirt" implies. A clean road cut along a highway confirms this. Stripes of different colors and textures reveal layers that vary in their proportions of soil's major ingredients: minerals, water, air, and organic matter. To read the soil in your backyard, dig a hole about two feet square and three feet deep, keeping one side as straight as possible. The exposed surface should look something like the cut shown here, typical of clayey soil in northern and central Virginia. Expect layers to differ in composition and depth: The United States has some 20,000 different soil types.

Soil layers are called horizons. The dark topsoil, the A horizon (here about 6 to 8 inches thick), contains organic material—leaves, roots, twigs—and animals ranging from microscopic bacteria to worms and burrowing shrews. These animals aerate the soil with their tunneling and process organic material in their guts. Earthworms have earned the epithet "intestines of the earth."

The E horizon, only a few inches thick, appears lighter in color than the A horizon. Minerals, which darken soil, leach downward from this zone to the B horizon, $1\frac{1}{2}$ to 2 feet thick. High iron content turns this layer red.

Soil is born in the C horizon, as water and temperature join to break down bedrock, volcanic ash, or sediment into smaller particles. The process is slow. It may take several hundred years for nature's weathering forces to make an inch of soil.

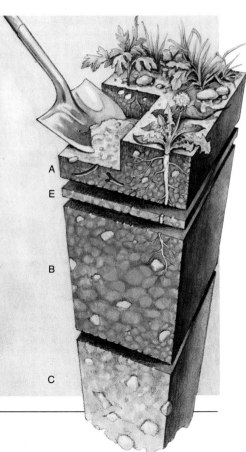

Eastern mole

Mite

Springtail

Nematode

Although not popular with lawn-proud suburbanites, the eastern mole shoveling through the earth does its part in mixing the soil. Because moles live underground, they are seldom seen. Their chief food is that prime topsoil processor, the earthworm. Moles may even store worms in their tunnels to eat in winter, immobilizing the creatures by biting off their front part.

Among the teeming microorganisms that help create garden soil are three groups—here enlarged many times—that can be examined with a magnifying glass. Mites and springtails feed on decaying vegetation and other soil creatures. Springtails get their name from a structure under the abdomen that catapults them into the air. Nematodes swim along watery channels between dirt particles. Useful decomposers of soil, they are also parasites on plant roots—a farmer's bane.

wilderness, amoeba-fashion, pouring their manicured pseudopodia into the woods and swamps, wildlife either adapts or vanishes. Such has been the pattern in suburbs all over the country.

When any wilderness area is developed, big animals are the first to go. In Florida it was bears, wolves, panthers, indigo snakes, gopher tortoises, bald eagles. How long could a six-foot-long eastern diamondback rattlesnake lie unmolested on the warm macadam of Heather Walk Lane? Or any snake, for that matter—although my father once spared a black racer that had taken refuge in his backyard grapefruit tree. (I guess 18 years of living with me must have counted for something.)

There are a few surprises, however.

I visited Naples, on the southwest coast of Florida, several years ago to see a bald eagle's nest in the crown of a front-yard pine. The nest was beautiful. Trumpet creeper, a woody vine with bright, trumpet-shaped orange flowers, wrapped around the tree, spreading snakelike up the trunk and out across the upper limbs. Vine-green, freckled with dozens of blossoms, the nest glowed in the morning light. A month earlier, when the vine had supported thousands of flowers, the nest could be seen a mile across the bay, framed against an arc of blue sky.

This was not a typical neighborhood for nesting eagles. BMWs and Mercedes-Benzes lined the street; the air was thick and sweet with lemon. Sanitation workers in (Continued on page 35)

Life in a Vegetable Garden

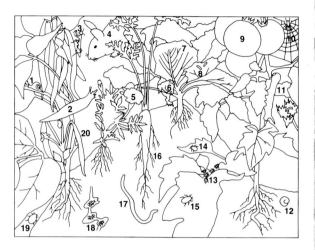

1 **Brown garden snail** *(Helix aspersa)*

2 **Spotted garden slug** *(Limax maximus)*

3 **European mantis** *(Mantis religiosa)*

4 **Eastern cottontail rabbit** *(Sylvilagus floridanus)*

5 **French marigold** *(Tagetes patula)*

6 **American toad** *(Bufo americanus)*

7 **Red cabbage** *(Brassica oleracea* var. *capitata)*

8 **Imported cabbageworm** *(Artogeia rapae)*

9 **Tomato** *(Lycopersicon esculentum)*

10 **Garden spider** *(Araneus diadematus)*

11 **Tomato hornworm** *(Manduca quinquemaculata)*

12 **Variegated cutworm** *(Peridroma saucia)*

13 **Potato aphid** *(Macrosiphum euphorbiae)*

14 **Colorado potato beetle** *(Leptinotarsa decemlineata)*

15 **Convergent ladybird beetle** *(Hippodamia convergens)*

16 **Carrot** *(Daucus carota* subsp. *sativus)*

17 **Earthworm** *(Diplocardia communis)*

18 **Black ant** *(Monomorium minimum)*

19 **Mexican bean beetle** *(Epilachna varivestis)*

20 **Green bean** *(Phaseolus vulgaris)*

The fertile soil, tender green leaves, and ripening vegetables of the home garden make the gardener unwitting host to a variety of animals—some pestlike, others beneficial. The Mexican bean beetle skeletonizes the leaves of green beans, while the Colorado potato beetle lays its cluster of yellow eggs on tomato foliage. These eggs will soon hatch into rapacious larvae. Beneath red tomatoes, the beneficial ladybird beetle devours aphids that feed on the plant's leaves and stems. Because each ladybug may eat more than 50 aphids a day, the species is often sold by the gallon to farmers and gardeners.

Few acorns lying on the ground in fall (opposite) will grow into new oak trees. Break open an acorn, and you may find a thriving ecosystem instead of a seed. An acorn weevil (above) attacks while the acorn hangs on the tree. With tiny teeth at the end of its hollow proboscis, the weevil bores a hole through the shell to the nutmeat. Females may lay an egg inside each hole. Once hatched, the larva feeds on the developing nut. When the acorn falls, the larva gnaws a round hole in the shell, pushes its head through and squirms its well-fed body after (above, middle and right), then burrows deep into the soil. It can lie dormant for up to five years.

Filbert worm moths (right) lay their eggs on growing acorns, and the hatched larvae chew their way in and out. Other insects use these holes to enter, lay eggs, or feed on the nut and on each other. Microorganisms such as fungi and springtails complete the nut's decay.

Acorns that survive intact are a favorite food of the chipmunk, here with cheek pouches stuffed full of nuts it will carry to a winter larder in its burrow. Chipmunks, mice, squirrels, magpies, and jays bury caches of acorns. Seeds that remain uneaten sometimes sprout as young oaks.

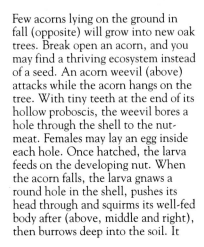

Watching Plant Succession

There comes a day when every homeowner is tempted to ignore the chores that keep a lawn looking neat and grassy green. Acting on this impulse could irritate neighbors, but it can also provide an opportunity to observe the slow, loosely predictable succession of plant life, called a sere, that occurs as nature reclaims a yard. Which species will overtake a lawn's grass—and, as time passes, each other—depends on the location. The yard illustrated here is typical of the Virginia Piedmont region. Let's see what happens when its owner forsakes yard work for a *very* long time.

In the scene labeled "Present" it is late summer, and the lawn of mixed fescue grass is in need of its weekly mowing. Dandelions, their seeds easily scattered by the wind, have already taken root. Visiting robins, sparrows, and squirrels may bring on their feet or leave in their droppings some of the seed beginnings of the next generation of plants.

After three years of neglect, wispy clumps of broomsedge dominate the scene, nearly obscuring the birdbath but not thwarting a curious grackle. Flowering plants such as the fuzzy goldenrods, pink-topped bullthistles, purplish

asters, yellow-crowned stalks of mullein, and brambly, white-flowered blackberries compete for space among the broomsedge. Yet the cool green presence of a Virginia pine and a feathery red cedar signal the end of grass dominance.

After 14 years, our sere shows a triumphant, 20-foot pine. Needles and branches that drop at its base create an acidic soil hostile to the growth of other plants. Broomsedge and thistles huddle outside the pine tree's realm. And while the pine will reign for years to come, the shoots of red maples lurking behind the birdbath, as well as the solitary seedling of a tulip tree, hint at a time—perhaps 60 years hence—when hardwoods will overtake the plot to produce the climax, or end stage, of the lawn's metamorphosis.

14 Years

Three years

Present

On Manhattan's West Side, seeds deposited by wind and wildlife have rooted on the gravel bed of an abandoned railroad track, producing a vigorous growth of grasses and wildflowers. If left alone, this track may eventually grow hardwood trees and shrubs, as plant roots grind up the gravel, decaying plants fertilize the soil, and the land reverts to the region's original woodland vegetation.

golf-cart-like satellites scooted up and down the driveways, collecting pails of garbage, which they then delivered to the mother ship down the street. Cuban royal palms and Norfolk Island pines, tufts of saw palmetto, pampas grass, and tightly pruned seaside grape decorated front yards, while the bay lapped at backyard dikes. Down the block, hotels and condominiums rose into the morning light.

A stream of people had arrived at the viewing site, a corner lot a hundred yards from the nest. Stunned by the spectacle, I stayed all day at the junction of Windward and Leeward Streets, eating warm oranges and watching eagles trail their shadows across the suburbs.

Although the presence of abundant lizards adds to my visit, it is not the reason my parents chose to live in Brooksville. My mother locks the front door at night because she's afraid lizards might get in. When a small anole does get in—which happens on occasion—it can mean only one thing, I tell her: ants under the sink. This she does not want to hear.

Most of my lizard watching is confined to the vicinity of the Heather Walk Villa communal Jacuzzi. Native green anoles, the most visible reptiles in Florida, roam the leafy branches of nearby pin and willow oaks, or rest like barrettes in gray-green braids of Spanish moss that hang down from the trees. They often sun on the smooth bathhouse wall, their weight supported by the friction of their toe pads, waiting for an insect or spider—or another green anole—to galvanize them into action.

Green anoles, natives of the Southeast, belong to the largest family of lizards, Iguanidae. Iguanids are the most visually oriented of all lizards, and anoles, because of overlapping habitats and ranges, have developed a wealth of showy, species-specific display behavior. Green anoles have pink fans called dewlaps on their throats and, when stressed, small neck and back crests and dark eyespots behind each eye. The histrionic anoles also engage in what looks like calisthenics: front-legged and four-legged push-ups, and head-bobs, all of varying tempo and significance. One herpetologist tallied 47 behavioral patterns for the green anole.

The 1950s were bad years for these animated little green lizards. They died by the tens of thousands, incarcerated in suburban homes. Every spring my mother took me to the Ringling Bros. and Barnum & Bailey circus at Madison Square Garden in New York City, and every spring I came home with a lizard. It seemed the circus sold more lizards than cotton candy. Each one was individually packaged in a small cardboard carton with air holes on the top and a cellophane window on the side so that children would know that their lizard was still alive. The word "chameleon" was printed on the side of the cage, so naturally that's what I thought I had bought. At 35 cents each, "chameleons" were the circus's bargain souvenir.

When I returned home, I watched my lizard change from bright green to brown to gray—a very limited color selection compared with *real* chameleons of the Old World—and handled it at every opportunity. Within a couple of months, inevitably, it grew lethargic

and then died. After losing four or five lizards, I became discouraged and stopped buying them.

Little green lizards and I went our separate ways until my sophomore year in high school. Then, during spring vacation, my parents sent me to Bermuda under the auspices of the school travel club. Although theoretically chaperoned by our young male history teacher and the future Mrs. history teacher, we saw progressively less and less of our guides. Even at 15, one can only ride a motor scooter in the wrong lane on a small island so many times before the thrill is gone, so eventually I took to the bush.

On the walls of our motel, two young boys caught little green lizards—relatives of the circus lizard whose name I now knew to be green anole—with a noose of thread that dangled from the end of a stick. I spent the rest of my vacation dropping loops over the heads of unsuspecting anoles, then snapping my wrists. After sexing the lizards (males have the larger, more colorful dewlaps), I let them go.

When I returned home from Bermuda, I visited the American Museum of Natural History in New York City, that enchanted house of science, to learn more about these lizards. I discovered that green anoles are the analogue of laboratory rats, the most studied lizards (perhaps the most studied reptiles) in the world. They had reached Bermuda as stowaways.

At the Heather Walk Jacuzzi, brown anoles—an introduced Caribbean species—hang face down from the patio wall, crossing at eye level in front of me whenever they spot an ant or beetle on the tiled floor. Browns have bright red dewlaps and are stouter than greens. Although they eat similar food, the two lizards hunt at different heights and generally ignore each other. Even in the laboratory, they do not interbreed.

Behind the wall, I hear anoles clatter through brittle saw palmetto fronds as large males chase smaller subordinates. On the wall, the lizards' behavior is easy to observe and easy to interpret. The larger the male, the more dominant, and dominant males occupy the most favorable perches—higher on the wall.

Hoping to forge an alliance between the anoles and my parents—both camps committed to ridding the neighborhood of ants—I look for my father. I find him with two friends, in conversation at the head of the driveway. Not wanting to interrupt, I stand listening. My hopes for the alliance fade as it gradually dawns on me that they

Flowers and greenery offer a welcome retreat from the city in a rooftop garden on New York's Upper East Side. Such plants must survive oil, soot, and dust that clog leaf pores. Birds, such as this mourning dove in a rain gutter, nest in crannies and ledges on city skyscrapers. Even cliff-dwelling peregrine falcons and other birds of prey swoop among these urban cliffs to hunt pigeons and sparrows.

Looking up warily from its dinner outside the kitchen door, this raccoon is making the most of city opportunities. These intelligent animals can pry the lid off almost any trash can. Our food scraps also feed house mice (opposite, upper) that nest in attics or walls. Prolific house mice inhabit cities worldwide. Females bear litters every four weeks.

Among interesting smaller house creatures is one we cannot see. Inside our furniture live dust mites (opposite, lower) that eat tiny flakes of dead skin shed by humans. Four dust mites can fit on a speck of dust.

are discussing the virtues of paving driveways with linoleum, to make it easier to clean up oil spots.

An hour after sunset, after the last orange contrail fades to gray, treefrogs come out. Dinner over, I grab my flashlight and a clean mayonnaise jar—its bottom filled with a half inch of water, its lid peppered with holes—and drift into the Florida night.

Pale-green squirrel treefrogs squeeze out through the clapboard seams of my parents' house and assemble around the porch lights—their busy, sticky tongues collecting insects that have come to keep the company of the lights. One frog lives in the drain of a backyard sink, another makes its home in the garden hose.

I see a larger frog, a two-inch green treefrog, silhouetted on a streetlight, its suction-cup toes fixed on a glass panel. Beyond the light, an armadillo roots for ants. Startled at my approach, it trundles off into the flower beds, hugging the villa wall. The quavering call of a screech-owl and the deep, rhythmic hoots of a great horned owl accent the suburban Florida night.

Down the street, an opossum sits by a front door eating from a cat's bowl. I walk over. It bares its teeth and grins. There's no death-

feigning from this opossum; it is too used to people. A friend in Clermont, Florida, told me about a mother opossum that had followed her cat through the garage cat-door, bedded down in the cat's bed, and given birth. Every night for nearly three months she used the door for egress and ingress. When her young were weaned, she left.

Opossums are adaptable and successful, perfectly at home in cities, although seemingly dim-witted and almost defenseless. Although their roots go back about 75 million years—and their family is one of the most primitive families of marsupials—Virginia opossums are not "living fossils." They are a recent species, less than 75,000 years old, that may have evolved from a small isolated population of neotropical common opossums.

It takes only a few opossums to found a population. The original ones wasted no time. It is believed that opossums expanded their range near the end of the Ice Age, about 12,000 years ago, moving north from Mexico. By 1600 they had reached the Ohio River; by 1900, the Hudson.

Nearly every aspect of an opossum's life predisposes it to suburban existence at a time when most native mammals are succumbing to

Standing in a dark garden, it is easy to appreciate the special adaptations of nocturnal creatures to this monochrome world of scents and sounds. A barn owl (opposite) glides in silent flight, muffled by soft wing feathers with serrated edges. Its large eyes and acute hearing detected the rodent it is carrying to its roost. The opossum (upper) probably relies on its sense of smell to locate edible plants and animals or garbage.

The summer night swarms with insects. Fireflies (lower)—flying beetles—send mating signals with flashing lights: Males signal in flight, females from the ground.

the siege of urbanization. These marsupials have catholic feeding habits, eating anything from puppy chow to venomous snakes, and they produce many young—2 litters a year with up to 13 young per litter. Opossums can endure maiming with little effect and rarely contract rabies. Ironically, it is not necessarily the most intelligent animals that adapt best to the humanscape, although many of our most familiar cohorts—rats, blue jays, crows—would certainly qualify for an animal Mensa.

Opossums are best known for feigning death when pursued by an enemy. This "playing possum" tends to follow the same pattern: The victim invariably falls over, tongue out and saliva drooling from its mouth; its lips curl, its eyes glaze and roll back, and a viscous yellow-green musk oozes from beneath its tail.

Most opossum references claim that feigning death is an involuntary reaction resulting from nervous paralysis. The animal faints, entering a state of shock. One writer recalled frightening a suburban Georgia opossum until it played dead. He then hid in the bushes to see if it would awaken when the danger had disappeared. While the author waited, a sanitation truck stopped, and a man hopped out, picked the animal up by the tail, and tossed it in the back.

There is controversy concerning the opossum's intelligence. After administering a series of tests to several animals, one biologist ranked opossums above dogs and on a par with pigs. He claimed that opossums aren't as stupid as they seem, but are simply inhibited by light. Naturalist Ernest Thompson Seton disagreed. He had no question about the opossum's mental capabilities. "As to intelligence," wrote Seton, "most observers agree the opossum has none."

The late Vernon Bailey of the U. S. Biological Survey produced incriminating evidence against the opossum's cerebral development. To test the brain size of several common mammals, Bailey filled the craniums of a red fox, a raccoon, a porcupine, a skunk, and an opossum with beans. The results: The fox held 198, the raccoon 150, the porcupine 70, the skunk 35, and the opossum 21.

I stand watching, less than ten feet from the Florida opossum as he consumes the cat food, and think that one obstacle he hasn't adjusted to in his conquest of the suburbs is cars. Almost every dark stain on Route 19 is an opossum. Now this one plods down Heather Walk Lane in the direction of the Jacuzzi, passing in and out of the incandescent glow of several streetlights before veering to another porch, another cat-feeding station.

I return to my parents' villa with two interned treefrogs, tokens of the night, gifts for my young son. At 18 months, Casey has plenty of enthusiasm but no formal training in herpetology. He laughs when the treefrogs jump.

I believe in touching the earth, in touching the wildness in our own backyards, to bond with the planet. A treefrog is a pathway to the indelible broadening of a child's landscape. I open the lid and remove it. Placing the treefrog on Casey's knee, I watch as his delicate, eager fingers move to meet it.

Woodlands

I hugged the tree, not because I loved it, but because otherwise I would probably have died. I could hear wind coming from the distance like a train.

I was perched high in the canopy of an old-growth forest, clinging for life and joy to the tapering trunk of an eastern hemlock. At ground level, where I first met it, the tree was a stalwart column a foot and a half thick. Up here, 45 feet from the ground, I could wrap one hand around it. Below, the forest was all shade and silence; up here it was exuberant, unfettered, filled with whispers and light. I hung on, and the wind blew.

These New England woods were, like all forests, a place of many moods and many scales of time. I had moved into this 200-acre grove in New Hampshire a few days earlier, coming to spend time in late summer and early autumn with one of the most intricate of America's many forests: the broad band of deciduous and coniferous trees that some foresters call the northern forest region. It extends from Maine to Minnesota and stands between the warmer mixed deciduous woodlands to the south and the austere boreal forest that blankets cold lands to the north with spruce and fir. It has some characteristics of both, and its own special qualities as well. It is no virgin: It has been logged, devastated by disease, and wracked by wind and fire. But it has survived and remains, by our cultural fondness for it and its own diversity, America's most traditional forest.

Yet even a familiar forest can seem strange. Many of us live in the open, and don't instinctively understand this shadowy place. When you first walk into the woods, the scene is all vertical lines more or less obscured by a green haze. It is overwhelming. What is going on here? What is all this thriving wood, this flood of leaves? But you don't start getting to know a forest in the branches. You begin below all that confusion of lift and chlorophyll, on—and in—the ground.

A forest is built on soil and landscape. What does the land look like? Is it sloped, flat, vertical? How does it face the sun? The latter is the most elemental question, upon which all else depends. In every forest, the balance of shade and sunshine makes the greatest difference. Almost all life on earth is a process of using the energy of sunlight, but this is most obvious in the forest, where the silence is so profound and the sun so deeply used that from the darkness below the canopy it appears the whole place is intent on the task.

Though it's direct, the relationship of trees to sunlight is not

Shafts of light penetrate the depths of a beech-maple forest. Woodlands feature marked vertical strata—each an ecological niche distinguished by its own community of plants and wildlife. The canopy is the forest's leafy roof. Below that stand the smaller trees of the understory, followed by a lower layer of shrubs, a layer of herbs, or nonwoody plants, and finally, the forest floor.

1

2

3

Leaf-shedding deciduous trees provide sure seasonal clues to their identity. While winter bares telltale silhouettes and twigs with buds, summer indicators include leaves and fruits. A round crown of spreading branches and a straight trunk with smooth, gray bark characterize an American beech (1). Its slender twigs have scaly, pointed buds, which give way to oblong, saw-toothed leaves. Small, triangular beechnuts are encased in a soft bur. The short-trunked sugar maple (2) has ascending branches that form a symmetrical oval silhouette. Glossy twigs bear characteristic tight, opposing buds. Its summer dress consists of five-lobed leaves and U-shaped, winged fruit. An irregular crown and a tall trunk with loose, shaggy bark identifies a shagbark hickory (3), its stout, hairy twigs tipped with large, scaled buds. Hickory leaflets—long, finely serrated, and stalkless—usually form clusters of five. In summer yellowish, thick-walled husks enclose elliptical nuts with four ribs.

simple. Different trees have different needs—some need more intense sunlight and some less; some need light for longer periods during the day and some for shorter periods. Ridges and canyons can lengthen or shorten the day. Topography also affects the amount of time water stays in the soil and the quality of the soil itself. The effects can be vivid: There are places in the West where south-facing slopes are grassland and north-facing slopes are forest; when you fly over, it looks as if the trees themselves are shadows on the land.

In the patch of old-growth forest I had come to visit, however, the land was almost level, a knoll left smooth-topped by glaciers barely 12,000 years ago but now receptive to the fall of water and leaves and the nurture of seeds. This was a democratic bit of land, so placed as to give every living thing the same first chance at light.

The composition and surface moisture of the soil on this gentle hill were almost as important to its forest as its orientation to light. This was moist, compact glacial till, full of boulders, gravel, and sand, and then a layer of hardness a few feet down, perhaps compressed by the weight of the glacier. Water drained reasonably well through the topsoil, but it did not pass easily through the lower hardness, so even on this knoll the ground stayed damp.

This type of soil, neither unusually dry nor unusually wet, generally supports the widest variety of trees; a plant has to be more specialized to feel at home in conditions that are drier or wetter. The dirt itself, as Robert Frost might have said when he came to his divergent paths in such a wood, makes all the difference.

The temptation is to tramp softly on this soft earth and look up. But the earth underfoot has intricate stories to tell. I dug a small hole, made an edge with my shovel, and looked at the soil layers, or horizons (see page 28). The top half inch was leaves, seeds, needles,

1

2

3

Most coniferous trees retain their needlelike foliage through the seasons. This complements silhouette as a year-round indicator of species. Fruited cones, present in the summer and fall, offer additional clues. A Douglas fir (1), distinctive for its height, displays a pyramidal crown; the branches on its straight trunk are irregularly spaced. Small needles, soft and flat, grow singly in a spiral around the twig. The reddish, woody cone of the male tree sports a collar of papery scales. Long, pointed bracts distinguish the female. Smaller in both stature and stem, the eastern red cedar (2) has a dense crown arranged in a tapered cone. Slender, scalelike leaves overlap on its twigs, and its fruit resembles small berries. Recognizable by an airy crown of horizontal limbs, the white pine (3)—the Northeast's largest conifer—produces slender, blue-green needles that grow in bundles of five. The long-stalked, cylindrical cone bears thin, rounded scales.

twigs, bits of bark: forest litter. This litter is vital to the forest. It protects against erosion and is the source of most of the nutrients that plants consume. The litter here could almost be peeled back in layers to reveal stages of decomposition: Clean, freshly fallen beech and maple leaves gave way to blackened skeletons of leaves, old maple seeds covered with a slime of microorganisms. And finally, beneath the litter, humus—here a black, loamy, rooty, rich mixture two to four inches thick.

You can tell if humus is acidic partly by its depth—acid tends to slow decomposition, so acidic humus will be thicker, up to three feet deep. This humus was acidic, typical of coniferous forests and of cool, moist climates.

Below that was a pale stripe, a grayness: the eluviated horizon, where acids that have leached from the trees and humus remove mineral elements, iron and aluminum oxides, and soluble organic matter from the soil. The E horizon, as soil scientists call it, was about an inch and a half thick. Below it was rich, brown, damp soil, where many of those oxides were deposited, and where the trees feed and drink.

Was this a silent place, this soil? Only to my ears. If one could shift scales and crawl among the grains as if they were boulders, the surroundings would become dramatic. This soil, ecologist J. P. Kimmins writes, is "a dynamic system in which the line between living and dead frequently becomes academic." If you were down in there, it would feel like a combat zone.

In the distance would be the thunder of voles, moles, squirrels, and woodchucks, all digging. Perhaps there would be the rhythmic earthquakes of a passing moose. Around you would be occasional millipedes, thousands of mites, springtails, potworms, and

Life in a Mixed Woodland

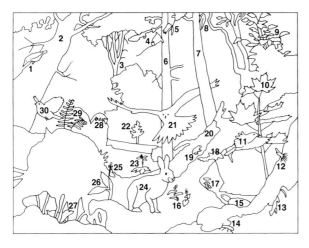

1 White-breasted nuthatch *(Sitta carolinensis)*

2 Sugar maple *(Acer saccharum)*

3 American beech *(Fagus grandifolia)*

4 Porcupine *(Erethizon dorsatum)*

5 Fisher *(Martes pennanti)*

6 Eastern hemlock *(Tsuga canadensis)*

7 Yellow birch *(Betula alleghaniensis)*

8 Hairy woodpecker *(Picoides villosus)*

9 Hobblebush *(Viburnum alnifolium)*

10 Sugar maple seedling

11 American redstart *(Setophaga ruticilla)*

12 Giant ichneumon wasp *(Megarhyssa* sp.)

13 Eastern red-backed salamander *(Plethodon cinereus)*

14 Ground beetle *(Pterostichus* sp.)

15 Wood turtle *(Clemmys insculpta)*

16 Wild lily-of-the-valley *(Maianthemum canadense)*

17 Broadgill *(Tricholomopsis platyphylla)*

18 Sulphur shelf fungus *(Laetiporous sulphureus)*

19 American toad *(Bufo americanus)*

20 Club moss *(Lycopodium* sp.)

21 Northern goshawk *(Accipiter gentilis)*

22 Eastern hemlock seedling

23 Indian cucumber-root *(Medeola virginiana)*

24 Snowshoe hare *(Lepus americanus)*

25 Leonardus skipper butterfly *(Hesperia leonardus)*

26 Yellow clintonia *(Clintonia borealis)*

27 Least weasel *(Mustela nivalis)*

28 Red fox *(Vulpes vulpes)*

29 Spinulose wood fern *(Dryopteris spinulosa)*

30 Black-capped chickadee *(Parus atricapillus)*

In each layer of the forest community, predator and prey are linked in a complex food web. Searching the canopy for hemlock twigs in early autumn, a porcupine may fall prey to the omnivorous fisher, an expert climber. Songbirds that frequent the understory seek food in different niches. While a white-breasted nuthatch probes the bark of a sugar maple for insects, an American redstart catches flying insects mid-air. On the forest floor, a snowshoe hare looks for succulent vegetation, always ready to flee a goshawk's talons.

Bark—an outer layer of dead tissue protecting an underlayer of new, living tissue—occurs in a variety of textures and patterns. Like fingerprints, it can differentiate tree species and is especially helpful in identifying winter-bare deciduous trees. Thick, dark-gray bark with deep, often diamond-shaped furrows and forking ridges marks a white ash (above). Curled and peeling layers of chalky-white sheets and orange inner bark help distinguish a white, or paper, birch (above, middle). A sycamore (above, right) displays its signature mottled bark—a colorful patchwork of molting old bark and new greenish white tissue.

nematodes working their way through the layers of litter and humus.

In their teeming numbers these animals might seem to be the workers of the forest floor, chomping and hacking the vast slabs of detritus that fall from above into digested lumps of soil. But they are not. They are only the consumers. The noble work of decay is done by the creatures these animals eat, creatures that even in your sand-boulder miniature world you would still find small: microorganisms—fungi and bacteria—that, in taking the sunlight from fallen leaves and wood, liberate the nutrients within them from their bonds of death.

There are killers here, too. The soil contains some of the organisms that feed on trees. Still with my head down, I saw, near the base of a lovely old sugar maple tree, a clump of brown-headed honey mushrooms, pretty mushrooms that come out in the New England fall to the delight of forest gourmets. But they were the fruit of a web of underground fungus, *Armillaria mellea,* and their presence meant that the sugar maple was doomed. Foresters call *Armillaria* a pathogenic infection; it spreads far beyond its small clumps of fruit to eat out the roots of trees. To the tree, that little clump of mushrooms was as lethal as a plague of insects.

I looked away from the *Armillaria,* emerged from the battleground of dirt, and found myself a little higher. No, it was not yet time to climb. I sat, instead, on a log. I was in the forest's herb and shrub layers, which reach from the ground to just over your head. You can learn much of the past, present, and future of a forest without ever looking up.

But what kind of forest is this? The Society of American Foresters lists 145 different types of forest cover in Canada and the United States, excluding Hawaii. Within the eastern hardwood forest are

Measuring a Tree

Trees define a woodland—the number and kinds of species proclaiming its essence, the individual trees providing details of its life history. From a naturalist's point of view, then, one *can* see the forest for the trees: In-depth knowledge of a single tree is a good first step to understanding any woodland. And a good first step to knowing a specific tree is to measure its height and canopy.

Pick a tree on level ground, preferably in a clearing. To measure the tree's height, you will need a straight stick about a yard long. Hold the stick vertically at arm's length. The distance from your eye to your hand should equal the length the stick rises above your hand, so adjust your grip as necessary. Keeping the stick straight and still, sight the base of the tree over your hand where it meets the stick. Now, moving backward slowly, align your sight over the top of the stick with the top of the tree. Stop. Check your sight lines, moving only your eyes: You should be able to sight the base of the tree at the top of your hand and the top of the tree at the top of the stick. Mark your position on the ground and measure your distance from the trunk to get the tree's approximate height.

To measure the tree's canopy area, place stakes in the ground in a rough circle directly beneath the outer tips of the branches. Depending on the size of the tree, 8 to 14 evenly spaced stakes should be sufficient. Then, imagining a line passing through the trunk of the tree, measure the distance between the two stakes that are farthest apart (x). In similar fashion, measure the distance between the two stakes closest together on opposite sides of the tree (y). Add the two measurements together and divide by two $(\frac{x+y}{2})$ to get the average width of the canopy. You can map the canopy by transferring the placement of the stakes onto a piece of graph paper and then connecting the dots. A lopsided canopy may suggest that a tree is buffeted by winds.

The vegetation within the staked area depends in part on the canopy's density of foliage. Noting how the species of grasses and wildflowers change with the seasons will add vital information to your tree's profile.

many variations; it is impossible to find a single acre that is identical to any other. The society's sober catalog of types speaks of "the seemingly chaotic mingling of species" in this region. How does one sort understanding out of that confusion?

Among the clues that naturalists use to classify a forest are certain species of trees, flowers, and wildlife. These indicator species may live elsewhere, but they are the major components in the woods they mark; the boreal forest of the north, for instance, is sometimes called the "spruce-moose forest," though both tree and animal disperse far beyond the territory they dominate. Indicators are often the trees and animals you first see when you go into the woods.

To limit the chaos, naturalists tend to look at small pieces of the woods. I informally marked off an area of about 30 feet by 30 feet. I made a list that began with my hemlock, a lovely tree whose short, dark evergreen needles look lacy against the sun. The hemlock was solitary here. It was not an indicator species, but its characteristically numerous and strong branches would make it ideal to climb.

Within my plot, though, there were plenty of indicators. There were two sugar maple trees, easy to identify by their dramatically

Flowering dogwoods (opposite, top) broadcast spring in a forest's understory with their annual display of white or pink "blossoms." The white or pink "petals" are not flower parts but modified leaves, called bracts, which surround the dogwood's true flowers. In winter the bracts protectively enclose the flowers (opposite, bottom left). As the weather warms, the bracts unfold, exposing the upturned, unopened flowers (opposite, bottom center and right). When fully open, the petal-like bracts advertise that the blossoms are ready for fertilization.

Most trees begin life as a seed, the fertilized egg produced by a flower. Each seed contains an embryonic tree complete with root, trunk, and leaves. There are two classes of seed-producing plants: gymnosperms, with naked seeds, and angiosperms, with covered seeds. A red maple's winged fruits (above) are examples of covered seeds. The cones of a balsam fir (above, right) bear naked seeds.

lobed leaves, familiar from the Canadian flag. They were accompanied by four red maples, whose smaller leaves have less dramatic lobes and a small-toothed edge; two red spruce trees; five yellow birches; and two beech trees. A spruce is recognizable by its sharp needles—"Shake hands with the tree," says Walter Graff, a naturalist for the Appalachian Mountain Club. "If it hurts, it's a spruce." There are other sensory clues: If you crinkle a fallen beech leaf in your hand, it feels like a paper dollar, and if you break a yellow birch twig, it gives off a startlingly powerful scent of wintergreen. The largest yellow birch had characteristically begun life on top of a boulder; now its roots gripped the big rock like talons.

I could recognize the trees without looking aloft at their leaves. Red spruce has a scaly bark; yellow birch has a shaggy, papery bark that peels off in shreds smaller than those of the famous white or

Making Leaf Prints

Exquisite examples of natural symmetry, leaves also celebrate nature's diversity. Making leaf prints is one way to create a permanent record of the myriad forms each year brings. Green leaves with distinct veins yield the best prints. (Maple and poplar are good choices.) You will also need a tube of printer's ink, two hard rubber rollers, and rice paper (all found in art supply stores), as well as plain paper and a smooth, nonporous surface—a pane of glass or the bottom of a glass baking dish—for rolling the ink.

With vein side up, place the leaf on a sheet of plain paper. Squeeze a little ink onto your smooth surface and spread it with a roller until the roller is evenly coated. Then roll ink onto the leaf until it is covered. Transfer the leaf, inked side up, to a clean sheet of plain paper and carefully tape a piece of rice paper over it. Pressing very firmly with a clean roller, roll the rice paper from top to bottom. Try to get the entire leaf impression in one firm roll. Then gently peel the rice paper from the leaf and allow the print to dry, inked side up.

Opposite, filtered rays find leafed-out shrubs and herbs in a stand of beeches, shedding light on a colony of foamflowers. In spring the greening of the forest proceeds from the floor up through successive strata.

paper birch; and beech is prominent for its sleekness, each trunk a gray column as smooth as water-worn stone.

Among those 145 types of forest covers listed, my choices were narrowed to one: the sugar maple-beech-yellow birch complex. The red maples in the sample were no anomaly. These trees, famous for their flaming foliage in the fall, prefer a little more moisture than the sugar maple, and so verified for me again the damp nature of the soil.

Indeed, tree cover is as much a clue to the ground as the ground is to the trees. It is the naturalist's fate to be entangled in linkages. When I asked one of New Hampshire's most respected silviculturists, the U. S. Forest Service's Bill Leak, how he recognized soil types, he said with a grin, "I look for the dominant species." If he sees a lot of big ash trees in a stand, for instance, he immediately knows the soil is unusually enriched—ash is a demanding tree.

Leak looks for other clues. An abundance of conifers may tip him off to poor soil, since evergreens thrive more readily on a lean diet. If he sees paper birch in abundance, trunks like white flags in the forest, he knows the woods have been disturbed. Paper birches, like pin cherry trees and aspens, can't tolerate the shade of a forest floor, but,

Female gypsy moths deposit their eggs on the trunk of a white pine (opposite). Each moth deposits a cluster of 400 to 1,000 eggs that hatch in spring. Nemesis of the Northeast woods, the larvae of gypsy moths feed on the young leaves of trees and shrubs. They have defoliated millions of forested acres and are expanding their range southward and westward at a rate of some 5 to 15 miles a year. Native to Asia, gypsy moth larvae were imported to the U. S. from France in 1869 by a Massachusetts naturalist trying to breed a better silkworm. Some of the larvae escaped and gained a foothold here.

helped by abundant, far-flung seeds, they charge into new openings like shock troops, throwing up a bivouac of new canopy, under which the more shade-tolerant trees—yellow birches and, especially, maples and beeches—will later raise their heads and win the war.

A fascinating part of getting to know a forest is learning the history of its development. The timeless calm of a wooded landscape is an illusion fostered by human haste. The forest seethes with change.

The species and shapes of trees, of course, reveal long-term changes. Paper birches tell their story of past fires or logging, while a balanced collection of trees of all ages, along with standing dead trees and the humps left by fallen logs and tipped-up roots, speak of long stability. If the oldest trees in the woods are unusually broadly developed, with branches spreading wide to gather the sun, it is likely that when they were young the forest was more open than it is

Various mammals, birds, and insects feed on the shrub layer, where thick growth often hugs the ground and provides a seasonal succession of edible fruits, berries, flowers, and seeds. Midsummer's sweet crop of wild raspberries (above, left) is a favorite food of bears, while eastern chipmunks will go out on a limb for bitter chokecherries (above, middle). Ants forage around jewelweed blossoms (above, right), an indicator plant of moist sites within forests.

today, and they didn't have to penetrate the canopy to find the light.

Large trees don't mean the forest is virgin. A big tree is not necessarily more than a hundred years old. Trunk diameter (traditionally measured four and a half feet from the ground) is a poor indicator of age, because so much of a tree's size depends upon individual access to moisture and sunlight. It may have shot up and grown thick in an opening in the forest in 75 years, or it may have stood slender and passive in the shade for almost as long, waiting for its chance. You can get a precise idea of how old a tree is by drilling out a core.

But a tree's age is less important to its future than the phase it has reached in its life cycle. Tom Lee, a professor of forestry at the University of New Hampshire, regularly reminds his students as they assess the condition of a forest: "Stage, not age."

The subtle progressions of forest life are often most visible in the understory. Some trees may appreciate other trees' shade: Maples sometimes appear to thrive best under beeches, and vice versa. There is a possibility—not researched definitively yet because of obvious difficulties of time—that a stable forest goes through cycles of species changes as the generations pass. If that is the case, a

Perennial sign of spring, a mass of great white trillium blankets the floor of an eastern forest (above). Damp and fertile, the woodland floor accumulates a cornucopia of plant and animal waste. This decomposes, nourishing a layer of wildflowers and other herbs, which—like the companionable foamflower and maidenhair fern (opposite)—frequently intermingle. In early spring, when the sun has sufficiently warmed the soil, woodland wildflowers bloom briefly under the open canopy. Afterwards most flowers wither, although the foliage of some, such as trillium, stays verdant throughout the summer. When the canopy has leafed out in late spring and summer, shade-loving ferns unfurl their fronds, transforming the forest floor into a green, feathery bed.

time-lapse movie of a forest that spanned centuries in a minute would show the colors and shapes of different species roiling through the woods like clouds.

I looked closely at the vegetation inside my 30-by-30-foot square near the solitary hemlock. Here were more plants typical of the northern hardwood forest: abundant fronds of wood fern; striped maple, with its huge leaves like ducks' feet; wood sorrel carpeting open areas with lovely leaves like oversize clover; shining club moss standing in tiny thickets of upright stems bristling with pointed leaves; the broad, parallel-veined leaves of clintonia; and an abundance of hobblebush, with its almost round leaves and red berries. Hobblebush earned its name because it tends to bend over and reroot itself, leaving loops of branches to trip the unwary.

Among these plants were the trees of the future: sugar maple, beech, and yellow birch saplings. There was no way of knowing which of the young trees would grow into the opening left when one of the larger ones fell, but meanwhile they all stood there quietly, like young actors aging in the extras pool, waiting for the big break.

There were also a couple of unexpected items: two tiny balsam fir trees and a higher percentage of red spruce saplings than in the present canopy. Later, I mentioned this to Bill Leak. He gave his ready grin, as if talking about woods he had studied for more than 30 years never ceased to delight him. "Over a long period of time," he said, "the soils push a forest in some direction. Sometimes you see hardwood trees in the overstory and spruce in the understory. Maybe it hasn't settled down yet and wants to be a softwood community."

I spent my nights in a tent about 65 feet from the hemlock, waiting for what the darkness might show of the forest's wildlife community. The silence was a mask, and I thought to use two of the

Vital to the forest, fallen trees serve a variety of functions for woodland wildlife. Downed limbs or trunks act as drumming logs for the male ruffed grouse (opposite) during mating season in April and May. Mounting his log stage, the grouse performs his ritual courtship dance, furiously and rhythmically beating his wings, which produces a muffled drumming sound intended to summon a hen.

Parasitic ichneumon wasps (above) depend on wood-boring horntail wasps as food for their larvae. Using her sensitive antennae, the female ichneumon—larger than the male—combs the surface of rotting logs for signs of burrowed horntail larvae. Then, inserting her long ovipositor into the bark, she deposits an egg into the body of the horntail larva host.

naturalist's most useful tools, time and patience, to hear the forest's whispered secrets. Most forest creatures only begin their day when the intricacies of the woods have faded into a black lace curtain against the luminous gray sky, so I was prepared to hear the scufflings and scratchings that haunt children's camping nightmares.

I thought I was ready for anything. At dusk I was prepared for the scolding of the red squirrel whose territory I had violated. After night came I was prepared for the red-backed salamander that came wading into the light of the camp lantern—it was another indicator of the moist quality of these woods. And I was almost prepared for the bouncing yellow flash of a woodland jumping mouse that shot past the fire one night about ten. But I was not ready for the moose. It wasn't that the animal was unexpected in these woods—quite the opposite. It was the way it announced itself.

When a tree falls—whether from wind, fire, lightning, or insect damage—the energy collected through photosynthesis and locked in its tissues is released slowly through a process of decay to support many communities of organisms.

The presence of particular species of fungi can suggest how long ago a tree fell. After five years (left panel), fungi such as sulphur shelf fungus (1)

and honey mushrooms (2), as well as bacteria, have begun to break down the dead plant matter. In so doing, they return nitrogen and other essential elements to the soil, encouraging the growth of poison ivy (3) and other green plants. The plants, in turn, attract fruit- and seed-eating birds such as the northern cardinal (4) and the rufous-sided towhee (5), which help to disperse the seeds.

It was almost midnight. The woods were a realm of peace. My light was out. The tent was black. Sleep was folding in. Then suddenly, right next to the tent, some kid picked up a bent trombone he had found in the attic and tried it out. *Ahhooauhum!* No, it was the sound of what might happen if you were to pin a tail on a real donkey. *Aiihaaaww!* No, it was a Klaxon sounding underwater. *Hoommargle!* It was a series of honks and groans that had me up and out of the tent with a flashlight long before I remembered that the way to observe animals is to move with patience and stealth. "The important thing in watching wildlife," Richard DeGraaf, principal wildlife biologist at the Northeastern Forest Experiment Station in Amherst, Massachusetts, had told me, "is to know that if you are careful, there is nothing out there to fear." I had forgotten that, too.

I was in these woods in late summer, during the moose rut, when

After about 15 years (middle panel), the log and stump host smaller fungi, including rosy-gill fairy helmets (6) and silkysheath mushrooms (7), as well as wood-boring insects and larvae that draw birds such as the pileated woodpecker (8). Mayapple (9) and partridgeberry (10) sprout in the rich soil around the log, their fruits and berries a food source for deer mice (11) nesting in the stump.

When 30 years have passed (right panel), autumn skullcap (12) grows in the spongy rot. Salamanders and newts (13) inhabit the damp recesses of the log, while the stump harbors insect prey for the northern flicker (14). A red oak sapling (15) sprouts from humus enriched by the parent tree and begins trapping energy from the sun, thus completing the cycle of death, decay, and regeneration.

Fairy helmet

Polyporous

Jelly fungus

Fungi, which feed on and decompose dead matter, are the primary agents in transforming floor litter into the dark, spongy organic layer called humus. Recognizable by their fruiting bodies—the variously shaped and colored mushrooms or toadstools that proliferate in autumn—fungi hide their working parts beneath the surface. Distinguishing features help in identifying fungi, such as the colors of *Russula* or the bell-shaped caps of fairy helmets. A large cap and black-tipped brown scales mark a *Polyporous*, while a gelatinous or rubbery texture indicates a jelly fungus. Tooth fungi have spore-bearing spines on the underside of the cap. Other identifying features of fungi include habitat, base, odor, underside, and stalk.

Russula (opposite)

Tooth fungus

cows and bulls call to each other through the trees. Bulls groan quietly or grunt, and cows utter the hoarse, off-key cross between a moo and a bray that had so stirred me (though not the way a bull moose is stirred). They sound, says John Lanier, the White Mountain National Forest wildlife biologist, "like elk with laryngitis."

Once I stopped dashing around, I stood apart and listened. There was no further sound. No crackling brush, no more broken trombones. Forest creatures are at home in the woods' quietness; even a moose, which can barrel along at 35 miles an hour if it wants, can also walk silently. The moose must have been no farther than 100 feet from me, but I heard nothing. It just dissolved. Much later there was a long, lonely sob in the distance that might have been the bull.

For most of us, seeing wildlife in the forest is a matter of accident. One day I wandered along an old logging road about two miles from the hemlock and startled two white-tailed deer, which went floating off through the forest like smoke, leaving only their sharp brackets of tracks in the mud to remind me that they were real. And twice in the early morning—a good time for wildlife-watchers—I startled black bears that were snuffling through the brush beside a road. It was bear-hunting season during my visit; on another early morning I heard a single shot, a reminder that the cycles of life and death in today's forests are never entirely free from adjustment by humans.

But there are ways to observe the forest's life more systematically. Tracks and scat let you know what's around: Look in the mud along streams and around puddles for the tracks of local inhabitants. Some animals mark territories with scat, or leave telltale droppings at den entrances or feeding areas. And there's nothing like coming upon a mound of warm bear droppings to make you look over your shoulder.

Smaller life-forms, the organisms in the soil, may be observed with a shovel or spade, a magnifying glass, and a Berlese funnel, which is covered at the wide end with wire mesh and burlap. You put the narrow end of the funnel into a jar, then pile a bit of soil on the burlap and heat it gently with a light. As the soil dries, the soil creatures dig deeper, until they burrow through the burlap and fall through the funnel into the jar, where they can be examined.

Larger life is more demanding. First, it requires odd hours, because most forest wildlife spends daylight hours in the shadows. Second, it demands a practiced stealth. Naturalist Tom Brown, Jr., suggests developing what he calls "splatter vision," a way of focusing in on detail and then allowing the "eyes to soften and take in everything in a wide half-sphere" like a wide-angle lens. Some of his other suggestions are stated as subtitles in one of his several books: "Let Go of Time," "Slow Down," "Sit Down," "Be Quiet," "Immerse Yourself in Nature," "Let Death Be Your Guide."

"Welcome and embrace minor discomforts," Brown writes. "They are the price of admission to the theater of the wilderness." The benefit of such effort is in seeing wildlife behave as if you weren't there. You see a red fox sleep in a patch of shade, as I did once while crouched uncomfortably in the edge of another one of

Like tracks in snow, distinctive bark markings signify the presence of certain birds and mammals, many of which can permanently damage or even kill a tree by destroying its first line of defense. A chiseled hole, for example, often tells where a woodpecker, such as this downy (left), has drilled for grubs. Nibbled twigs and small-toothed gnawings low on a willow shrub (opposite, top) are evidence of a snowshoe hare's winter feed. Porcupines, which go for the tender tissue under the bark, leave telltale bare patches and toothmarks, such as those on a lodgepole pine (opposite, bottom). As protection against animal damage, some thin-barked trees, such as yellow birch and Scotch pine, have developed thicker bark near the base.

FOLLOWING PAGES: Deciduous trees—mainly maple, birch, and beech—interspersed with dark green conifers provide the color in this autumnal New England landscape. The leaves of deciduous trees turn color and fall sequentially by species—first, red maple, followed by birch, beech, and sugar maple. Temperature and moisture determine the complexity and brilliance of the color cycle.

those 145 forest types, the California coast live-oak woodland. Or you see a great horned owl pluck a snake from the forest floor, as I did once in Idaho when a picnic had kept me still for half an hour.

Of course, the best way to know a forest would be to live in it for years, but few of us have that option. I spent many early autumn hours in my patch of woods, but missed the joys of other seasons: winter's leafless brightness; the race of flowers in spring to grow, blossom, reproduce, and die before the forest canopy closes out the sun (that's why many flowers actually start growing under the snow—to get a head start). I missed the summer's throb of heat and energy and the roar of insects (though not their bites). I missed the spring waves of returning birds and the symphony of their courtship.

Knowing the birds in a forest is often a matter of hearing rather than seeing them, but this season was relatively quiet. Once an

All manner of wildlife thrives where it can find abundant food. A forest provides amply for many species, from the plant eaters, or primary consumers—low on food chains—to the predators, or secondary consumers, which feed on the plant eaters. Nesting birds, such as this mourning dove (above), are prey for corn snakes (opposite), which can glide straight up tree trunks, using skin and muscle to grip the bark. Also agile climbers, martens (above, right) prey mainly on birds and on squirrels and other rodents.

ovenbird strolled through camp; ruffed grouse often went blasting off from nearby as I hiked among the trees; there was the occasional isolated cry of a blue jay; and I saw groups of flickers shooting among the trees like loping torpedoes. But most of the birds were already on their way south.

Other sounds had ended, too. The American toads and wood frogs I found hiding in the litter were mute now, long after their spring courting season.

But at least I was among the northern hardwoods during their hour of fame: the color season.

When I arrived in the woods, all was green; by the time I left, in late September, the sugar maples were blazing, and all the rest were beginning to "color out," as the people of northern New Hampshire put it. The actual process is more a matter of getting the green out. The varied pigments in the leaves are there all year, but, as naturalist Peter J. Marchand writes, "they are swamped by the sheer abundance of chlorophyll." As the weather cools and the days shorten, the trees abandon their leaves, cutting off the supply of water and minerals. Chlorophyll breaks down, letting pigments of yellow and

A bull moose (opposite) strips a downed birch branch. Denizen of northern forests and wetlands, the ungainly and solitary moose thrives on a diet of shrubs, seedlings, bark, and a variety of aquatic plants. Were it not for its main predator in the wild, the gray wolf (right), with which it shares parts of its habitat, the moose would ravage the vegetation within its range. Undaunted by the formidable size of their prey, the carnivorous wolves usually attack the large animal in packs, thereby keeping the moose population in check.

brown shine through. In some species, sugar left in the leaves turns into the pigment anthocyanin, which is bright red.

This blaze of color reveals the chemical tools a tree has been using all summer but has now abandoned. To us this show is both an industry and a joy. Among the indicators of this time of year in northern New Hampshire and Vermont are tour buses jamming the highways and "No Vacancy" signs on all the motels.

Late in an early fall day, drawn upward by the high color, I at last climbed slowly up into the hemlock, and the forest changed. It was like rising from the depths of the ocean. As I hoisted myself from branch to branch, the light grew, until the sun shone warm on the leaves all around me, and on my face. At the forest's surface, everything was different.

The top was a new world—a frothy place, all light and movement. The solemn trunk of the yellow birch that had such a grip on the boulder below had exploded into 15 rising branches, all swaying gently. The maple that had the *Armillaria* at its base was bravely putting out its winged seeds by the thousand. When I looked over my shoulder at the top of a beech tree I could see it covered with spiked burs. No wonder the lower trunk of that tree and many of its sleek gray neighbors had been scarred with neat arcs of five holes each: Black bears had made tracks up into the canopy to snack on the nuts.

After an hour up there I felt a bit like a black bear in autumn myself: sore, hungry, and sleepy. But I couldn't relinquish this place. Who would have expected such exuberance? Life exploded all around. I couldn't see the ground. I might as well have been living on a planet made entirely of leaves and wood.

"That's where the factory is, up there," Bill Leak had said. "The input of solar radiation is right up in that layer. Most of the water

exchange takes place up there. You see trees positioning themselves, because so much of the competition is for light and warmth. Some people think trees grow faster on a slope: It's like a football stadium when everybody stands up, craning to see."

A gust of wind passed over, and the whole world swayed. It was a dance. I felt friendly toward my tall partners. Tree species are like human characters, each looking out for Number One with a different strategy. The red maple to my right was an example of one way trees arrange their leaves to catch the most sunlight. In this pattern, called multilayering, the individual leaves are relatively small and arranged randomly from branch to branch so the sun can percolate to lower layers. A nearby sugar maple had another approach: monolayering. Its leaves were closer together and larger, so that each branch cast a deeper shadow and consumed a larger percentage of

Large tracks tell of a snowshoe hare's trail through a snowy wood (right). Among the various signs left behind by often elusive forest animals—signs that both record their comings and goings and provide clues to their habits—track patterns are the most common. In woods, animal trails are most readily visible in snow.

Additional signs of life often lie on the surface of the forest floor, including pellets of indigestible material (above) regurgitated by some birds and often found beneath their roosting perches. A pellet's size, shape, and contents, such as bones and fur, offer clues to the species. The pellets above suggest the presence of a great horned owl.

Reading & Casting Animal Tracks

Most wild animals lead lives hidden from human view. But many species leave clues about what they are, where they live, what they eat, and how they interact with other species. These clues might be bits of fur or feathers, leavings from meals, droppings—or tracks.

Look for tracks in mud, dust, sand, and snow. A mouse scurrying over a leafy forest floor leaves no distinct trail. Neither does a jackrabbit hightailing it across stony ground. But a raccoon at pond's edge, a gull on the beach, a hare in the snow, a deer strolling in fine dust through a forest clearing will likely leave prints.

Identifying a species from a single print can be tricky. But tracks tend to come in patterns, making identification somewhat easier. To read a track pattern, first note the size of the footprint and, if possible, count the number of toes and look for claw marks. Also note the distance between tracks and the width of the pattern. With these details, plus a sketch of the print and its pattern, you should be able to identify the species with the help of a field guide.

For more tangible evidence, you can make a plaster cast of the track, using a strip of plastic about two to three inches high, such as the rim of a cottage cheese container; a paper clip; and some plaster of Paris with a coffee can to mix it in. Choose a distinct print and gently clear it of debris. Make a ring of the plastic strip, push it into the ground around the track, and fasten it with the paper clip. Mix the plaster of Paris with water until it reaches the consistency of cake batter. Quickly fill the mold to an inch below the rim. Allow the cast to dry as long as possible—at least 15 minutes. If you must leave the site before the mold dries, carefully dig it up along with the surrounding earth and take it home in a plastic bag. When the cast is solid, remove the plastic collar and clean the dirt from the track with water and a toothbrush. With skill and some luck, you should end up with a good imprint of the animal foot that made the track.

The tracks in the illustration show a five-toed animal with claws that do not retract when it walks. The prints of its front feet alternate with those of its longer hind feet. You may find the same prints in the soft earth of your yard, clues to the presence of that old masked bandit, the raccoon.

The stillness of a lodgepole pine forest (opposite) belies the vitality of the winter woods. Life goes on, adapted to survive the season's rigors. Temperature lowered and metabolism slowed, chipmunks hibernate underground (above, right), waking only now and then to feed on caches of stored food. They and other small rodents are prey for the winter-active bobcat (above).

the sunlight. Monolayering is probably an adaptation to the shady depths of mature forests, in which you have to get what you can at the top. Multilayering is useful in more open environments, and allows the tree to plunder up to two or three square feet of sunlight for every square foot of ground it covers.

Of course the most dramatic difference in strategies I could see in the canopy was between the deciduous and evergreen trees, particularly now that the color had begun and the spruces, hemlocks, and white pines farther down the hill stood out darkly from the flushed crowd. In this matter trees have been compared to investors: The evergreen is conservative—the money-market tree—investing in leaves that last several years, heavily protected by a waxy covering. The deciduous tree is more daring: It puts its entire nutrient bank into building a glamorous new leaf each year that blooms all summer but goes dazzlingly bust in the fall.

I sat up in the factory for two hours. The sun began to fade. The wind died away. The forest became hushed, as if concentrating all its effort on drawing the last energy from the sun. In the still air and silence the leaves quivered.

Suddenly a tree fell. Fifty yards away, beyond my view, an old leaning sugar maple had broken fifteen feet up. The top had fallen to the ground. *Boom!* The crash rang through the woods like a bell. I gripped my hemlock, stunned.

Out there sunlight poured into the new opening, as if a levee had broken. In the understory, the young maples, beeches, spruce trees, and hemlocks felt the full flood of light for the first time. Who would fill the gap? In 20 years I would have to return and see.

I sat in the tree. The crash died away, but the silence that returned was not as quiet to my mind as it had been.

Grasslands

I hate to mow the lawn. It's a wearisome chore I perform under the weight of the summer sun. When the dew lifts, which in my valley in east-central Vermont can be as late as noon, I set my course and begin. The blades spit out pieces of green, green, green—Timothy and Kentucky bluegrass—then a spray of purple, red, and yellow as vetch and hawkweed bow under the mower. A monotonous and seemingly endless wave of green stretches ahead of me, beyond the stone wall and across my neighbor's meadow.

In the eastern third of North America most grasslands are pastures and meadows, ephemeral plant communities that depend on people to survive. Without mowers or livestock they slowly choke. If a hay meadow is left uncut or a pasture ungrazed, a transition community crowded with perennials—goldenrods, milkweeds, asters, fleabanes, cinquefoils, clovers—slowly gives way to other communities and, eventually, to forest monarchs such as sugar maple, beech, and hemlock. I mow a third, nonutilitarian grassland—3,000 square feet of pedigree grasses, carefully bred and randomly planted—which supports my view, enhances my house, and tires my back.

I mow several times a summer, just enough to stem the rising tide of seedling willow and aspen that drift in as seed from the edge of the woods. I've just returned from a trip to the vast grasslands of the West and Midwest, and although it takes me two hours to mow my lawn, I now know it could be much worse. If I had to mow the original North American prairie—more than a million square miles of grass—it would take me about nine million years working steadily for eight hours a day. If I volunteered to add the desert grasslands of the Southwest, the Palouse prairie of southeastern Washington, and the interior grasslands of California, all isolated climax grasslands, I would be busy for another million years. Fortunately, other arrangements were made for maintaining the grasslands—drought and fire and grazing.

Grass has probably been around for 65 million years, appearing about the time mammals scurried out from under the shadow of dinosaurs. Of the 7,500 extant species of grasses, most are characterized by long, narrow, parallel-veined leaves attached alternately to a jointed stem. The base of each leaf wraps around the stem to form a sheath, while the blade spreads out and up from the side of the plant. The stem, or culm, is hollow—except at each joint, or node, where a single leaf originates. On the end of the fertile stem, clusters of

A sulphur butterfly clings to a blade of canary grass in an Iowa meadow. Grassland ecosystems, from the great prairies west of the Mississippi to eastern fields, tend to vary according to soil and climate. Though these regions are dominated by grasses, they support other herbaceous plants and scattered shrubs or trees as well, along with myriad animals—many of them small and well concealed.

tiny, feathery flowers are borne in spikelets. Each spikelet bears one to many pairs of odorless flowers without petals. No frills are needed to attract insects, for grass flowers are attuned to the restless, shifting prairie wind, which posts both their pollen and their seeds.

The characteristics of grasses that allow them to tolerate mowing have allowed them to survive drought, fire, and a galaxy of grazers, from prehistoric horses and mammoths to cows, bison, and prairie dogs, from grasshoppers to microscopic roundworms. Most of the biomass of grass is below the surface. Roots and rhizomes—those creeping, underground stems that send grass sideways into my garden, no matter how many times I yank up the shoots—account for more than 60 percent of the weight of big bluestem, a grass so tall it can hide a man. If placed end to end, the grass roots in a square yard of prairie soil four inches deep might run for up to 20 miles.

With all that underground growth, grass has an advantage over forbs—nongrass herbs such as daisies—whose seeds have trouble penetrating the sod and competing for nutrients and soil moisture. Big bluestem may extend its roots 12 feet down into the prairie soil. Short grasses, which have comparatively deeper roots in relation to their height, can survive two or three years of severe drought. Grasses have ways of conserving water, too. In Kansas I saw the leaves of Canada wild rye and Indian grass rolled into tubes to reduce the surface area exposed to the hot, dry wind. In South Dakota, mats of buffalo grass and blue grama, brown and shriveled, curled close to

Fire, whether ignited by nature or by man, plays a crucial role in maintaining the prairie. Periodic burning (above) clears old growth and invading shrubs and trees, leaving unharmed the deep roots and the buried buds of certain grasses and forbs. Stimulated by the release of nutrients and additional sunlight, prairie vegetation often returns quickly (left), lusher than before.

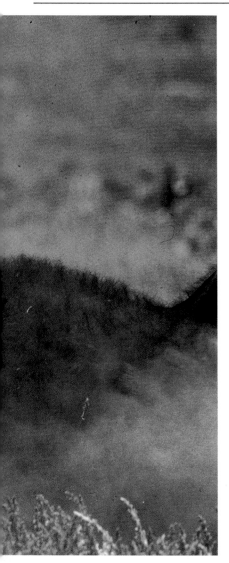

the ground. With rain, all four species of grasses began to uncurl.

In most varieties of flowering plants, meristems—the tissues that produce new stems, leaves, and branches—occur at the tips of growing shoots. Meristems rise with the plant as it grows. In grass, the growth occurs at the *base* of the leaves and stems. New tissue thus pushes the leaves and stems above it higher into the summer sun. Mowing or grazing, which cuts off the growing tips of most plants— and drought, which sears them—leaves grass practically unharmed; the large meristem at the base of the plant, hidden by a blanket of soil, simply sends up new shoots.

Some of my neighbors torch their fields in spring to remove old growth. In doing this, they unknowingly do for their meadows what nature does for the prairie. Fire destroys last year's brown, withered stalks, encouraging the growth of new shoots, while it scorches invading trees and shrubs.

Climax grasslands are prone to burn. Fire is part of their history. By autumn, grass stems and leaves stand brown, dry, and very combustible, while the roots and rhizomes live on underground, insulated below the soil. The Eurasian steppes, the Argentine pampas, the South African veld, the East African plains, and the North American prairies have all been shaped by fire. The older grasslands, such as the African plains, support a few species of trees that have adapted to wildfire. But at 20 million years old, our prairies are the youngest of the great grasslands and are without fire-adapted trees.

Following a decreasing rainfall gradient from east to west, plant geographers divide the prairies into three broad units named according to the height of the dominant grasses. In the east, tallgrass. In the west, shortgrass. Mixed grass, a wide band with boundaries that move west with excessive rain and east with drought, is a broad transition zone. All three prairie types burn, but they burn differently.

When I was a graduate student in west Texas, my fire ecology class burned 800 acres of shortgrass—the grassland in the rain shadow of the Rockies, which extends east across Montana to western North Dakota, and south through the Llano Estacado, or Staked Plain, of

Seeking relief from tormenting flies and mosquitoes, a bison rolls on the mounds of a prairie dog town. Years of bison wallowing have left the prairie pockmarked with shallow basins (left)—which, when filled with rain, serve as watering holes for other kinds of animals.

In this nearly treeless habitat, burrowing owls (right) display adaptations unusual for birds, going underground to nest in deserted prairie dog chambers and badger holes.

Life in a Mixed-grass Prairie

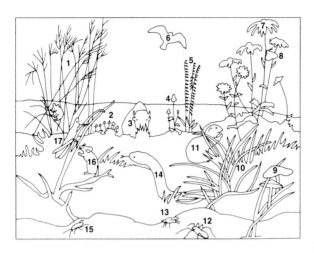

1 Needle-and-thread grass *(Stipa comata)*
2 Purple coneflower *(Echinacea angustifolia)*
3 Bison *(Bison bison)*
4 White prairie clover *(Petalostemon candidum)*
5 Side-oats grama grass *(Bouteloua curtipendula)*
6 Swainson's hawk *(Buteo swainsoni)*
7 Black-eyed Susan *(Rudbeckia hirta)*
8 Painted lady butterfly *(Vanessa cardui)*
9 Fairy ring mushroom *(Marasmius oreades)*
10 Buffalo grass *(Buchloe dactyloides)*
11 Thirteen-lined ground squirrel *(Spermophilus tridecemlineatus)*
12 Grass spider *(Agelenopsis naevia)*
13 Dung fly *(Scatophaga stercoraria)*
14 Bullsnake *(Pituophis melanoleucus)*
15 Field cricket *(Gryllus pennsylvanicus)*
16 Western harvest mouse *(Reithrodontomys megalotis)*
17 Two-striped grasshopper *(Mermiria bivittata)*

Survivors of drought, fire, grazing, and nibbling, a wide variety of sturdy grasses prevail in the mixed-grass prairie. Species such as buffalo grass and side-oats grama grass are favored by grazing animals, including the majestic bison, which once roamed the prairie in vast, thundering herds. The spiky awns on the seeds of needle-and-thread grass may discourage grazers, but not western harvest mice, which feast on the seeds. Some prairie grasses owe their success to the aggressive growth of their roots and rhizomes, which form dense sod virtually impenetrable to other kinds of vegetation.

Common reed

Crested wheatgrass

western Texas. This is dry country, only a heartbeat from desert.

On a cool March morning, with the wind blowing lightly toward a fork of the Brazos River, we lit the grass. The river was to be our firebreak. Flames leaped and raced in twisted orange lines, moving back on themselves with every whoosh of the wind. This shortgrass fire, fed by a scanty source of fuel, did not produce a lot of heat. A horned lizard flattened out as the fire passed over its back, then got up and crawled away. A jackrabbit bounded ahead of the flames, moving at a more leisurely pace than if it had been chased by a predator. Just for the record, I jumped a line of fire.

To some creatures, the fire was a disaster, to others an invitation. Harvest and deer mice lost their cover, grasshoppers their perches, as plumes of smoke alerted red-tailed hawks, turkey vultures, and loggerhead shrikes to the instant vulnerability of their prey. The acrid smell of smoke aroused coyotes. Cholla and prickly pear withered in the heat. Mesquite burned. But a few days later, green tobosa shoots poked through the ash as an overgrazed range was brought back to grass. Even earthworms benefited, increasing their population as the grass increased its production of roots and rhizomes.

On my recent excursion, I saw lightning spark a mixed-grass prairie in South Dakota's Wind Cave National Park. Safely seated in my car, I was watching a thunderhead build above a busy village of black-tailed prairie dogs when the sky suddenly ripped open, and three white flickering shafts like electric harpoons appeared to drive straight down to earth, striking behind a knoll about a half mile from where I was parked. The prairie dogs never stopped feeding, barking, or kissing. Twenty minutes later, after the storm had passed south toward Nebraska, tendrils of smoke rose into the evening sky as fire purified an acre of mixed-grass prairie. The Park Service arrived and extinguished the fire. According to Plains Indian lore, I had just witnessed the calving of a wildfire, the birth of a "Red Buffalo."

Tallgrass prairie, richest in fuel, burns the brightest and hottest. Its deep, black soil, watered by up to 40 inches of rain a year, supports ranks of big bluestem 5 to 10 feet tall, switch grass, and Indian grass that once ran from northwestern Indiana to east Texas and north into Manitoba. Lightning fires stopped forest from advancing along the prairie's eastern front and restricted gallery forests to river valleys. Fueled by tall sun-cured grass and fanned by hot, dry winds, fierce tallgrass fires were arrested only by rivers and by rain.

Driving west on Interstate 70 through the Flint Hills of eastern Kansas, I saw dark green forests covering what had once been tallgrass prairie. Here the Red Buffalo had been slaughtered. Where fire was employed as a range management tool, however, wands of tallgrass replaced the trees. The carpet of black ash that results from a spring prairie fire here absorbs heat and warms the soil, stimulating an early and vigorous growth of grass. Tallgrass that had stood unburned and ungrazed for more than six years was clogged with standing dead vegetation and was only half as productive as burned sites.

As much as I dislike mowing, setting fire to my lawn is not a

Foxtail barley

Most grasslands support dozens of grass species, depending in part on the availability of moisture. Foxtail barley, a relative of domesticated barley, grows like a weed on wet prairies. Bristlegrass thrives in sites disturbed by human activity. The cosmopolitan common reed favors moist environments, such as marshes or the banks of lakes and streams. Adapted to survive periodic droughts, crested wheatgrass grows on cool, dry prairies.

Bristlegrass

A young black-tailed prairie dog nuzzles a watchful adult (opposite) on the earthen roof of their underground town. Ever alert to predators such as night-prowling bobcats, coyotes, and badgers (above), prairie dogs stay close to home, ready to dive for cover into a convenient hole. Prairie dogs collectively excavate elaborate burrows, constantly digging and repairing their subterranean lairs (above, right), which can extend for hundreds of acres and house thousands of animals. The labyrinths include grass-lined nesting chambers that serve as both sleeping quarters and nurseries, as well as turning bays, which provide refuge from hawks, eagles, and other daytime predators.

consideration. My house, pine with cedar shingles, is crisp and dry, sits in the middle of the lawn, and would flare in a second. There are safer, less tiring ways to keep the grass short. My wife suggests sheep or goats, maybe dairy cattle. I prefer bison, but with only 3,000 square feet of grass, my yard would soon be pulverized by their hoofs.

After trailing a herd of 200 bison around Wind Cave National Park for two weeks, I can unequivocally say that having "a home where the buffalo roam" would be difficult and dangerous, especially in July and August during the rut. Bison are large—some bulls weigh more than a ton—unpredictable, and fast. They can reach speeds of 35 miles per hour.

Bison society has a matriarchal bent. During most of the year, females and young form large nomadic groups that wander across the plains, grazing and resting, never staying too long in any one spot—which is just fine for prairie grasses because this gives them the opportunity to regrow. Mature males are solitary or, at best, loosely associated, except during the rutting season.

I always kept watch for wayfaring bulls, for they would appear out of nowhere, lumbering up from a crease in the prairie or from the shadow of a ponderosa pine. I learned to plot escape routes and to recognize a good climbing pine in case I had to get off the ground in a hurry. If a bull headed toward me, I moved. I'm not proud. Or fast. Out of sight, out of mind was my motto. Fortunately, just ducking below the horizon, down a gentle prairie undulation, would make the bison lose interest in me.

When bison rut, the plains tremble. Their collective voice, wafting on the prairie breeze, can be heard for miles. A park ranger told me that at least once a summer an irate camper, rudely awakened, reports loud snoring neighbors.

Lines of excited bulls, three or four, sometimes more, attach themselves to each ripe cow. She's like an uncommitted Pied Piper, paying no attention to the male train behind her. The bulls are consumed with a single purpose—mating. They bellow and wallow and fight to determine who gets breeding privileges. The readier the

North America's swiftest mammals, pronghorn bound across the prairie. Adapted to a browsing life in open country, their long legs and large heart and lung capacity enable them to cruise tirelessly for miles in search of forage and, when danger threatens, to sprint at more than 50 miles an hour. Especially vulnerable to predators, a fawn (left) knows instinctively to hide while its mother grazes a short distance away.

cow, the louder a bull bellows, sticking out his long, fat, black tongue while making a noise that sounds like an airplane full of sick passengers. And the louder bulls bellow, the more they wallow.

A wallowing bull flops on his side, legs flailing spastically in the air, raising a smoke screen of brown prairie dust. Bison cannot roll over. The hump of a mature bull is shaped by neural spines, large vertical processes that rise from the thoracic vertebrae to anchor the enormous neck muscles that hold its huge head erect; the spines get in the way of a complete roll. A wallowing bull rolls up to his hump, then helplessly rocks back.

Wallows are naked depressions in an otherwise continuous mantle of prairie grass. Some are used over and over for generations until the soil is so compacted they become temporary pools during the spring rains. When vegetation reclaims an abandoned wallow, shallow-rooted forbs—which can penetrate the hard, compacted soil—often take over, not grasses. I saw old wallows in the Flint Hills that still maintain their shape, dimpling the land a century after the last bison kicked up his heels there. After all those years, tallgrass has still not moved in: It stops at the edge, while forbs, sedges, and shorter grasses fill the basins.

The more the bulls wallowed, it seemed, the more they fought. Except for earthquakes and volcanoes, nothing in North America rivals the force and power of rutting bison. Two bulls charge, generally from a short distance—like opposing football linemen—and crack their thick, flat triangular faces together, raising a thunderhead of dust. I watched one bull drive his 2,000-pound antagonist back 40 yards at a speed faster than I could sprint. It was as though nothing was in front of the bison. Nothing.

I found an articulated bison skeleton on the plains, an old bull with grass-worn teeth. Calcified ribs marked the site of an old injury, and several cervical vertebrae had fused together in an arthritic lump. The vertebrae, compressed under the enormous force of shoving bouts, and the ribs, broken when a contestant's head had rammed the bull's side, testified to the power of the procreative urge.

Besides tearing up the grassland with their fighting and compacting the soil at wallows, bison wear footpaths through the prairies as the herd follows ancestral routes from one grazing site or water hole to the next. The prairies at Wind Cave are crisscrossed with red-brown lines that mark the paths of roaming herds. A dozen years ago in South Dakota's Badlands National Park, I wandered off a park trail and onto a bison trail that was so wide and so well cut that I hiked for several miles before I realized my error.

Bison have positive effects on grasslands, too. During the rut, they unleash their aggression on invading ponderosa pines, thrashing and gouging off the bark with their horns and sometimes breaking the small trees in half. Wherever a mammal urinates and defecates, nutrients are added to the soil. Both bison and their domestic analogue, cattle, constantly add nitrogen to grasslands, improving the growth of grasses. Studies have shown that both animals

prefer to feed on greener, more nutritious tufts of grass—tufts fertilized with their own nitrogenous wastes.

Because grasslands are uniform habitats—compared to a stratified deciduous forest, for instance, with its varying heights and branch patterns—they support a less diversified group of animals and plants. What prairies lack in diversity, however, they make up for in numbers. In addition to an estimated 40 million roving, snorting bison, the interior grasslands of the early 1800s probably supported about the same number of pronghorn. A single prairie dog town that stretched across 25,000 square miles of Texas around 1900 housed more than 400 million prairie dogs. In the mid-1900s, an average square mile of mixed-grass prairie near Fort Hays, Kansas, contained 2,462 prairie voles per square mile, 1,952 thirteen-lined ground squirrels, 1,728 deer mice, 716 plains harvest mice, 614 least shrews, 337 short-tailed shrews, and 185 black-tailed jackrabbits.

All of these animals eat and scatter seeds. Jackrabbit pellets I found in South Dakota held fertile seeds. According to one study, seeds that travel this route are more likely to germinate than seeds merely freighted by the wind. West Kansas jackrabbits are credited with depositing almost eight pounds of seeds per acre each October.

The bison is also an agent of seed dispersal, as awned, barbed, and sticky seeds hook into its thick mane and chaps. I examined mats of wool that littered a popular wallow: Each was festooned with seeds.

Bison, pronghorn, and black-tailed prairie dogs, the three most visible grazers at Wind Cave, have an interesting feeding alliance that contributes to the diversity of mixed-grass and shortgrass prairies. The herd of bison that I trailed often lingered at the edge of a dog town, grazing the newer, softer, nitrogen-rich shoots that had been clipped by grazing prairie dogs. Of course, the converse is true also: Prairie dogs benefit from grazing bison. Pronghorn, however, prefer browse. They select forbs and dwarf shrubs over grasses, visiting the center of old overgrazed dog towns where grass has lost its competitive edge. These sites are gray-blue with fringed sage and Louisiana sagewort, favorite pronghorn foods.

The distinctive handiwork of spiders decorates grasslands and meadows, each web type designed to trap a particular kind of food. Orb weavers spin their wheel-like webs on tall supports, such as wild parsnip (opposite), to snare flying insects. The low-slung hammocks of sheet-web spiders (above left, middle and bottom) catch leaping and flying insects with silken scaffolding threads. The funnel webs of grass spiders (above left, top) similarly trap insects on a blanket of silk that covers a funnel, where the spider waits in ambush.

FOLLOWING PAGES: Rays of sunshine break through a meadow glade. Distinguished as moist grasslands within a forest belt, meadows occur in areas deforested by humans and other animals, as well as in places where natural physical factors, such as flooding or salt accumulation, prohibit forest development. Where forest has been cleared, grazing and mowing keep trees at bay.

My lawn is too small for even a hundred-pound pronghorn, but it does support a legion of grasshoppers, particularly Carolina locusts, which rise from the grass like popcorn from a hot skillet as I press forward with the mower. Actually, grasshoppers consume more grass than all the other aboveground grazers combined. Only root-hungry nematodes—microscopic roundworms whose populations number in the millions per square foot—eat more grass. I'm not sure how many species of grasshoppers live in Vermont, but the more extensive the grassland, the greater the variety found there. No state in the prairie region has fewer than a hundred species. Kansas alone entertains about three hundred.

During a dry summer—which favors grasshoppers—there may be as many as 30 individuals per square yard. At that density, an acre of grasshoppers can consume as much grass as a bison. When successive years of drought have scattered bird predators and inhibited grasshopper disease, Rocky Mountain locusts—migratory grasshoppers that periodically plagued the prairies during the last century—have been recorded at densities of 1,000 per square yard. One living cloud, measured with surveying instruments, hit Nebraska on a 100-mile front that was a mile high and 30 miles deep.

Rocky Mountain locusts have been extinct for more than 80 years, but there are still plenty of prairie grasshoppers to watch, some as big as mice. Green and brown and slow grasshoppers. Red grasshoppers and gray grasshoppers. Striped grasshoppers. In South Dakota, I even saw my old friend the Carolina locust, part of an assemblage of insects that cut, nip, drain, saw, chew, and mine the leaves of grasses and forbs. I turned my binoculars around, using them as a magnifying lens, and looked through the wide end at the busy and careless world of grasshoppers. Some species ate just grass, others just forbs. They sliced through the greenery with sharp, sliding mandibles that moved from side to side—the left always overlapping the right—dropping as much as they ate.

I grabbed a fat lubber off some needlegrass and held him firmly in my hand as he scratched against my palm with spiked feet—the desperate kicks of the dispossessed. At three inches, this grasshopper was a handful. I finally understood how kestrels can subsist on grasshoppers; an early morning lubber, heavy with dew and stiff with cold, is easy prey for the robin-size falcon. Once or twice a day I spotted a kestrel peeling off the tough exoskeleton of a fat lubber.

"Tobacco juice," a grasshopper's last line of defense, dribbled from the lubber's mouth, staining my fingers an inky brown. He could not fly away from me; this species' wings have atrophied and no longer function as organs of flight. He just kicked and scraped and twisted in my hand, a corkscrew with a shell. I placed him on the ground, and he bounded away with short little hops.

My late summer mowing does more than just displace the Carolina locusts; it disrupts their mating rituals. Two or three feet above the lawn, male grasshoppers hover on long, broad black wings edged with yellow along the rear. A slow buzzing sound made by the

Apparently empty of wildlife at first glance, a meadow reveals its hidden life on closer scrutiny. Above, a katydid matches the leaves of the plants on which it lives, its camouflage concealing it from predatory birds, snakes, and frogs. Inconspicuous in the cup of a milkweed leaf, a gray treefrog (opposite, upper) can sit motionless for hours awaiting its unsuspecting prey. The crystallized breath of mice frosts a patch of grass (opposite, lower), betraying the entrance to a burrow.

vibrating wings fills the air—a sound altogether different from the fiddling a male grasshopper makes by rubbing projections on its hind leg against a scraper on its wings. Both sounds attract females and other males that compete for the attention of the ripe females. Whenever a grasshopper lands, three or four others move toward it. If I get too close, they snap into the air.

I have never visited a prairie in late summer, but I imagine it rocking to the tune of grasshoppers. This music may have accompanied the age of dinosaurs. Nowhere is the chorus louder than in grasslands. From egg to egg, the chorusing insects hop the length of their days under the high suns of a single season. Last year's eggs hatch when the prairie grows warm, each nymph a wingless miniature replica of its parents. The young add size and wings as the grasses ripen, and now, as the maple blushes, they scrape and scratch those wings until silenced by frost.

As animals influence the development of grass, grass molds the evolution of animals. Each species is a distillate of the action its environment has had on its anatomy, physiology, and behavior. Most grasses contain silica—the abrasive ingredient in sand—which stiffens their long, narrow leaves. Silica also erodes teeth and is difficult to digest, so only certain animals can eat grass. To graze, mammals need strong, resistant teeth. From horses to voles, grass-eaters show a similar dental pattern: the presence of high-crowned teeth with alternating folds of dentine and enamel—teeth resistant to erosion. Grasshoppers that cut grass have bulkier mandibles than those that cut forbs. It's like comparing wire cutters with scissors.

After teeth chew up the tough, fibrous grass, a specialized stomach and intestine digest it. Only microbes can digest cellulose, the principal component of cell walls. My neighbor's cows and sheep swallow grass, let it ferment in the first chamber of their four-chambered stomachs, then spit up the cud, chew it, and reprocess it. Jackrabbits eat soft, bacteria-filled fecal pellets directly from their anuses, recycling the microbes back into their stomachs. Vole intestines expand and fill with symbiotic bacteria and protozoa.

The shape and behavior of a prairie animal are clues to its long association with grass. Rattlesnakes, products of the High Plains, as American as apple pie, evolved amid rivers of prehistoric bison and pronghorn, horses and camels. One theory holds that the resonators they developed—loosely attached keratin rattles at the end of their tails—helped them avoid being stepped on. The trick works. I've seen horses flinch when a rattler, hidden in tallgrass, began its song. I, too, take the buzzing at face value, back up, and walk around.

Without trees for shelter, many small mammals have become

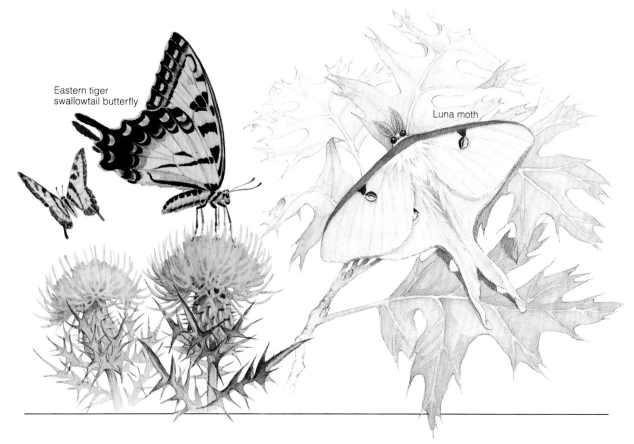

Eastern tiger swallowtail butterfly

Luna moth

adept at burrowing. The tunnels of ground squirrels, prairie dogs (a type of ground squirrel), pocket gophers, and mice protect them from most predators. Rodents asleep in their burrows have little to fear except badgers, which are the fastest, strongest diggers of all, and weasels and bullsnakes, both of which prowl below the ground. Last spring I watched a seven-foot bullsnake emerge into the California sun, its sides swollen with ground squirrels. I counted four separate bulges. An entire family, I suspect.

Burrows also provide a constant environment that protects the inhabitants from fire and from prairie weather, which swings from boiling hot to frigid. Western spadefoot toads spend the hot, dry summer in tiny burrows dug with the horny tubercles on their hind feet. The gopher tortoise, too, is a burrower. Even larger animals, coyotes and swift foxes, dig deep whelping dens in the prairie soil. All this digging, by all these diggers, loosens and aerates the grassland soil, offsetting compaction from the hoofs of grazers.

If you cannot dig, you can always freeload. Gopher tortoises share their burrows with cottontails, opossums, eastern diamondback rattlesnakes, indigo snakes, gopher frogs, and Florida mice. The roster of animals that live in prairie dog towns is long. I watched desert cottontails on the edge of dog towns take refuge in abandoned burrows whenever the dogs were alarmed. I saw a bullsnake and a western rattlesnake sunning on the lips of two different prairie dog mounds. When I ventured too close, they disappeared down the tunnel as though inhaled by the earth.

Another adaptation among grassland animals is running. Clocked for short bursts at close to 60 miles per hour, the pronghorn is the fastest mammal in the Western Hemisphere. Its lungs and windpipe are oversize for deep, fast breathing; its large heart, twice as big as that of a domestic sheep, quickly pumps oxygenated blood through its body. Its huge, wide-set eyes have excellent peripheral vision and see eight times more detail than our own. I never caught pronghorn unawares. As soon as they saw me, their semaphore rumps, flashing white like giant powder puffs, broadcast my presence.

Swift foxes reach speeds of 25 miles per hour, jackrabbits 33 miles per hour, and coyotes 40 miles per hour. Among snakes, coachwhips and racers are fast, diurnal predators, which often cross my car's path as I slowly drive prairie back roads. In the tallgrass of east Kansas, I saw collared lizards rear up on their hind legs to run from danger. Greater roadrunners prefer to run. So do northern bobwhites and ring-necked pheasants, depending on the nature of the threat.

The social system of black-tailed prairie dogs is a response to life on the plains, where a thousand pairs of eyes are better than one. Nepotism is the order of business in prairie dog towns. Each town is divided into family groups called coteries, which usually consist of a male, several females, and their pups, all living together in a labyrinthine burrow. I watched coterie members kiss when they met, saw them play and groom and squeal with exuberance, leaping high in the air as though sprung from a trampoline. Except when danger

Common denizens of meadowlands, moths and butterflies belong to the order Lepidoptera, which includes insects with scale-covered wings. Certain characteristics tend to distinguish the two types of insects. At rest, most butterflies hold their wings above their bodies, while moths usually spread theirs flat. Slim and smooth-bodied, butterflies have knob-tipped antennae. Moths, stouter and furry, tend to have feathery antennae without knobs. While most butterflies conduct their business by day—recognizing mates by wing patterns and colors—most moths are nocturnal and dull-colored, relying on the long-distance sensing of chemicals rather than visual stimuli to locate mates.

1

2

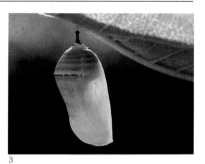

3

4

5

6

Unlike creatures that hatch from eggs as miniature adults, the butterfly undergoes a miraculous metamorphosis: From the time it leaves the egg as a tiny caterpillar, or larva, the monarch spends its first few weeks devouring buds and leaves, periodically shedding its skin to accommodate its rapid growth. When it reaches maturity, the larva finds a sheltered place, such as a leaf or twig. There it spins a silk "button," to which it attaches itself by hooks on its abdomen (1). After molting for the last time (2), the monarch becomes a soft pupa, or chrysalis (3), the skin of which soon hardens into a protective shell. The chrysalis hangs motionless for 9 to 15 days. Inside the shell, the monarch completes its transformation, the larval body dissolved and refashioned into a butterfly, visible through the pupa shell (4). When the mature monarch is ready to emerge (5), the shell cracks and the monarch works its way out head first, its wings moist and crumpled. Hanging upside down (6), it pumps fluid through its wings to expand them. Then, once its wings have hardened (left), it sails off for life as a butterfly.

Sepal
Petal
Stamen — Anther / Filament
Pistil — Stigma / Style / Ovary

Flowers typically consist of four main parts (above): Sepals, often green and leaflike, protectively enclose the petals in the bud stage. Stamens, or male reproductive organs, make the pollen used to fertilize the ovules, which are produced by the female organ, or pistil. Flowering plants reproduce sexually through pollination—the transfer of pollen from stamen to pistil, which allows fertilization to occur. Some plants self-pollinate, but most require wind, insects, or birds to carry pollen from one flower to another. Animal agents feed on particular flowers, attracted by their odors or colors. Busy pollinators, bees have a keen sense of smell that leads them to fragrant blossoms. As they feed, pollen grains stick to their bodies, traveling with them to other flowers. Hummingbirds, drawn to red and orange blossoms such as those of the wild lily (opposite), carry pollen from flower to flower on their long bills as they gather nectar.

threatens—when a badger or coyote appears, for instance—coterie members drive unrelated prairie dogs away from their burrows.

Prairie dogs have one alarm call for coyotes, another for golden eagles. When a coyote appeared one afternoon on the edge of a Wind Cave dog town, alarm calls spread until everyone was alerted; those prairie dogs closest to the coyote dived into the nearest burrows; those farther away stood erect and watched. The coyote kicked up a cloud of dust as it ran across town, stopping here and there to sniff and paw at the ground. For the moment, the dog town was a ghost town—hundreds of prairie dogs, silent and hidden. A town gripped by a demon. A town in need of an exorcist. Then the coyote left. With periscope eyes set high on their heads, prairie dogs peeked from their burrows. Assured that the coast was clear, a dog barked. Another and another, until a discordant babble filled the air.

Birds, too, have been affected by the grasslands. In breeding sites where food is so abundant that females can feed their young without the help of males, the members of some species are polygynous. Male red-winged blackbirds, bobolinks, eastern and western meadowlarks, lark buntings, dickcissels, and marsh hawks spread their seed to several females. Because perches are scarce, many prairie birds sing from the air. The haunting song of the upland sandpiper followed me from the prairies of South Dakota to Kansas. I came to expect the notes at dawn as one expects the rising sun. For me, it was the voice of the prairie, no less thrilling than bellowing bison.

Fruiting heads of long-plumed purple avens waft in the spring breeze (opposite). In profusion, these members of the Rose family resemble a haze of purple-gray; hence their other name—prairie smoke.

Another sign of springtime, a greater prairie-chicken (above)— lively resident of the tallgrass prairie—performs his spectacular, noisy courtship dance on a communal display ground, or lek.

Not all grassland birds perform in the air. More than a dozen years ago, I crouched in the dark and cold in a blind on the Texas Panhandle waiting for lesser prairie-chickens. Male prairie-chickens—both the lesser, a denizen of shortgrass, and the greater, at home in tallgrass—gather before dawn, when the wind is still, to boom and strut. To the west, the sky was black; to the east, gray-blue. A meadowlark sang. I strained my eyes, trying to resolve shadowy silhouettes of bunch grass into bulbous prairie-chickens. Suddenly, a robust, dull brown, streaked bird walked in front of the blind, not 15 feet away, and began stamping his feet. Then he leaned over, raising and fanning his tail and slightly lowering his wings. The stiff feathers on his neck stood up, and a pair of plum-colored gular sacs on each side of his throat filled with cool Texas air as hollow notes rolled out across the shortgrass. Booming had begun. Half an hour later, 12 other prairie-chickens, each evenly spaced from its neighbor, had joined in. Together their booming rolled like distant thunder. When the sun rose and the wind picked up, the dance ended.

Prairie forbs have also been shaped by long association with grass. Purple prairie clover drives a taproot six feet through the sod, spreading most of its branches at the lower end of the root to avoid direct competition with the network of tallgrass roots that crowd the upper level of the soil. The knee-high purple coneflowers have eight-foot unbranched taproots, and compass plants prospect for water and nutrients straight down fourteen feet.

Some forbs discourage browsers with chemical warfare: the bitter juice of milkweed, for example. Others, such as bluestem prickly poppy, have spines or stiff hairs. The leaves of rattlesnake master, reinforced along the margins and veins with tough lignified cells, tax the biting power of insects. Grasshoppers and caterpillars, whose mandibles slide from side to side, not up and down, have difficulty cutting through these leaves.

As I follow the mower around the house, I see bits and pieces of the interior grasslands that have followed travelers—native and European—to the East's lilliputian prairies. Black-eyed Susan and blue-eyed grass, both prairie forbs, grew more abundant with the clearing of the deciduous woods. So did cowbirds, which fly up from the lawn at the sound of the mower. Their commitment to the avian foster parent program—laying their eggs in the nests of other birds, which then incubate the eggs and fledge the chicks—once freed them to follow the wandering herds of bison that stirred up insects and seeds for them to eat. So closely tied were the two that Plains Indians knew them as buffalo birds.

I saw cowbirds milling around bison in the mixed-grass prairies of South Dakota. I see them milling around cows at home in Vermont. They're in my yard, across the meadow, and in the pasture, plump little birds that watch me push my mower across the lawn with the attention they once lavished on the hulking bison. Then here they come to follow my mechanical bison, which emits its own sexless, Saturday morning bellowing.

By David Rains Wallace

Deserts

After walking up the canyon at Willow Spring for less than an hour, I found myself gravitating to its south side, where a cliff cast a narrow band of shade. The April morning sun already felt like a caustic substance on my skin. I crouched gratefully against the cool stone and squinted at the blazing expanse of desert scrub covering the canyon's north side. Here in central Arizona's Tonto National Forest, the classic Sonoran Desert vegetation of saguaro cactus and paloverde was near its northern limit, but that didn't seem to blunt its thorny vitality.

Although people associate giant saguaros with American deserts, these cactuses do not extend far into the United States. The Sonoran, the only place where they grow, stretches from Mexico's Sonora State and Baja California peninsula to the lowlands of south-central Arizona and extreme southeastern California. Different plant communities—those of the Great Basin, Chihuahuan, and Mojave Deserts—cover a vast area to the north and east. They contain no giant cactuses and few large shrubs. Saguaro, paloverde, and many other Sonoran species cannot survive the cold winters. These other American deserts are also drier, being separated from the oceans by high mountains or long distances. Like all true deserts, the Sonoran averages no more than ten inches of rain a year and has a high rate of evaporation. But parts of it get both winter rain from Pacific storms and summer rain from moist air off the Gulf of Mexico. This two-season rainfall and consistently warm climate contribute to an unusual diversity of desert-adapted life. The Sonoran is North America's richest desert—and an alluring place for a naturalist.

The canyon, about 40 miles north of Phoenix, was living up to the Sonoran's reputation for biotic wealth. A steady rain had fallen the week before, and the canyon's creek was running copiously. A lush carpet of bunch grass, yellow monkey flower, and Indian paintbrush covered the banks, and patches of owl clover, gilia, lupine, and desert marigold still bloomed on the higher ground. Red and yellow blossoms covered chollas and prickly pears, and the saguaros were beginning to bud at their tops. Their waxy white blooms would appear in a few weeks.

At least three thriving generations of saguaros covered the canyon's north side. Many-branched, 40-foot-tall giants must have been well over a century old, since it takes a saguaro that long to

Traces of a rabbit in the sands of Death Valley, California, belie the myth of the desert as an empty wasteland. Thousands of species of plants and animals have adapted to the harsh environment of North America's deserts, among them mammals such as rabbits, mice, and shrews. Active mainly in the cool of night, these creatures often leave signs for the alert observer.

reach full maturity. Olive green columns about half as tall as the giants and half their age were just putting out their first branches. A third group of saguaros, roughly 45 years old, was unbranched and stood about 10 feet tall. The distinct generations probably represented years of ideal weather conditions and low rodent populations, when many saguaro seedlings were able to survive. The big mature cactuses produce great numbers of seeds—an average of almost 450,000 a year—but insects, rodents, and birds usually eat most of them. Woodrats and other animals even eat the spiky seedlings. Only one in about 40 million seeds eventually replaces its parent. Because the species yields so many seeds and lives for so long, however, it manages to propagate new generations.

The saguaros rose from the dense matrix of small trees and shrubs in which these cactuses usually grow. Spreading paloverde trees formed an open, lacy canopy above leathery-leaved jojoba, spiky ocotillo, and bristling patches of other common cactuses, such as cholla and prickly pear. This wiry tangle wasn't confined to the protected canyon. The silvery columns of the saguaros, deceptively soft-looking in the distance, stretched far up the red granite peaks through which the canyon led.

The saguaros looked as though they had always been part of the landscape. Yet the cliff above me told a different story. Red mudstone topped with layers of gray volcanic rock showed that this place had once been a lake full of sediment, then a scene of volcanic activity, of lava flows and ashfalls. From what I knew of past climates in the Southwest, it seemed likely that woodland or grassland had surrounded the lake and volcano rather than the present Sonoran Desert scrub, which developed only recently in geologic time—since the end of the last glaciation some 12,000 years ago. The region was cooler and wetter before that, and the vegetation lusher.

When I left the cliff's shade and continued up-canyon, I was surprised at the abundance of wildlife in and around the creek. Topknotted Gambel's quail fussed everywhere in the scrub, and the air was seldom without the headlong flight of mourning and white-winged doves. Male Costa's hummingbirds sounded like steaming teakettles as they swooped in mating display, flashing the iridescent purple feathers of their throats and crowns. The plain green female hummingbirds fed busily at the scarlet paintbrush blossoms. Gila woodpeckers and gilded flickers sailed among the saguaros, looking

A rare snow dusts giant saguaros in Arizona's Sonoran Desert. Models of successful adaptation, these cactuses have shallow roots and expandable skins that enable them to absorb water after rain or snow. They hoard it in their large, spongelike trunks, accumulating as much as several tons. Tough and hardy, saguaros can live up to 200 years and grow to heights of 50 feet.

Desert Life by Day

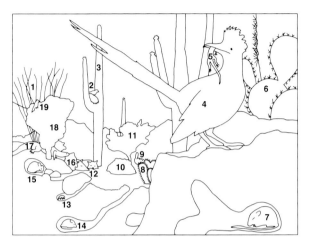

1 Ocotillo
(*Fouquieria splendens*)

2 Harris' hawk
(*Parabuteo unicinctus*)

3 Giant saguaro
(*Carnegiea gigantea*)

4 Greater roadrunner
(*Geococcyx californianus*)

5 Zebra-tailed lizard
(*Callisaurus draconoides*)

6 Prickly pear cactus
(*Opuntia phaeacantha*)

7 Desert pocket mouse
(*Perognathus penicillatus*)

8 Hedgehog cactus
(*Echinocereus fasciculatus*)

9 Harris' antelope squirrel
(*Ammospermophilus harrisii*)

10 Jimsonweed
(*Datura wrightii*)

11 Foothill paloverde
(*Cercidium microphyllum*)

12 Collared peccary
(*Tayassu tajacu*)

13 Desert tarantula
(*Aphonopelma chalcodes*)

14 Merriam's kangaroo rat (*Dipodomys merriami*)

15 White-throated woodrat (pack rat)
(*Neotoma albigula*)

16 Brittlebush
(*Encelia farinosa*)

17 Chuckwalla
(*Sauromalus obesus*)

18 Teddy bear cholla
(*Opuntia bigelovii*)

19 Cactus wren
(*Campylorhynchus brunneicapillus*)

Birds, lizards, and heat-tolerant mammals dominate the daytime world of the Sonoran Desert. These animals tend to seek shade at midday, hunting or foraging only in the morning or late afternoon. The roadrunner, with its sturdy legs and feet shaped like an X, sprints at speeds of up to 15 miles per hour in pursuit of zebra-tailed lizards and other prey. Cactus wrens search for beetles; Harris' hawks scan the desert floor. After a meal of prickly pear or tubers, collared peccaries bed down in the soil, while such rodents as pocket mice and woodrats remain in the cool of their middens and burrows.

Desert Life by Night

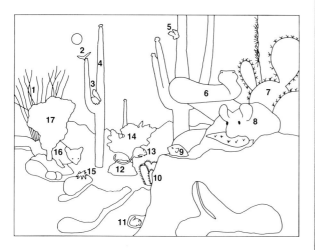

1 Ocotillo
(*Fouquieria splendens*)

2 Sanborn's long-nosed bat (*Leptonycteris sanborni*)

3 Harris' hawk (*Parabuteo unicinctus*)

4 Giant saguaro (*Carnegiea gigantea*)

5 Elf owl (*Micrathene whitneyi*)

6 Western diamond-back rattlesnake (*Crotalus atrox*)

7 Prickly pear cactus (*Opuntia phaeacantha*)

8 White-throated woodrat (pack rat) (*Neotoma albigula*)

9 Desert pocket mouse (*Perognathus penicillatus*)

10 Hedgehog cactus (*Echinocereus fasciculatus*)

11 Harris' antelope squirrel (*Ammospermophilus harrisii*)

12 Jimsonweed (*Datura wrightii*)

13 Merriam's kanga-roo rat (*Dipodomys merriami*)

14 Foothill paloverde (*Cercidium microphyllum*)

15 Desert tarantula (*Aphonopelma chalcodes*)

16 Ringtail (*Bassariscus astutus*)

17 Teddy bear cholla (*Opuntia bigelovii*)

The desert at night belongs to reptiles, rodents, and other creatures that are roused from their tunnels and dens by darkness and lower temperatures. A western diamondback rattlesnake poises to strike a woodrat nibbling on a prickly pear. Near a night-blooming jimsonweed, a kangaroo rat leaps into mid-air, its keen ears detecting the sound of predators. The diminutive elf owl hunts for scorpions and centipedes, while the catlike ringtail, a relative of the raccoon, ambushes a desert tarantula—one that has crawled from its burrow to feed on insects revealed by the light of the moon.

Enduring the heat of a scorching sun presents a great challenge to desert animals. The kit fox (right) and jackrabbit (below) have evolved similar adaptive features: nocturnal habits and oversize ears that radiate excess body heat. By day, these creatures lie low in the shade of a rock, plant, or den; by night, they hunt or forage, their scooplike ears serving to augment their hearing. Opposite, a chuckwalla seeks the safety and shade of a rock crevice at midday. Like other diurnal lizards, members of this species change their skin color during the day from dark to light, to reflect the sun's rays.

for likely sites for nest holes (a search they conduct at least once each breeding season), or trying to protect the ones they had made from being usurped by one of the 14 other bird species that nest in saguaros. In the scrub below, glossy black phainopeplas, cardinals, cactus wrens, mockingbirds, and curve-billed thrashers darted about on nesting errands. Turkey vultures, ravens, and red-tailed hawks circled overhead.

Other animals were equally numerous. Lizards were everywhere: Tree lizards sprawled on boulders; western whiptails slithered through the grass; zebra-tailed lizards scuttled over the sand with their banded tails curled over their backs. Some earless lizards were gorgeously colored, with pink throats, blue bellies, and sides dotted with pink and orange and barred with black and yellow. Desert cottontails bounced out of the shade of mesquite trees on creek-bottom flats. Numerous trotter marks on the creek sand indicated the presence of a band of collared peccaries, the piglike creatures that range from South America into our Southwest.

The creek water was full of aquatic insects—striders, backswimmers, water bugs, and beetles—and of smaller creatures such as mites and copepods. There was even an abundance of hydras, the tentacled freshwater relatives of jellyfish that one often encounters in biology textbooks. This pale brown species, about an eighth of an inch long, attached itself to plants and rocks to wait for small animals to swim within reach of its tentacles.

I hadn't expected to find hydras in the desert. As far as the creek's aquatic creatures were concerned, it seemed, the canyon might as well have been in forest as in desert. While I camped there during the next two weeks, however, I saw that this abundance was not a permanent feature. It arose largely from the seasonal presence of

Capacious saguaros provide a spine-guarded shelter for nesting western screech-owls—and prime birding sites for naturalists. Bluebirds, cactus wrens, pygmy-owls, Lucy's warblers, and ash-throated flycatchers also nest or take refuge in saguaros, often in cavities originally excavated by woodpeckers. Within such holes, temperatures on hot days can be 20°F cooler than outside air and 20°F warmer on cool nights. A saguaro's massive arms—and the bedding of an abandoned hawk's nest—help protect the eggs of a great horned owl (above), as well as its young, from marauding rodents, snakes, and other birds.

surface water. When the creek dried up in the summer (its level fell noticeably in the two rainless weeks I was there), much life would disappear. Many birds would emigrate, having fledged their young. Water bugs and beetles would fly away in search of other waters, while the copepods and hydras would remain only in the form of eggs and cysts in the dry creek bed. Similarly, many of the wildflowers would persist only as seeds or underground roots and stems.

At its seasonal peak of activity, the canyon was a good place to see some of the ways that desert creatures adapt to their harsh environment. So much was happening that I was kept busy finding and observing wildlife with the binoculars, headlamp, hand lens, and field guides I had brought in my backpack.

My time in the canyon became an object lesson on the basics of desert life—on the need to get water and on the equally pressing need to keep from losing it to the sun's evaporative power. Even the most adapted desert organisms require water to carry on respiration, photosynthesis, and other life processes. They simply get and keep it more efficiently than do transient desert organisms, such as the migratory birds and annual wildflowers that dodge the desert's heat and dryness by living in it only when seasonal water is available.

Some of the adaptations of full-time desert organisms are extraordinary for their ingenuity. Mesquite, a small tree common in the Sonoran, has been known to put its roots down 160 feet into the ground to reach water, an impressive depth for a tree that usually grows no more than 30 feet above ground. A stout root protruding near the foot of a cliff probably belonged to a small mesquite at the top of the 30-foot height. With its delicate pale green foliage and small spikes of creamy blossoms, the mesquite hardly seemed powerful enough to break through rock. Saguaro roots, on the other hand, form a wide, shallow mat that fills much of the space around them. Whenever it rains, this mat rapidly absorbs the water as it sinks into the soil, thus taking full advantage of the annual rainfall.

Birds that live in deserts year-round have high tolerance for heat and aridity, even those that belong to species not usually considered desert-adapted. With their relatively high body temperatures, birds expend less energy cooling themselves than do mammals. Mourning doves, common in most North American habitats, can lose body moisture amounting to 20 percent of their weight without ill effect and can drink enough to replace the loss within five to ten minutes. (That's like a 160-pound man downing more than three gallons of water.) Gambel's quail can lose moisture equaling half their body weight and recover. Though they will drink water when it is available, they can manage without it, getting all the moisture they need by eating succulent vegetation.

Many desert mammals, too, drink only rarely or not at all, fulfilling their water needs from food. Woodrats take moisture from cactus pulp, while the kangaroo rat can subsist on a diet of dry seeds. During digestion, the starch in the seeds breaks down chemically into hydrogen and oxygen, some of which recombines into the hydrogen and oxygen molecules of water. The rat's digestive system then absorbs the water.

Compared with other animals, the kangaroo rat loses very little water through respiration or excretion, and it spends hot, dry periods in its cool, moist burrow, loosely plugging the entrances with soil. Its exhaled breath and the moisture from the soil serve to humidify the burrow.

Similarly, the ability of saguaros to absorb scarce rainwater rapidly is reinforced by adaptations that allow them to hold it. Their fluted stems expand like accordions for water storage, and the waxy cuticle covering their spongy water-holding tissues permits little evaporation. This cuticle is thickest on the sunny side of the cactus. Most plants lose water through their leaves. Cactuses have no leaves; photosynthesis is carried out in their green, chlorophyll-bearing stems.

Over the millennia, desert plants have evolved reduced leaves or thorns that minimize evaporation and discourage animals from browsing. A century plant's funnel-shaped leaves (above) conduct water down to the root of the plant; its thorns prevent animals from getting at the precious liquid. The inward-curving spines of the barrel cactus (above, right) also channel water toward the plant's roots. The thorns of prickly pears (opposite) deter most animals, but the fruit-seeking Harris' antelope squirrel uses them as ladder steps.

Throughout the canyon, I found the effort to retain water more in evidence than the effort to find it. The only animals I saw drinking were the bats that swooped down to skim creek water at twilight, but the abundance of burrows and nests attested to the general need to avoid the sun's desiccating heat. I couldn't watch plants absorbing water with their roots, but their tough, spiky stems and branches made it clear that little of the water they absorbed was evaporating into the air. I myself certainly spent more time finding shade than I did filling my water bottle from the creek, flitting from the vanishing shade of this boulder to the dwindling shade of that one and sometimes winding up stretched full-length in the creek.

As I was cooking dinner on my second night, a loud snort beside the creek announced that a band of collared peccaries had discovered me. Social creatures, peccaries move in herds of 6 to 30 closely

associated individuals that feed, travel, and rest together. The long-snouted animals seemed a little disgruntled at my presence and eyed me myopically for a moment before galloping away up the canyon wall. On the rim, they stopped to eat cholla buds before wandering off, as though to demonstrate that this was still *their* place, even if they had relinquished it temporarily.

The next morning I found a reason for their apparent disgruntlement. I had camped on a sandbar just below a boulder-filled gully, and when I pushed past a shrub screening the gully, I came on a deeply trampled little trail that led a few feet to a large, overhanging boulder. I could see from the compacted soil under the overhang that the peccaries probably spent hot afternoons lying beneath it. The presence of ferns, mosses, and liverworts indicated a consistently cool microclimate under the thick granite. I had usurped one of their favorite spots for beating the heat. With the high temperatures of summer, collared peccaries become more and more nocturnal, moving about and feeding on mesquite beans, bulbs, and cactus fruit and stems at night; resting in the shade during the day.

I subsequently moved my camp upstream to the shade of the only juniper tree on the canyon bottom, where I encountered other water conservation strategies. The resident tree lizard, a delicate black-and-brown mottled creature about five inches long, took over my pack as a daytime shelter, remaining in one or another side pocket even as I rummaged for objects. I would have thought the tree's

Virtually drought-resistant by design, the barrel cactus draws up even scant moisture through its shallow roots and vascular tissue to the central pith, where it stores excess moisture and conducts photosynthesis. Water loss is reduced by the plant's thick skin, shading spines, and squat shape, which presents the smallest possible surface area to the sun's rays.

Spines

Skin

Vascular tissue

Pith

Roots

shade was sufficient, although lizards are less resistant to solar radiation than birds or mammals because they lack insulating feathers or fur. Lizards will overheat and die if exposed to direct sun for long, so they are careful to stay near shelter. The tree lizard might also have been trying to avoid the hot surface soil. Or it may have resorted to my pack for other reasons than need for shade and heat relief—protection from predators, for example—but the fact that it stayed there in the afternoons suggested a temperature regulation strategy.

A pair of verdins nesting in a nearby thorn bush found my presence less useful than did the lizard, and let me know with harsh "tut-tut" cries that seemed loud out of proportion to the size of the three-and-a-half-inch gray birds. The yellow-headed verdins, a male and a female, didn't require a man-made shelter for the nestlings that I could hear squeaking as their parents relayed caterpillars into the thorn bush. They had made a perfectly adequate one themselves, a carefully roofed mass of thorny twigs in the center of the bush that evidently kept predators and harmful radiation from the naked and helpless chicks, even though the roof of the nest was fully exposed to sunlight and my prying eyes.

Such water conservation strategies were obviously successful: The mammals, reptiles, and birds that employed them were everywhere in the canyon. Because these strategies resembled my own ways of avoiding overheating, they were easy to understand. The relationship of other canyon dwellers to the sun, however, seemed less

Its thick, leathery skin protects the desert tortoise from the spines of a prickly pear as it devours the plant's low-growing and succulent fruit. This endangered reptile gets much of the water it needs from the vegetation it eats. It can store up to a pint of fluid in its large bladder; its carapace minimizes evaporation of this reservoir during the long dry season.

straightforward. I would have expected a colony of canyon treefrogs living on the granite walls above a deep pool to avoid the midday sun entirely. Frogs are amphibians. Unlike reptiles, birds, and mammals, their skins are not waterproof. Whereas higher vertebrates lose water only through exposed mucous membranes or sweat glands, frogs lose water to direct evaporation all over their bodies. To avoid dehydration, most species live in moist places or in water. It would have been easy for these canyon treefrogs to have remained in the shade: The pool was in a steep gorge where the canyon entered the mountains, and parts of the granite walls above it were shady all day. Yet the frogs sometimes seemed less inclined to seek respite from the sun than did lizards or peccaries.

I first encountered the treefrogs one morning when the walls were all in shade. Looking at the near-vertical pink granite above my head, I suddenly realized that one of the pink knobs was a frog resting with its legs tucked neatly beneath it despite its cliff-hanging position. It stayed motionless as I explored the pool, which contained native desert minnows called longfin dace—a species that can survive short periods without water, taking refuge beneath wet mats of algae and debris—as well as crayfish, water scorpions, and large dragonfly nymphs. Before leaving, I noticed another treefrog in a crevice just above the first, almost touching noses with it.

I returned to the pool in late afternoon and found the second frog in the same position. By that time, the wall was baking in full sunlight, and the first frog had disappeared. The crevice protected the remaining frog from the hot sun, but I noticed that a ray was creeping into the crevice, touching the tip of the frog's nose. The frog remained motionless as the sun spread to its leg, but when the light reached the top of its head, it backed up so that only its snout remained in sunlight.

I kept an eye on the two frogs in the crevice during the next few days. They were fairly active—one of them kept calling and following the other around as though trying to mate—but neither stayed in full sunlight for more than a moment. Then one hot afternoon, I noticed a third frog on the wall at the far end of the pool. It was in a crevice too, but in full sun. The frog just sat there, eyes closed. It remained so still, and its skin was such a deathly pale color, that I wondered if it was alive.

I swam the pool to get a better look and watched the baking frog

Capricious cloudbursts bring rain to the parched Sonoran Desert. This shower will feed shallow-rooted cactuses, but may not benefit more deeply rooted plants. Deserts receive an average of no more than ten inches of rain a year, and lose much of this moisture to evaporation. Giant red velvet mites—the size of a pea—emerge after brief summer rains to eat breeding termites.

for perhaps 45 minutes, long enough to drive me out of the sunlight into the shade on the other side. I was beginning to feel like a large pink frog among small pink frogs as I clambered over the rocks and hopped from the icy water to the stovelike granite. I was about to splash the frog when it suddenly opened its eyes and marched vigorously across the wall to another crevice that was partly shaded. Unfortunately, the shade was on the wrong side of the crevice, and the frog wound up hunched again in full sunlight. There it stayed for another 20 minutes. Finally, it crept into a crevice that shaded about half of it, remaining there until the sun had gone.

At least one treefrog evidently could tolerate long exposure to solar radiation. I wondered briefly if the sunbathing frog remained in its inadequate crevices because its two neighbors had excluded it from their better protected ones, but this seemed unlikely. There

The desert blooms sporadically year-round, but saturating rains flood the landscape with colorful blossoms. California poppies and goldenbush (opposite) gild California's Mojave Desert in spring—at the same time the teddy bear cholla (above) puts forth its flowers in the Colorado Desert. Some blooms wither in a day; others linger until drought conditions return.

FOLLOWING PAGES: Bursting with color and pollen, blossoms of a barrel cactus flare briefly after summer rains. Once pollinated, this cactus produces an edible fruit that ripens in the fall.

was plenty of shade around the pool. I found later that even the first pair could be careless about exposure. The last time I visited the pool, I found one frog crouched deep in the shade of a large crevice while the other crouched in full sunlight below, though there was plenty of room in the crevice. Its skin was the same deathly pale gray as the sunbather's, a color that blended well with the sunlit granite.

I got some insight into the frogs' behavior by talking to the curator of herpetology and ichthyology at the Arizona-Sonora Desert Museum and consulting the biology sections of libraries. The canyon treefrog has an unusually thick skin for a frog, and since frogs can absorb water through the skin as well as lose it, it may be that the frogs were insulated by literal "skinfulls" of water absorbed while they were in the pool. I had noticed that their skin did sometimes seem to exude moisture when they were in sunlight. There was only one problem with this explanation: I never saw the frogs in the water. In fact, canyon treefrogs have a reputation for going into water only to breed or to escape enemies, and then only briefly. There is more to be learned about these amphibians; the literature doesn't have much to say about them. Such a paucity of information about a common species is not unusual. It's one of the frustrating—and fascinating—aspects of studying natural history.

The behavior of some close relatives of the canyon treefrog was less perplexing. A population of red-spotted toads in the canyon responded to the sun's heat simply by finding shade in burrows. They stayed underground in daytime, but their resonant trilling echoed along every few feet of creek at night. The calls were powerful enough at close quarters to set off a vibration in my ears like the ringing of a cake mixer's rotors against a bowl.

It took a while to locate the source of the noise, but my headlamp

Wind-sculptured sandstone in the Colorado Plateau captures rainfall to create a reflecting pool. Such temporary oases, as well as intermittent streams, creeks, and springs, provide desert wildlife with much needed water. Herbivores, such as the desert cottontail, rely on the moisture in plants, but drink when they can.

eventually picked out treefrog-size, reddish toads in the black water. When the light angle was right, their eyes shone an eerie red. There was nothing of the sunbather's languor about the red-spotted toads. Their inflated white throats shook with the enthusiasm of their calling, and they kept pivoting and climbing on things as if to broadcast their message. When one caller neared another, they would charge and shove each other like tiny sumo wrestlers.

During desert nights, animals and plants make the most of the respite from daytime heat. Kangaroo rats and other rodents emerge from their nests to seek food or mates, and predators follow to take advantage of them. Saguaros and other plants open the pore-like stomata on their cuticles to absorb carbon dioxide and release oxygen, the waste product of photosynthesis. Night-flying bats and insects pollinate saguaro flowers.

In the canyon, curve-billed thrashers and mockingbirds continued calling long after sunset, the thrashers filling the scrub with a peculiar, interrogative "whit-wheet?" On the tops of mudstone buttes, great horned owls threw themselves into the act of hooting, leaning far forward as they called, like speechmakers projecting over the banquet table. After each strenuous "hoo *hoo* hoo hoo," an owl would pause to peer around, as though to see how the local rabbits had taken its remarks.

The canyon got noisier as it got darker. Coyotes yelped on mesas; barn owls shrieked overhead. Poorwills whistled tremulously on the

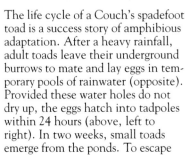

The life cycle of a Couch's spadefoot toad is a success story of amphibious adaptation. After a heavy rainfall, adult toads leave their underground burrows to mate and lay eggs in temporary pools of rainwater (opposite). Provided these water holes do not dry up, the eggs hatch into tadpoles within 24 hours (above, left to right). In two weeks, small toads emerge from the ponds. To escape the midday heat, the toads use the horny projections, or spades, on their hind feet to burrow in the sand. At the onset of drought, they burrow one last time for the season and begin a period of hibernation that lasts until the next rainstorm, usually 9 to 11 months.

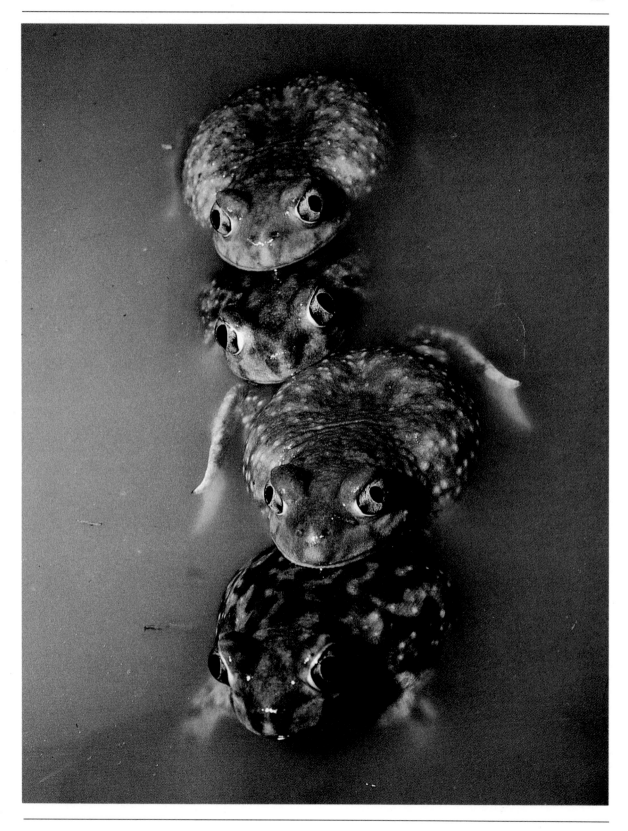

canyon slopes, and even the toads didn't drown out the chirps and buzzes of crickets and shield-backed grasshoppers. I recognized these calls, but there were other, unfamiliar ones—high-pitched squawks, descending whistles, hoarse yelps.

Not being a nocturnal animal myself, I found it hard to get around in the nighttime desert. The footing was tricky, and the prospect of being pierced by invisible cactus spines or treading on a snake was not a happy one. Western diamondback rattlesnakes are common in this area, but as it happened I didn't encounter a single snake in the canyon. This isn't all that surprising: Snakes are vulnerable creatures, lacking the metabolic heat-regulating mechanisms of birds and mammals, so they are active only under the most favorable conditions. I was told that many rattlesnakes would be hunting in the canyon on warmer nights in June.

Staying in camp wasn't necessarily a disadvantage. One of the animals I most wanted to see was the elf owl, a tiny species measuring only five inches long. This smallest American owl is common in saguaros, nesting in abandoned woodpecker holes, and I thought its calls might be among those unfamiliar night sounds. I spent much

As the sun sinks below the horizon, the desert comes alive with a bevy of nocturnal pollinators drawn to plants such as the jimsonweed (opposite). A long-tongued bat (above) pollinates a saguaro as it laps up sweet nectar from the blossoms. Within the unfurled bloom of a jimsonweed, a sphinx moth (left, bottom) collects pollen as it aims its long proboscis toward the blossom's deep reserve of nectar. In a remarkable case of symbiosis, a yucca moth (left, top) deposits its eggs into the ovary of a yucca plant, then stuffs some pollen in on top. The resulting plant seeds serve as food for the newly hatched moth larvae.

time walking among the saguaros, shining my headlamp at holes, but I didn't see any elf owls.

When I returned to camp and got into my sleeping bag, peevish-sounding squawks suddenly surrounded me, but I couldn't tell where they were coming from. On the third night, a squawk came from the juniper directly above my head, and although I still caught nothing in my light, I heard a faint, receding whir of wings.

Elf owls are known to make a whirring sound when flying, unlike the more silent larger owls. I shone my flashlight at the tree every time I heard a squawk. After many fine views of bare branches, and a few glimpses of vague flitting shapes, a sparrow-size owl finally sat still for me while it took the last bites of what was probably an insect, the elf owl's staple food. It was definitely an elf owl, yellow-eyed, short-tailed, and round-headed.

Another nocturnal mystery remained unsolved until my last night in the canyon. I had often walked past a saguaro containing a head-high hole from which an untidy mass of straw protruded. It was clearly something's nest, but I couldn't tell what. On that final night I gave the straw a gentle tug. A small mouse sailed out, landed at my feet, and took shelter under a prickly pear. After some crawling around, I saw enough of its coloring and features to figure that it was a cactus mouse, a relative of the deer mouse that is known to nest in saguaro holes—occasionally in holes as high as 20 feet above ground. Cactus mice have lighter coloring and larger ears than their forest relatives, common desert adaptations for avoiding overheating. Light coloring reflects solar heat, while large ears radiate body heat back into the air.

I felt ashamed of disturbing the mouse. Outside its nest, the tiny creature's life was at risk.

Desert ecosystems are not always as easy to observe as was the canyon in Tonto National Forest during spring. The day after leaving the canyon, I took a walk in Saguaro National Monument about 150 miles to the southeast. I saw very few animals or wildflowers there. The Tucson area gets most of its rain from summer thunderstorms, and those had not arrived yet, so much life was dormant. The monument's bone-dry creeks looked an unlikely breeding place for toads, but I knew they would emerge to mate if I waited long enough.

Aspiring naturalists shouldn't get discouraged when the desert shows its desolate side. A modicum of patient observation will almost always reveal much of interest. While many desert animals are light-colored, blending into the background of sand or rock, careful observation can pierce that camouflage. Even if an area seems empty of animals, their tracks, burrows, scats, and other signs reveal their hidden presence. And even if an area *is* virtually empty of plants and animals (as alkali flats and mudstone badlands may be), soil and rock hold fascinating information. Important fossils that provide windows into the past have been discovered in desert badlands. Although I didn't find any fossils in the canyon's mudstones, I kept a lookout for them. There is no such thing as an empty desert.

The hot and shifting sands of the desert cause a special set of problems for plants and animals alike. To move rapidly across the torrid sand, the sidewinder throws its body sideways in a flowing **S**-curve that creates sufficient friction for locomotion. Incapable of movement, this dune flower of the family Compositae will disappear beneath the sand, contributing its roots, leaves, and seeds to the soil of a dynamic landscape.

Mountains

There was so much light when I awoke beside Emerald Lake that I thought dawn was breaking. High-pitched "kek kek" sounds came from surrounding rocks, the cries of awakening birds, I presumed. When I looked at my watch, however, I saw that it was only 2 a.m. The landscape in the Sierra Nevada at 9,000 feet may look Arctic, but the late August sun in California doesn't rise on Arctic time. The light wasn't moonlight either: I had seen the moon set before I fell asleep.

I glanced up at the sky and discovered the light's source. In the clear air the stars shone with an intensity that momentarily dazzled me. The Milky Way formed an almost solid band of white across the zenith. This brilliance overwhelmed the stars' remoteness and gave me a palpable sense of the earth's connection to the heavens. The gleaming cliffs around the lake seemed cooled, solidified starlight.

As I walked the heights around Emerald Lake during the next two weeks, I saw other connections between earth and sky, past and present, that might have seemed less clear in the lowlands. With their elemental remoteness, mountains foster a long view of natural history. There are no better places to study the geological processes that shaped the earth. Mountain uplift and consequent erosion expose bedrock over vast areas, revealing geological phenomena elsewhere buried by soil, vegetation, or civilization.

Mountains also reveal much about life's origins and development. Charles Darwin's discovery of seashell fossils on Andean peaks contributed to his ideas about evolution. Naturalists often resort to highlands to observe plants and animals because the rugged terrain is less disturbed by human activity than are gentle lowlands.

The area around Emerald Lake is particularly good for studying the natural history of mountains. Here in the canyon of the Kaweah River, the Sierra range rises from 500 feet above sea level in the San Joaquin Valley to crests above 12,000 feet—in only 30 or so miles as the crow flies. Increasing elevation causes striking changes in temperature and vegetation within this relatively short distance. As part of Sequoia National Park, the area's ecosystem is little disturbed. Only the grizzly bear and California condor have disappeared from its native fauna.

The Sierra Nevada is one of the greatest expanses of exposed granitic bedrock in the world. The fundamental material of continents, granitic rock tells much about how land is formed. In Tokopah

Scooped out by a glacier in Washington's Cascade Range, Gnome Tarn mirrors Prusik Peak and the golden larches on its timberline. These deciduous conifers grow at about 7,000 feet amid mosses, evergreens, and shrubs such as huckleberry and juniper. Varying soil, terrain, moisture, temperature, and exposure to wind and sun determine what plants and animals live in such alpine zones.

Valley, a higher part of the Kaweah canyon, most of the bedrock is granodiorite. This granitic rock is grainy, formed of pale crystals of quartz and feldspar peppered with dark crystals of mica and hornblende. It takes different forms in different parts of the valley, and this diversity helps to explain how the rock originated.

In many places I found bits of granodiorite in which the individual crystals were quite small, embedded in masses of coarse-grained rock. Elsewhere, I saw masses of small-grained granodiorite adjoining masses of the coarse-grained rock. According to United States Geological Survey scientist James Moore, who has mapped the area's rocks, these variations in grain size mean that the rocks cooled from their original molten state at different rates. Large crystals show that rock has cooled slowly, because crystals have more time to grow during slow cooling. Coarse-grained granites generally form deep within the earth, where cooling is slow. Small-grained granites tend to form closer to the surface, where magma cools quickly.

The once molten state of the granodiorite offers a clue to how the western part of our continent came into being. The Sierra Nevada is part of a belt of peaks and volcanoes that runs from Alaska to Tierra del Fuego. Geologists believe that movements of the earth's crust created these mountains. According to the theory of plate tectonics, the earth's crust is broken into rigid plates made of basaltic and granitic rock from the planet's molten interior. These plates, which carry both continents and ocean floor, are not stationary, but ride

Hardy tundra plants, lichens and mosses can tolerate stressful conditions at high elevations. Both hold moisture well and can go dormant in extreme weather. Orange *Xanthoria* and other lichens and cushiony mosses (above) hug the ground and rock faces, where temperature is warmest and wind minimal. Yellow-green wolf moss (right), a lichen, clings to conifer limbs and trunks in the Sierra and elsewhere.

Most lichens consist of fungi and algae living in symbiosis. Algae produce carbohydrates for both through photosynthesis. Fungi shelter the algae and capture moisture and minerals from the air and from the surface to which the lichen is attached.

over the viscous mantle. Granitic continental crust is more buoyant than the denser basalt of ocean floor crust.

The granite of Tokopah Valley originated about a hundred million years ago, during the Cretaceous period, when a series of plates underlying the Pacific Ocean collided with a plate underlying the North American continent. The lighter North American plate overrode the Pacific plates, which dragged quantities of surface material down into the hot mantle. This rock melted, grew lighter, and rose toward the surface again, erupting as volcanoes or cooling below the surface as buried masses of magma. The Tokopah Valley granite was one such mass.

But how did rocks formed deep within the earth's crust reach their present elevation at 9,000 feet? About 20 million years ago, a Pacific plate began moving northwestward in relation to the North American plate, scraping sideways against it. The stress of this movement, along with other geological forces, thrust up the Sierra—slowly at first, then more rapidly over time. Today the range is still rising.

Mountains are short-lived in the scale of geological time: Once uplifted, their rocks erode quickly, coming under relentless attrition from rain, streams, ice, wind, sunlight, and vegetation—forces capable of wearing them down thousands of feet within the geological moment of a million years. The Appalachian Mountains once were higher than today's Sierra; now their highest summits are less than 7,000 feet—lower than Emerald Lake.

A succession of life zones scales an idealized mountainside in the southern Sierra. As temperature decreases with higher elevation, and amounts of moisture fluctuate, open grassland and oak woodland give way to mixed forests of ponderosa pine and other conifers. A thick subalpine forest of red-fir yields to an alpine meadow, capped by a snowy summit. Climbing up through progressively colder ecosystems may be compared to traveling north toward the Arctic.

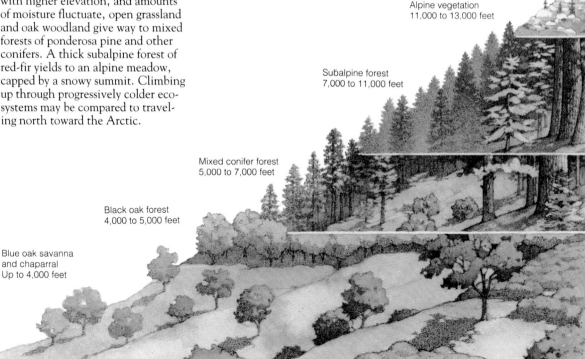

Snowfield

Alpine vegetation
11,000 to 13,000 feet

Subalpine forest
7,000 to 11,000 feet

Mixed conifer forest
5,000 to 7,000 feet

Black oak forest
4,000 to 5,000 feet

Blue oak savanna
and chaparral
Up to 4,000 feet

Gentle contours of the Great Smoky Mountains covered with fall foliage (above) contrast with the bare, saw-toothed grandeur of the Sierra Nevada (opposite). The Smokies are part of the ancient Appalachian Mountain system. Thrust up by tectonic activity some 300 million years ago, the Appalachians may once have rivaled today's Himalaya in height. Erosion by rain, wind, ice, and

stream has worn them down to rolling ranges with broad river valleys.

Uplift some 20 million years ago tilted the massive granite block that forms the Sierra, raising jagged peaks on the eastern edge. Rivers flowed swiftly, cutting deep canyons. Glaciers scoured the rock and carved some canyons into **U**-shaped valleys such as Yosemite. In time, erosion will blunt these sharp young peaks.

In Tokopah Valley I found a dramatic example of one kind of erosion. About two million years ago, for reasons little understood, global climate began to undergo periods so cool and wet that sheets of unmelted snow accumulated at high elevations and latitudes. Under pressure of their weight, these snowfields compacted into ice and began to flow. Some became glaciers, ice rivers of enormous power that scraped and plucked soil and rocks, even entire cliff faces, from their paths.

Before glaciation began in the Sierra, the Kaweah River's Marble Fork probably had eroded the Tokopah Valley into a **V** shape. As climate cooled over millennia, glaciers formed in the shadow of high peaks, where snow lasted longest. Becoming deeper and heavier, the glaciers first carved out amphitheater-like cirques below the peaks, then flowed down into the valley, carrying away soil and forests. There they coalesced into a huge glacier believed to have been 1,000 feet deep in places. This glacier eventually descended to a 6,000-foot elevation.

After the climate warmed some 12,000 years ago, the glacier melted, but its tracks remain clear. At middle elevation, between 6,000 and 7,000 feet, the Marble Fork now runs between two massive, elongated hills. These are lateral moraines, formed as the glacier deposited the rocks and soil it had carried down conveyor-belt fashion from the heights.

I realized just how much material the glacier had removed from the high country when I followed the canyon of the Marble Fork above 8,000 feet. Instead of a **V**-shaped, forested valley, I found a shining, dizzying expanse of granite cliffs and waterfalls. The highest cliff, the Watchtower, rises 1,600 feet. The glacier has carved today's canyon into a **U** shape, with a level floor and vertical walls.

Nuzzled protectively by its nanny, a mountain goat kid grazes on sparse herbage. Adapted to survival in the high, rugged terrain of the northern Rockies, kids develop fast. They can stand up ten minutes after birth and soon make wobbly attempts to climb and jump. A four-month-old goat (above) can leap confidently between crags on its short, strong legs.

The hoofs of mountain goats, hard-rimmed with nonskid pads under each toe, spread wide to grasp rocky footholds. Hollow guard hairs over a fluffy inner layer of wool give the animals double insulation in winter. To reach grasses, sedges, and other food, they paw the snow away.

Related to the chamois of the European Alps, mountain goats are not true goats but members of the goat-antelope family.

Steep, rocky chutes lead upward from the canyon floor to the cirques where the glaciers began. These cirques now contain tarns—lakes such as Emerald—which formed as the glaciers melted.

Much of the canyon floor is still bare granite, in places polished as smooth as a tombstone by the glacier's abrasive burden of sand and gravel, or scratched and grooved by transported boulders. (Many rocks and boulders left behind when the glacier melted still litter the floor.) Subsequent erosion has begun to erase some of these marks; I saw sheets of glacial polish flaking away. Yet glacial tracks grew clearer as I climbed higher, so that I seemed to be traveling back toward a prehistoric age of ice.

Climbing mountains is the equivalent of traveling hundreds of miles north, since average temperature drops 1°F for each 300-foot rise in elevation, and reduced temperature causes major changes in flora and fauna. U. S. Biological Survey scientist C. H. Merriam observed this phenomenon in the 1890s. While climbing Arizona's San Francisco Mountains, he noted that the series of habitats he encountered (which he called life zones) corresponded roughly to the series of habitats one would encounter in traveling from Mexico to Canada. Subsequent work has shown that Merriam's life-zone concept can't be applied to all mountains, but it remains useful in studying western North American ranges such as the Sierra Nevada.

Below 5,000 feet, the Kaweah canyon passes through a warm, semiarid landscape resembling that of northern Mexico, with oak woodland and California brushland, or chaparral. Lining the river between 5,000 and 9,000 feet is a forest of big, mainly coniferous trees, similar to forests along the Pacific coast. Above 9,000 feet, the river's headwaters drain a landscape like northern Canada's, with small conifers scattered over stretches of treeless, tundralike habitat.

At 7,000 feet, where I started my climb to the high country, the dense forest of pine and fir covering the lateral moraines made the glacier seem long ago and far away. The present, relatively mild climate of Sierra mid-elevations combines with adequate soil and precipitation to make this one of the most diverse and impressive coniferous forests in the world. The giant sequoia is the largest of the forest's species, with individual trees up to 300 feet tall and 3,200 years old. Some of the pines I saw on the moraine, although dwarfed by the sequoia, had trunks five or six feet across. Sugar pine, which has purplish bark, blue-green needles in fascicles of five, and cones up to 18 inches long, is the world's tallest pine, reaching heights of up to 200 feet. Jeffrey pine, with reddish, jigsaw-patterned bark and needles in threes, grows nearly as tall.

Animal life wasn't highly visible in the dense forest. Dark blue Steller's jays and reddish Douglas squirrels were the most conspicuous inhabitants, scolding me as I passed. Both species are abundant throughout western coniferous forests because they feed largely on conifer seeds. Occasionally, groups of chickadees, nuthatches, and creepers trooped through the trees, seeking safety in numbers from hawks and other predators. These birds occupy the forest all year,

Fossils are a window on prehistory. Trilobites (top) scavenged ocean bottoms 500 million to 225 million years ago. Found high in the Canadian Rockies, trilobite fossils helped prove that violent geological activity there thrust up an ancient seabed. Palm and freshwater fish fossils (above) from the Wyoming-Utah basin region show that 50 million years ago this was subtropical lake country.

PAGES 144-145: Indian paintbrush and mountain daisy splash vivid summer color over a subalpine meadow. Soil moistened by snowmelt, lakes, and streams supports these grassy habitats within drier alpine zones.

finding enough to eat by gleaning insects from bark and foliage.

I found one sign of a larger forest dweller, the scat of a black bear. It contained mostly manzanita berries. Evergreen manzanita ("little apple" in Spanish) is a typical shrub of California chaparral. Evidently the bear had traveled through the forest after feeding in brush. Black bears move up and down the mountains through the year, seeking food at different elevations as it becomes available. They climb trees readily, but get most of their staple berries, roots, insects, acorns, and herbs on the ground. When days shorten and deep winter snow makes food scarce, bears retire to tree-hole and rock dens to sleep for periods of weeks or months, insulated by thick layers of body fat.

On the cliffs above the moraines, I encountered a forest adapted to more stressful conditions. Although still impressive in size, the trees were no longer giants, and there were fewer species. Uniform stands of red-firs covered slopes where the glacier had failed to scrape deep soil away. Their blue-green foliage cast such a shadow on the ground that it was bare of undergrowth. Lodgepole pines with flaky bark and needles in fascicles of two grew in the moist soil by streams and lakes. Western white pines with bark in deep red plates stood in the rockiest, most exposed sites. Their elongated cones and fascicles of five needles indicated a relationship to the sugar pines below, though the western white pines were smaller.

Trees generally decrease in size as one moves from temperate or mid-elevation habitats to northern or high-elevation ones, where winters are colder and growing seasons shorter. Such conditions reduce size by allowing plants to survive only in certain forms, or growth habits. For example, large broad-leaved trees such as oaks grow among mid-elevation conifers in the southern Sierra, but they are rare above 6,000 feet because their spreading growth habit makes them vulnerable to breakage during heavy snowstorms. Smaller broad-leaved species such as aspens and bush chinquapins survive at higher elevations. Conifers become bent and twisted from high-elevation winds and from the weight of winter snow. Average annual snowfall at 7,000 feet is more than 200 inches. Such a burden would shatter broad-leaved trees such as oaks, but short, drooping branches and soft, flexible wood allow conifers to withstand heavy weight. Waxy, evergreen conifer needles continue to photosynthesize food throughout the winter.

Animal life also changed as I ascended. The high-pitched, nasal "craaa" of the Clark's nutcracker replaced the raucous "shook shook" of the Steller's jay. Like jays, the gray-and-black nutcrackers belong to the crow family and feed mainly on conifer seeds and insects. Yet Steller's jays seldom wander far from dense tree stands, while the nutcrackers of the southern Sierra stay in the scattered forest above 9,000 feet, except when winter storms temporarily drive them to lower elevations. Nutcrackers survive winter in the high country by feeding on seeds, which they store in communal caches on the ground or in bark crevices. They show a good memory for

Finding Fossils

Nothing compares to that first fossil find, when you hold in your hand the remains of a creature that lived millions of years ago. Fossils occur when something organic dies and is buried by mud, sand, or other sediment. The organism's soft parts may decompose, leaving only its hard parts—scales, shells, bones, and teeth—or just an imprint or mold.

To find fossils, consult a fossil guidebook, a geological map, or a local museum or fossil club. Head for sedimentary rock formations, especially limestones and shales. Look for places with exposed rock: cliffs and streambeds, road and railroad cuts, construction sites, quarries, sand pits. Plan your hunt carefully. Get permission to explore private land. For laws regarding federal and state lands, check with a state geologist. To search a highway road cut, contact the state police.

A fossil hound needs a good, tempered steel *geologist's* hammer—ordinary hammers may fracture, sending out a spray of metal splinters. Also, a rock chisel, newspaper, felt-tip marker, notebook and pencil, tape measure, knapsack, and protective clothing—safety glasses, leather gloves, sturdy shoes, and a hard hat.

At the site, scan the rock for clues: discolored areas, mineral traces of fossils glinting in the sun, or hard fossil parts protruding from weathered rock. Check the rocks on the ground. Crack open

large ball-shaped rocks with the flat side of your hammer. Then work smaller pieces with the chisel end. Find a spot along a distinct layer of sediment, tap it with the chisel end, and then pry open the rock. You may uncover a fossilized seed fern (shown here).

Record your find by sketching the different exposed rock strata, noting the depth of each, and marking the layer from which your fossil came. Then wrap the

fossil in newspaper and label the contents. Some fossils need extra preparation before being transported. Consult a fossil text for techniques. At home, clean your fossils by scrubbing them with water and an old toothbrush. To chip away at the rock matrix, use old kitchen knives, sharpened crochet hooks, or dental tools.

If you hit a fossil jackpot, report your find to a museum or university paleontology department.

Windflowers

Arctic hares

Animals and plants of Arctic and alpine tundra show adaptations to their similar environments. Found in both habitats, cottongrass and windflowers spread through underground rhizomes. In fall, the rock ptarmigan, its legs feathered for warmth, molts from speckled brown to snow white. The Arctic wolf keeps its white coat year-round. So do Arctic hares in the far north. Besides acting as camouflage, the absence of dark pigment in fur and feathers allows for more air space; hence more insulation.

recovering the seeds even when several inches of snow cover the caches. This food supply enables them to start nesting in March and April, assuring that the fledglings will mature before the end of the brief alpine summer.

Above 9,000 feet, trees became increasingly scarce. On the rocks of many slopes and ridges the only growing things were crusts of bright-colored lichens. Lichens can survive at higher elevations than other organisms because of enormous resistance to cold and dryness, and because they require no soil. Composite organisms of green algal cells in matrices of threadlike fungal tissues, they are self-sufficient, requiring only minerals and water absorbed from rocks and the atmosphere. The algal cells use the water to photosynthesize food for both alga and fungus. The fungal matrices protect the algal cells from dryness and cold.

Arctic wolf in cottongrass

Rock ptarmigan

As lichens grow and die on bare rock, they form small amounts of soil, which mosses, ferns, and flowering plants colonize. I saw this process at work everywhere in the upper reaches of the Marble Fork canyon. Although the rocky slopes appeared barren, a great variety of tough little plants grew in the interstices: low shrubs of gooseberry and elderberry; yellow mats of sulphur flower, a relative of buckwheat; fragrant tufts of pink-flowered coyote mint.

Meadows occupied level parts of the canyon floor, with trees growing in isolated groves. High Sierra meadows develop when glacial lakes and ponds fill with silt. These soils tend to be too wet for tree growth, so water-tolerant meadow plants such as rushes and sedges dominate them. As plant material accumulates and meadows grow drier, more species of plants invade them, including grasses and wildflowers and eventually trees.

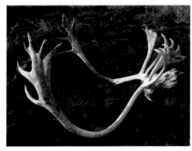

Backlit by the midnight sun, the branched arms of reindeer lichen (above)—magnified many times—mirror the forking of caribou antlers (left). Caribou, called reindeer in Europe, graze heavily on this two- to three-inch-high plant of the Arctic tundra. Such similarity of form does not result from chance. Antlers and lichens follow a growth pattern based on a **Y** shape, repeated in smaller and smaller units. In plants, branching limbs and roots expose larger surface areas to sun and moisture within a space scaled to the plant's size.

"In matters of visual form we sense that nature plays favorites," observes Peter S. Stevens in *Patterns in Nature*. "Among her darlings are spirals, meanders, branching patterns, and 120-degree joints. Those patterns occur again and again."

Because of their wildflower diversity, moist Sierra meadows produce successions of blooms throughout the growing season. Melted snow usually provides ample water for lush growth. It was an unusually dry year, so the upper basin meadows were past their peak, but they still bloomed with masses of waist-high flowers. Most conspicuous was pink-flowered fireweed. It grows in mountains and at high elevations throughout the Northern Hemisphere and is named for its ability to colonize burned areas with its millions of wind-driven seeds. There hadn't been a fire in the Marble Fork canyon recently, so fireweed grew scattered among other flowers such as sunflower-like sneezeweed and deep blue monkshood.

The open landscape brought changes in fauna. Marmots and pikas replaced the forest's Douglas squirrels. The steepness of the habitat seemed to bother them not at all. As I walked along the most dizzying stretch of trail, a ledge with cliffs above and below, a pika appeared over the lip of the lower cliff and scampered without hesitation up the higher one.

Pikas are small, round-eared relatives of rabbits. They inhabit mountains of western North America and Eurasia, surviving alpine winters by feeding on stores of sun-dried herbs in rock shelters. In summer, they cure this "hay" in little piles by turning it so that it doesn't get moldy. When snow covers their rocky habitat from October to May, they remain active and healthy beneath it.

Pikas prefer the fields of rocks called talus that pile up at the base of cirque cliffs, and sizable colonies may develop there. It was actually pikas that made the "kek kek" sounds I thought were dawn birdcalls at Emerald Lake. I learned this the next morning when one appeared and called in my camp. Pikas call back and forth to one another to assert ownership of territories and food supplies. They also call when predators or other intruders appear, but they are selective about this. If a predator small enough to enter their dens appears—a weasel, say—they keep quiet.

Marmots, large ground-dwelling rodents related to woodchucks, survive mountain winters by hibernating, entering a state of extreme physiological torpor in which body temperature may drop from 98°F to 40°F, and breathing and heartbeat decrease drastically. A hibernating animal will remain unconscious even if dragged from its den. Marmots remain in this state for six to nine months of the year, awakening only occasionally to urinate. Thick body fat accumulated during the summer serves as insulation and energy. It lasts throughout the winter, when the rodents' slowed metabolism uses little energy. After awakening in spring, marmots burn this fat quickly.

Some animals are able to survive high-country winters without storing food or hibernating. Blue grouse, which I found common around Emerald Lake, spend the winter roosting in red-fir groves and feeding on the needles. Feathers insulate their legs in snow.

Most mountain carnivores remain active during the winter. The shortage of meat makes these predators scarce, but they sometimes occur in the Marble Fork canyon. I heard coyotes during my stay.

Mammals of the High Sierra, Rockies, and Cascades, marmots (above) and pikas (above, right) often mount lookouts to sound the alarm when predators approach their rocky domain. These include birds of prey, weasels, and occasionally bobcats like this one streaking downhill with a red squirrel in its jaws. Barely twice the size of a domestic cat, the shy, nocturnal bobcat usually hunts in lower terrain.

The marmot mother and her six-week-old baby will fatten up on grasses and flowers until fall, then hibernate for as long as nine months. Pikas, known as "haymakers," cure piles of plants in the sun to eat in their winter dens among the rocks. They stay alert even under the snow.

Park naturalists told of a family of fishers seen playing beside one lake, and a marten was observed chasing a ground squirrel at another. Members of the weasel family, martens and fishers inhabit mountain ranges throughout much of North America. They survive by seeking food almost everywhere—from the treetops, where they hunt squirrels and songbirds, to the talus, where they find both pikas and ground squirrels.

Some animals leave the high country in winter. A pair of golden eagles I saw circling the peaks in search of marmots would move down to the foothills after the summer. A peregrine falcon I glimpsed at one lake would follow its duck and shorebird prey to the valleys or seashore once the high lakes froze. Heavy animals such as deer move downhill because deep snow hinders their movements and buries their food supply.

My sense of traveling back to a glacial age deepened as I followed the canyon above 10,000 feet. Sometimes I thought I smelled snow in the air. This was fanciful; snow lingered only in a few dirty patches under the peaks in this dry year. Even the river held water only in ponded stretches, and I could climb waterfalls as though they were staircases. Yet severe weather is never far away in the High Sierra. After a few clear days, thunderheads began massing above the peaks. I climbed a dry waterfall at the start of one morning hike and found myself nervously climbing back down an increasingly wet one at the end. A four-hour thunderstorm that afternoon turned the river from a string of ponds into a torrent.

I was glad that only rain fell. In autumn, snowstorms often drive hikers out of the high country. It was easy to see how a significant increase in average precipitation could deposit more snow in the canyon than the summer could melt. In most years, snow remains until July. Parts of the Sierra are still buried under some 60 small glaciers.

The sky was cloudless one morning at 9 a.m. when I arrived at Table Meadows, a two-hour hike upward from my camp at Emerald Lake. Headwaters of the Marble Fork, Table Meadows lies in a bowl surrounded by low ridges on the north, east, and south. After resting

a moment by one of the last trees in sight, a lodgepole pine, I climbed the ridge to the north. As I neared its top, the biggest jackrabbit I'd ever seen loped away across the rocks. It was a white-tailed jackrabbit, an uncommon species that manages to survive Sierra winters up to 12,000 feet by feeding on vegetated ridges swept bare of snow by wind. Unlike its abundant lowland relative, the black-tailed jackrabbit, the species turns white in winter, an adaptation it shares with snowshoe hares.

Beyond the ridgetop, I entered a landscape that might well have been in northern Canada. This was the Tableland, a small plateau that lies under the crest dividing the watersheds of the Kaweah and Kings Rivers. I crossed winding hillocks crowned with house-size boulders to a sparkling lake surrounded by meadows in which rushes and sedges barely reached above my bootheels. Trumpet-shaped white gentian blossoms, toe-high, peeped out here and there. Gentians are among the latest blooming of mountain flowers, something that suggested the plateau's growing season was almost over. The ground-hugging vegetation indicated that conditions here resembled those of Arctic tundra.

Yet when I looked up at the crest, I saw a scattered grove of small trees halfway to the top. They came as a surprise above the treeless plateau, so I started climbing again to see what they were, although the clear skies of 9 a.m. were a thing of the past. Little cumulus clouds drifting over from the east had coalesced with startling speed into towering thunderheads. These produced ominous rumbles as I toiled upward, heart and lungs laboring in the thin air.

Hail began falling as I reached the grove, but the climb was worth it. The trees were foxtail pines, an unusual species that grows only at high elevations in the southern Sierra Nevada and the northern California coastal mountains, where a little more rain falls than in other California ranges. Foxtails have deep red bark and fascicles of five needles like western white pine, but their round, bristle-tipped cones and slightly pendant branches make them easy to distinguish from the more common species. Probably as an adaptation to their harsh environment, in which new growth is limited, foxtail needles remain on branches for many years.

Like the closely related bristlecone pines, which grow isolated at high elevations in the Rockies and Great Basin, foxtail pines are long-lived. Some are two thousand years old. The largest tree I

Elk descend from high elevations to winter at feeding grounds in Yellowstone National Park. They will return to higher pastures in summer. Huge herds join in seasonal migrations. Most birds and nonhibernating herbivores, such as mule deer and bighorn sheep, migrate downslope from alpine zones in winter. In rare contrast, blue grouse migrate upslope, where they feed on fir needles.

Fir trees at the timberline on the Sierra's Mount Whitney (right, upper) begin to thin out under harsh weather conditions. The lower branches of the subalpine fir—a species found in the Pacific Northwest and the Rockies—may root beneath a blanket of snow, forming an evergreen skirt (above). On exposed ridges, severe winds produce dwarf trees and contorted shapes. An ancient bristlecone pine (right) displays a condition called "flagging," with branches growing only on its sheltered side.

found was only twenty feet tall and two feet in diameter, but it must have taken many centuries to reach that size. Its top was scarred and gray from wind and lightning, as was that of every tree in the grove.

In climbing from the ancient giant trees at the foot of the Sierra to the ancient dwarf trees on its crest, I felt I had closed a circle, and 12,000 postglacial years seemed insignificant.

Enough hailstones were accumulating to turn the ground white in places. I still hadn't reached the crest, so I climbed on. It wasn't far, a jumble of boulders presided over by a marmot so fat it wobbled as it jumped from rock to rock. I looked eastward at the Kings River watershed, and beyond that, at the endless stretch of Sierra peaks. A desire for those far horizons struggled briefly with a more sensible wish for shelter from impending lightning strikes; then I started back toward camp.

Streams, Lakes, Ponds & Bogs

Blood Brook is a humble stream. For more than three miles its waters curl through a single narrow valley in east-central Vermont, draining three and a half square miles of woods and meadows before emptying into the north end of Lake Fairlee. I live high in the narrow valley, on a hill a hundred yards above the rushing water. From my front yard I see Blood Brook blinking in the sun as it coils through ranks of golden-rod and cattails, flanked by a dark wall of pine and the somber trunks of November maples. The brook quickens my curiosity far out of proportion to its size.

Before me lies a handsome topographical map of the United States Geological Survey, the Fairlee quadrangle of 1981. Blood Brook is a crooked blue line running south from the 1,400-foot contour on Spaulding Hill to the lake. Two hills parallel its course— Bald Top on the east, an unnamed ridge on the west. On the east, the brown contour lines crowd close. Here, on steep land, four inter-mittent streams—each a fractured blue line—feed the brook. From the west, three others enter. A permanent stream joins Blood Brook from the west, an eighth of a mile upstream from the lake.

On the map, a half mile down Spaulding Hill on the 1,100-foot contour, Blood Brook finally gains some measure of credibility with the cartographer, who connects the dots to declare it a year-round brook. On its short course, it descends 721 feet, guaranteeing riffles and little falls. At Lake Fairlee's outlet, a fork of the Ompompanoo-suc River's East Branch begins an eight-mile run toward its union with the West Branch. The Ompompanoosuc then joins the Con-necticut, New England's largest river, another four miles down-stream, at the town of Pompanoosuc. I recently drove south to Old Lyme, Connecticut, to see the big river filter through a maze of fer-tile salt marshes as it enters Long Island Sound, the end of my extended watershed, 200 miles from its roots.

Now, walking upstream along the flank of Spaulding Hill in No-vember, I search for Blood Brook's headwaters. I'm pushing the term to its limit. To my surprise, I find not one source but many sources scattered over the south side of the hill, all mere puddles in the spongy soil. These seeps, as hydrologists call them, are sites where groundwater, forced up by an impenetrable layer of rock, trickles to the surface. A spring is formed in the same way, but has a greater flow. The water in my muddy puddles, forced to the surface by some

At Jay Cooke State Park in Minneso-ta, turbulent rapids create one of many distinct aquatic habitats along the St. Louis River. Shifting mixes of current speed, oxygen, nutrients, and suspended sediment give rise to an immense variety of life. Richness defines fresh waters, moving or still: In the United States alone, these habitats sustain myriad plants and some 10,000 invertebrate species.

invisible geologic configuration, began as rain or snowmelt—perhaps years ago. Absorbed by porous soil, it has threaded its way through fissures in the rock to emerge at my feet on Spaulding Hill. I am reminded of this each winter as I drive along the interstate, admiring those great ice formations that decorate the sheer granite walls where the highway department's blasting has broken into underwater streams.

There are so many headstreams to Blood Brook, so many avenues and seeps, that my primitive field sketch begins to look more like a network of capillaries than a brook. Eventually, I give up searching—and drawing—and settle on a more productive task instead: exploration farther downstream in my valley.

Here, where the brook is a brook, I step into my waders, adjust the straps, and walk upstream toward my neighbor's meadow, a quarter mile above my house. In the pines behind my house, the brook funnels through a notch in a slippery, water-polished ledge, then drops in a wavering curtain over the edge to a pool below. I can hear it lilt from my front yard. A pool above the ledge holds three sculpins. Alarmed by my shadow, they dart for safety in a ball of roots in the shade of an undercut bank. I probe around with a stick. Two high-strung little fish, no more than two inches long, propelled by wing-like pectoral fins, scoot across the bottom, leaving an expanding line of sediment in their wake. I keep probing. The sculpins keep fleeing, and six plumes of silt spread out and merge into a thick, brown

Observations gleaned afield render the naturalist's journal a vital record, shaded with personal meaning. Sketches and notes from an outing illustrate the role current plays in the distribution of organisms. Rapid flow erodes material that is later deposited downstream in slower-moving reaches—in turn creating shallow, aerated riffles rich in insect larvae and deeper pools hospitable to fish.

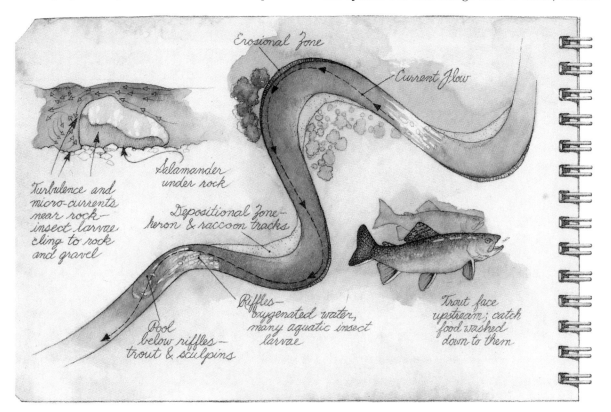

Erosional Zone

Current Flow

Turbulence and micro-currents near rock—insect larvae cling to rock and gravel

Salamander under rock

Depositional Zone—heron & raccoon tracks

Pool below riffles—trout & sculpins

Riffles—oxygenated water, many aquatic insect larvae

Trout face upstream; catch food washed down to them

screen. The pool is so stirred up that I can no longer follow the fish.

Another gathering of sculpins convenes in some riffles 50 yards upstream. Not wishing to disturb them, I watch from the bank. A sculpin is an odd-looking fish. It looks as if someone had stepped on its head, flattening its forehead and forcing the eyes to pop up like a frog's. This is a fish designed for life among the stones of cold, swift-water streams. Each sculpin faces into the current, tight in the riffles, its head flat on the bottom, its large pectoral fins pressed against the stones. Together with the tiny pelvic fins, set close together and far forward on the body, the thick leading edges of the pectorals form a friction plate that keeps the sculpin from being swept downstream. Slowly the little fish forage along the bottom for aquatic insects. Sculpins have large mouths for their size—big enough to engulf stonefly and mayfly nymphs.

They also eat brook trout eggs, usually those on the outside of the redd—the nesting area or spawning ground. These are the eggs most likely to be infected with fungus, and the feeding of sculpins and other fish keeps the disease from spreading to the healthy trout eggs deeper in the redd. Sometimes, too, sculpins eat trout fry, but turnabout is fair play: Adult brook trout eat sculpins, swiftly picking off the little fish as they clamber over a riffle or dart across a pool.

Sculpin eyes, perched on top of the fish's head, scan the water with what seems to me an almost mechanical beat, swiveling back and forth, up and down, like a pair of periscopes on ball-and-socket

Tendrils of the Yellowstone River vein an encroaching depositional zone in Montana. Over time, rivers often develop sinuous curves, or meanders. Between the bends in a meander, the main current switches sides and riffles often develop, such as those in the lower right of the photograph. In these shallow riffle areas, algae thrive, producing abundant food for aquatic animals.

joints. I lean out, my shadow stretching across the brook. Sculpins sense it and scatter.

Several days later, I march downstream through the brook. A dozen water striders skate across a pool, in and out of my shadow. With long, hair-thin legs, these insects glide, hop, and stand on the water, supported by the surface tension. This tight, stretchy film of water molecules occurs at the interface of air and water. Water striders use the upper side of the surface film for support, but other creatures use its lower side. I've seen rafts of mosquito eggs and larvae suspended upside down from it, as well as a hydra, tentacles stretching into the water below. Once I watched a little snail creeping along the under-surface of a glass-smooth pond as though it were an aquarium wall.

Long legs distribute the strider's weight, and tiny pads of waxy hairs repel water so that the animal's feet dimple the surface without breaking through. The apical claw, usually at the end of an insect leg, is set back so that it does not penetrate the surface film. If a strider wets its feet, it crawls out of the water and dries off before resuming its skating.

I remember lying on a small wooden bridge once, my head hanging over a Long Island stream, caught in the spell of dancing, balloon-like shadows that striders made on the shallow, sandy bottom. The shadows formed where a leg depressed the surface, curving it to make a lens. As striders glided by, coordinated and effortless, their attendant balloon shadows twitched and jerked, revealing some subtle interplay between air and water and insect.

The dark, rocky bottom of Blood Brook makes it hard to follow the water striders' shadows. I watch them glide instead. The longest pair of legs, the middle pair, rows the insect forward while the hind pair trails and the short front pair rests on the surface, waiting to grab prey. Through sensory organs in its legs, the insect receives surface tension vibrations. These are generally used to orient the strider to its prey, but in spring, each male vibrates the surface with his middle legs, sending a rippling species-specific love note to anxious females.

I drop a mosquito on the water. A strider skates over, grabs it with its forelegs, drills it with its stylet mouth, drains it dry, then discards it. A mosquito husk drifts downstream, an inconsequential loss.

I leave the striders and pass through a neighboring pasture, following a cow path downhill onto a broad, grassy plain. An intermittent stream enters the lower pasture from the east. There it drips from a culvert and is ground into a long, muddy swath by cattle. Two unmapped tributaries, both heavily trampled, enter from the west, adding to the widening belt of mud. Blood Brook itself flows deep and swift through the pasture, as though in a hurry to leave.

The cattle spot me, take the initiative, and move toward me. Having once spent time with bison, I'm too nonchalant about domestic bovines. Their pace quickens; mine too. I'm running now, my hands pinned to my shoulders, supporting my chest-wader straps, binoculars banging my chest. I glance over my shoulder. This is not a pastoral scene of the Vermont, Holstein cow T-shirt ilk—these are

Summer brings together two fresh-water denizens in an Alaskan stream (opposite): a black bear and a salmon migrating inland to spawn. Wolves, as well as scavengers such as gulls, benefit from the bear's fishing ability, remarkable for terrestrial animals. But few mammals can match the fishing skills of river otters (above). Though their ancestors lived on land, the otters' adaptations to aquatic life—streamlined bodies, webbed feet, waterproof fur, and the ability to stay submerged for up to three minutes—assure them a preferred diet of fish, frogs, and other freshwater prey.

The spring-fed waters of Florida's Ichetucknee River host spiky spring-tape leaves (top) free of epiphytes, which, in abundance, can signal ecological disturbance. The pearly mussel (above), another index of water purity, accumulates toxic metals in the annual layers of its shell. With too much pollution, the mussel dies out. The federal government lists more than 40 freshwater mussel species as endangered.

squat Herefords, bovine vigilantes, and they're charging. I win the race to the gate. Half vaulting, half kicking, I scramble over the top.

Under hemlocks below the pasture, Blood Brook takes on a wild, wondrous aspect, tumbling down terraced ledges and rushing around boulders. In the tree-cooled waters, I see brook trout fingerlings—no more than a few inches long. In summer they gathered in the shadows of the overhanging bank and patrolled nearby pools for terrestrial insects trapped by the surface film or for mayflies leaving the water. At the riffles, they checked for larvae of algae-feeding caddisflies, for nymphs of mayflies and stoneflies, and for damselflies—maybe even sculpin fry. Now suspended in the current, exposed and hungry, trout wait for what little November has to offer. They spot me. They're gone, passing through my field of vision so quickly that I'm not sure whether I saw fish or specks of sunlight.

It's hard to appreciate the color of a brook trout while peering into running water. Sure, I see the clean white stripe on the leading edge of the lower fins—a definitive characteristic; the dark squiggles over an olive-green back; the blushing flanks of spawning males. If they move into the light, I see the large yellow spots that pepper the trout's sides. But when a live brook trout rests in someone's creel— then I see the subtler colors; the iridescent aqua sides spiced with a few small, blue-haloed red spots; the orange-tinted fins.

Brook trout are actually char, members of the genus *Salvelinus*, which includes lake trout. The two species descended from a

The array of organisms that live on a stream bottom can shed light on the stream's health and water quality. An even mix of bottom-dwelling invertebrate species, such as the larvae of stoneflies (left), caddisflies (center), and mayflies (right), often indicates a healthy stream. Pollution or other disturbances that reduce oxygen levels in water can alter the balance of species, allowing tolerant species to gain a competitive edge. Some kinds of stoneflies need highly oxygenated water; their absence may be a first sign of pollution. Certain caddisfly species, on the other hand, are more tolerant of low oxygen levels and can "ventilate" by undulating within their twig cases, increasing water flow over their gills.

common ancestor in eastern North America during the Pliocene epoch, about two to five million years ago. According to the fossil record, lake trout have changed very little since then, confining themselves to relatively stable, deepwater lakes and rivers where baitfish thrive. Their range now sweeps across the northern half of the continent from coast to coast and beyond the Arctic Circle. Although native brookies remain an Atlantic drainage fish, they adapted long ago to a much wider range of habitats than their larger cousins. They live in beaver ponds and cold-water lakes, in streams ranging in size from Blood Brook to the Connecticut River. In Maine and the Canadian Maritimes, an anadromous race of brook trout, shiny as a silver dollar, comes to spawn from the sea.

Trout line up in the current behind the submerged trunk of an old white pine. One. Two. Three . . . Eleven. Twelve. They wait for food, paying no attention to me. Water spills over the smooth, bare wood. The fish hold their position, inhaling the current as it pours over them.

I splinter a white pine twig, chipping little pieces, and flick them into the brook. One trout rises. Another. And another. One takes the wood in its mouth, settles in front of the trunk, and then realizes it has been tricked. My wooden lure floats to the surface.

Brook trout, because they live in swift water, must be adept at holding position in the current or be swept downstream. Unlike sculpin, they don't hug the bottom, sprawling over stones. A

Homing in on their birthplace, two sockeye salmon swim up British Columbia's Adams River to spawn at the end of their lives—having traveled perhaps 2,000 miles in the past year. So purposeful is the migration from ocean to natal waters that adults easily cover 25 miles a day, undeterred by waterfalls or sandbars, eating nothing, surging over one another's backs in narrow streams—and then dying soon after eggs are laid and fertilized in nests called redds. Translucent alevins emerge some three to four months later; juveniles spend up to three years in fresh water before starting their ocean-going migrations. Their remarkable odyssey calls for major physiological adaptations as the fish bridge the vast gulf between freshwater and marine environments twice in a life cycle.

Summer spawning run in Alaska

Salmon eggs

Newly hatched alevins

Alevin (with yolk sac)

streamlined body, tapered at both ends, widest just in front of the dorsal fin—a little more than a third of the way down its length—makes for perfect ballast in rushing water. A trout need only undulate its body against the water and fan its broad, square tail to hold position. Its fin and tail margins trail to reduce drag, yet are tough enough to withstand abrasion against the brook's rocky bottom. Its fine body scales—so fine that most people eat trout unscaled—form an almost frictionless surface in the rushing water, while an extended dorsal fin stabilizes the fish.

Even the brook trout's respiratory system helps to maintain its position in the current. When a trout—or any other species of fish, for that matter—breathes, it opens its mouth and expands its mouth cavity, creating a strong negative pressure. Water rushes in, passes over the gills—which extract the dissolved oxygen—and then is forced out under the opercula. The position of these hard gill covers is such that the exhaled water propels the trout slightly forward before it runs smoothly over the fish's body. This smooth envelope of exhaled water, a pattern called laminar flow, reduces drag and turbulence by softening the eddies of water pushed up by the brook.

Slowed by beaver dams, a Minnesota stream flows into ponds surrounding beaver lodges. A whole watershed may undergo radical transformation from beaver activities as flooded trees die, marshes and bogs emerge, and organic muck builds up. Consumed with dam building, a beaver is itself a marvel of aquatic engineering, with oil-coated fur, valvular ear and nose flaps, and a paddle-shaped tail.

FOLLOWING PAGES: Cattails fringe the still waters of a Minnesota beaver pond—and its grassy shallow-water habitat, which attracts muskrats, herons, frogs, and spawning fish.

Family life at the beaver pond picks up its pace in summer as focus shifts to the year's young. A cutaway of the domelike lodge reveals the female nursing newborns in the chamber. Temporarily displaced, her mate and yearlings may have to find alternate quarters until the family reunites when the kits are two weeks old. In the meantime, yearlings hover nearby. Those at far left and in right background carry leafy branches for their mother to eat; a third, diving out of a lodge tunnel at right, has just made a delivery. But summer also means relative ease: While one yearling surfaces, another grooms itself on the lodge's roof.

Brook trout capture prey at all levels in the water. Their eyes furnish excellent binocular vision in front and above. They have good lateral vision, too, and can scan the bottom. Sneaking up on a brook trout is an acquired skill.

I get an idea. If hungry trout come to wood, they'll love cluster flies. I pick 20 or so from my office window, where a congregation gathers in the sun, and surgically remove a wing from each so that when the flies hit the water they will spin in a circle, broadcasting concentric distress signals as they head downstream.

I check my topo map for the easiest access to the trout, gather up the flies in a baby food jar, and drive down the road toward Lake Fairlee. I park and enter the woods, the flies buzzing in my pocket, cross a wet meadow, and intersect Blood Brook below the smooth white pine. A hundred yards downstream stands a big pine. Its bent and scoured roots guard a grotto in the undercut bank, keeping out all but the most skillfully cast flies. A seven-inch male brookie with belly and sides washed in red and a slightly enlarged lower jaw tended a five-inch female there last week.

I lean straight down the bank, my feet hooked on pine roots, my

right hand wedged against a yellow birch, and peer over the lip of the bank. No big red trout. Perhaps he's deeper in the grotto. There are fish, however—fourteen trout that range in size from two to four inches. They gather two and three abreast. I shake out the cluster flies. A trout rises. Hits. There are two flies. Then one. As I stare at the remaining fly, a trout shoots up from the grotto, striking it. As a method of pest control, tossing flies to brook trout is less efficient but infinitely more satisfying than vacuuming them off my windows.

I walk a hundred yards downstream. A patch of riffles that in early May had entertained unnumbered spawning white suckers now is quiet by comparison. I turn over a stone. A dusky salamander launches into the current and quickly disappears. I turn another. Nothing. A third yields two flattened mayfly nymphs. Unlike the salamander, they're not in a hurry and creep over an adjacent stone.

Last spring these shoals seethed with suckers more than a foot long, so many that I caught them with my hands. One swollen female discharged a fusillade of sticky, yellowish orange eggs as I held her. To hold their place in the current, sucker eggs stick to everything—rocks and roots, my waders. Three weeks later, while adult

On Montana's Medicine Lake, a trio of western grebes rises up in a "rush-ing" display. Courting birds may race across the water's surface side by side for 20 yards or more before diving. Awkward in the air but agile in wa-ter, grebes make floating nests, often anchoring them to shallow bottoms or reed clumps. An ample, meticu-lously built nest supports a trumpeter swan (above) during breeding sea-son. This largest of North American waterfowl also lays its eggs on aban-doned beaver or muskrat lodges.

Life in a Pond

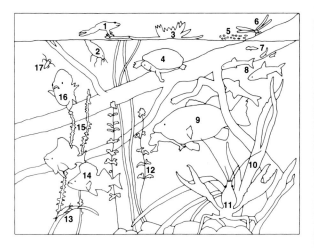

1 Northern leopard
   frog (Rana pipiens)
2 Predaceous diving
   beetle (Dysticus
   sp.)
3 American water lily
   (Nymphaea
   odorata)
4 Painted turtle
   (Chrysemys picta)
5 Common duck-
   weed (Lemna
   minor)

6 Green darner
   dragonfly (Anax
   junius)
7 Bullfrog tadpoles
   (Rana
   catesbeiana)
8 Shiner minnows
   (Notropis sp.)
9 Largemouth bass
   (Micropterus
   salmoides)
10 Sweet flag (Acorus
   calamus)
11 Burrowing crayfish
   (Cambarus
   diogenes)
12 Water milfoil
   (Myriophyllum sp.)

13 Mayfly larva
   (Caenis simulans)
14 Yellow perch
   (Perca flavescens)
15 Canadian water-
   weed (Elodea
   canadensis)
16 Bluegill (Lepomis
   macrochirus)
17 Water boatman
   (Sigara sp.)

A pond's shallow waters and muddy bottom support a teeming world of plants and animals woven in an intricate food web. Largemouth bass, among the pond's larger carnivores, consume leopard frogs, insects, burrowing crayfish, and smaller fish—all seeking food and protection amid waterweeds and milfoil. With few predators to contend with, adult largemouths may grow longer than 2 feet and weigh more than 15 pounds. Most never reach this size, however, since newly hatched fry and fingerlings fall prey to bigger fish, dragonfly nymphs, diving beetles, and giant water bugs.

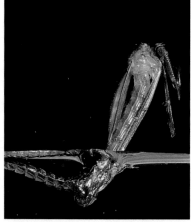

Heads down, mosquito larvae hang from a pond's still surface. This pose allows the larvae to feed on microorganisms and detritus suspended in the water while taking in air via their snorkel-like breathing siphons. The final transition to adulthood occurs at the pond surface, as the mosquito breaks out of its pupal skin (right, top) and dries briefly before taking flight (right, bottom).

suckers vacuumed food off the bottom of Lake Fairlee, sucker fry hatched in the brook.

Beyond the riffle, the brook widens and slows. A gray sandbar reaches into quiet water. Deer drink here and leave deep, cloven prints, sunk down to the dewclaws. One trail comes down an unnamed hill, another crosses the meadow. A raccoon has passed down the west bank, walked out on the bar, reached into the brook with its sensitive forepaws, and then moved on. A pileated woodpecker laughs in the distance.

On the Fairlee quadrangle, the lake looks like a giant tadpole, its tail swung to the north to meet Blood Brook, its head feeding the fork of the Ompompanoosuc's East Branch. I secure my kayak on the car, drive to the lake, and park where Blood Brook empties its freight. The land is flat and sandy, worn by shifting water.

Three feet off the road is a snapping turtle nest—a six- or seven-inch hole in the sand—dug last July by a resident of the cattail marsh. Digging, I uncover scraps of eggshells, curled along the edges, but no whole eggs or turtles. A skunk has prowled nearby, teased the sand with its long claws, and left some scat, now dried. Had the turtles hatched?

I break apart the scat: apple skin and apple seeds, beetle parts, pieces of yellow jackets, but no snapping turtles. Three dark spots on the paved road—two-dimensional baby turtles, flattened by traffic—suggest an answer. Some turtles, at least, had hatched.

Ceiling for some, platform for others, the water's surface provides habitat for specially adapted insects called neuston. A water strider (1) skates across the surface to take its insect prey. A whirligig beetle (2) also hunts from above, peering downward with a unique second pair of eyes. The water boatman (3) can swim underwater by storing air in a thin film held by hairs on the underside of its body. The extensible air siphon of the rattailed maggot (4) allows it to rest and feed four or five inches below the surface. Both the giant water bug (5) and the water tiger (6)—here devouring a tadpole while hanging from the surface—can carry an air supply underwater, but must rise up periodically to replenish it.

Last summer I lay in the grass and watched a nonchalant mother turtle dig this nest and methodically lay 27 round, white, leathery eggs—one at a time at three- or four-minute intervals. Then she covered her clutch with sand, packed solid by her hind feet, and lumbered back to the brook, an animated Sherman tank.

The temperature of the nest will determine the embryos' sex: 84°F or hotter produces females; 80°F or cooler produces mostly males. In between, either sex may develop. Somehow this arrangement must produce a balance of males and females in the population, for snapping turtles have been around for a long time. They are among the most primitive of living reptiles: Their ancestors go back more than 150 million years.

During mild September weather, young snapping turtles emerge from their nest and crawl straight to the marsh; harsh weather keeps them in the nest until spring, either in or out of their shells. To learn their winter plans, I check for road kills; the greater the number, the larger the exodus.

Once in the marsh, turtles pass the winter buried, insulated from frost by a layer of ice and snow, their metabolism slowed.

Winter in the nest is unpredictable. One year 80 percent of the turtles might perish, the next, none. The difference between life and death is snow depth. Deep snow insulates the turtles. Without it, they freeze, ice crystals rupturing their cells.

In my kayak I paddle to a muskrat lodge on the edge of the marsh,

a three-foot-high stack of cattails and water lilies, plastered with mud and decorated with red cigarette packages. The lodge is at the center of a patch of stubby cattails, each stalk neatly cut below the waterline—as though a barber had delivered a vegetative crewcut. The muskrats had cut the cattails for insulation and carried them back to the lodge in their forepaws. Unlike beavers, muskrats don't fill pantries. They're busy all winter digging roots, tubers, rhizomes, and the occasional clam below the ice.

One January morning while lying on black ice, I watched a muskrat swim below me. He held a tuber in his forepaws. His fur shed streaks of shiny silver bubbles that rose and stuck against the undersurface of the ice like strings of pearls. Following, I slid on my belly until the muskrat dived from sight.

Although I see little movement in the marsh today, I know that

First light on a Maine lake unfurls petals of an American water lily as a bullfrog hunts for snails, worms, and insects that inhabit pads and underwater stalks. Water lilies benefit wildlife in a multitude of ways. Leaves—as well as stems and flowers—provide a favored browse for white-tailed deer (opposite, top). Ducks and other wildfowl eat the seeds. Large floating pads offer shade and shelter to fish, which in turn become prey for a green-backed heron (opposite, bottom).

life still courses at a frantic pace below the surface. Several weeks ago, in September, I paddled the marsh by moonlight, out beyond the reeds where the water deepens. A beaver towing an alder through a bar of reflected moonlight slapped his tail and dived. All around me, phantom midge larvae rose toward the surface, twisting and snapping their thin, half-inch, transparent bodies. With one sweep of a small dip net, I caught several dozen and transferred them to a jar for a closer look. My flashlight revealed the dark air bladders at each end of the body, nothing more. At night, billions of phantom midges bubble up from the sediments to harpoon zooplankton—rotifers, mostly—on short, bristly antennae. To watch this, I use my dissecting scope, for rotifers are even smaller than dust.

In a laboratory at Dartmouth College I glimpsed another slice of life below the surface of Lake Fairlee. A graduate student working on

Red-spotted newts (opposite) feed around submerged spatterdock leaves in Ginnie Springs, Florida. Under waving canopies of sedges, pondweed, eelgrass, and other aquatic plants are microhabitats where many organisms flourish. Taking cover in a tangle of vegetation, a mudminnow earns its name from the silty bottoms of lakes and ponds where it burrows. Water itself becomes a snare for the prey of a webless wolf spider, clinging upside down from a leaf with her egg sac. A water-lily leaf-cutter caterpillar incises a rough round for its new home, then swims away with it.

Eastern mudminnow

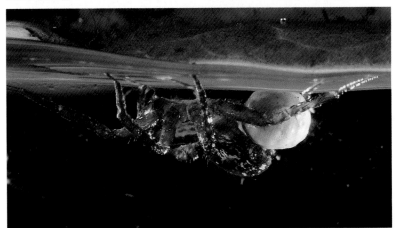

Wolf spider *(Pirata)*

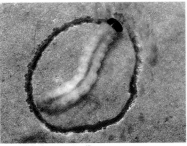

Water-lily leaf-cutter caterpillar

Tiny but treacherous, saclike traps stud underwater stems of the carnivorous bladderwort plant (top). Aquatic organisms browsing in the vicinity trip ultrasensitive trigger hairs, which in turn spring the bladderwort's one-way trap doors, sucking in prey. Fish fry and other large victims—such as the mosquito larva in the lower photograph—meet doom in stages, nabbed first by head or tail, then gradually digested.

predator avoidance behavior let me watch her experiment. She was studying the way damselfly nymphs position themselves on bulrushes to avoid the brightly colored pumpkinseed sunfish that methodically search each stalk for food.

She anchored sections of bulrush stems vertically to the bottom of six aquariums—four or eight to a tank; then blocked the sunfish from the stems with a plexiglass panel and released damselfly nymphs into each tank. After the nymphs swam to the stems, she freed the fish.

When a pumpkinseed approached the bulrushes, all the nymphs crept in unison to the back sides of the stems. Out of sight, out of mind. The sunfish almost never pursued them around the stem. The more nymphs per aquarium, the quicker they detected the sunfish and the quicker they sought cover. Tanks with only two or three nymphs had a higher rate of predation than tanks with four or eight. I flicked a bulrush, dislodging a nymph, and a pumpkinseed arrived on the spot, devouring the twisting little insect. I left the college with an insight: Whenever my kayak paddle strikes a cattail stalk and dislodges an aquatic insect, an attentive sunfish gets a meal.

I paddle around the far end of the marsh, looking for whirligig beetles, which just last week had gathered by the thousand in tight, oblong-shaped rafts. I count three; the rest must be in the mud, each with a bubble of air from which to breathe—a beetle Aqua-Lung, of sorts—that comes from a reservoir of air beneath its wing covers.

I drifted close to that crowd of whirligigs last week. At 20 feet away, their collective engines revved. I drifted closer. The raft disintegrated, beetles exploding in all directions, spinning, darting, and whirling on the surface like so many tiny bumper cars. I drifted away. They reconvened.

In spring, whirligigs swim back to the surface and mate. After the females attach their eggs to submerged plants, they die. The eggs hatch in about two weeks, and the larvae remain in the water for two or three months, hunting small aquatic animals along the bottom.

By early August, mature larvae crawl out of the water and pupate on the stems of aquatic plants. A month later, a new generation of shiny black adult whirligig beetles erratically scoot across the surface of Lake Fairlee, pushing a wake of ripples ahead of themselves.

A whirligig is built for life on the water. Oval and flattened, a whittled-down version of a June beetle, it has two pairs of eyes—one set sees above the surface, the other below—and short, flat middle and hind legs, which stroke the water 50 to 60 times per second for rapid propulsion. Plates at the end of these legs come together like the cupped hand of a swimmer on the power stroke, and then open on the upstroke, allowing water to pass freely through. The long, thin front legs, suited to grab insects off the surface, fold up under the head, and a pair of short antennae rest at the surface to detect the slightest ripple.

So sensitive are the whirligig's antennae that a beetle in a tightly packed raft—which may sponsor close to a quarter of a million nervous beetles—never brushes against its neighbors, even when every one is moving helter-skelter. Much like a bat that reads returning sound waves in the air, the whirligig uses a form of echolocation to avoid collisions and to locate food. Its antennae read the echoes of its own ripples as they bounce back from objects in the water.

Whirligigs may congregate because their toxic secretions are thus more concentrated and more likely to repel predators. At night they disband to hunt along the lake's surface film, sometimes commuting a mile away. When dawn comes, they join other beetles in the area to form a new raft. Whenever I slapped a mosquito, I dropped it in the water and watched by flashlight as racing beetles headed for their dinner.

As Lake Fairlee cools, something more than whirligigs goes below the surface: The heavier, cooler surface water sinks, too. Because water density increases as temperature falls, warm surface water floats on cold deeper water until it cools to 39.2°F—the temperature at which water attains maximum density.

In summer, a deep lake such as Lake Fairlee stratifies into three distinct zones: the top, the epilimnion; the middle, the metalimnion; and the bottom, the hypolimnion. Each zone circulates

Making a Pond Viewer

Life found on a pond surface is fascinating, but it only hints at the world of organisms flourishing below. Attempts to observe this watery realm are often thwarted by reflections or the sun's glare. A pond viewer will correct these problems and may bring you eye-to-eye with a curious minnow. Find a used plastic container—a small wastebasket, for instance. Cut out the bottom carefully with a utility knife. Apply a waterproof adhesive about halfway up the outside of the basket. Then stretch a large piece of clear, heavy-duty plastic wrap over the new opening and up onto the glued sides. Further secure the plastic by wrapping strong, waterproof tape around the edges. Hold the viewer by the top and tilt it slightly as you immerse it just below the surface of the pond. Then straighten it and allow pond life to adjust to its presence. For the best results, try to keep the shadow of your body over the viewer.

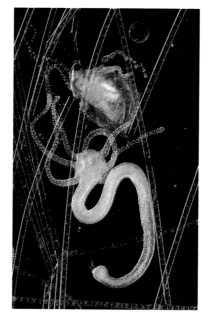

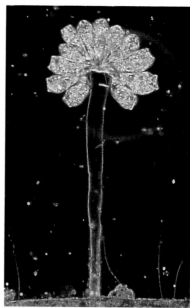

Unseen by the naked eye, freshwater life reveals itself under a microscope, with help from color-enhancing camera filters. Among the most complex organisms, a gammaridean amphipod—or scud—(right) bears a family resemblance to better-known saltwater crustaceans, such as shrimp. Likewise, the hydra, with its stinging threads that paralyze a hapless water flea (above, left) with potent venom, is distant kin to jellyfish. Freshwater habitats hold countless numbers of microscopic creatures. A single-celled animal called a protozoan blooms elegantly (above, center). Although most protozoans are harmless, some species spread diseases such as African sleeping sickness. Green algae (above, right) lack specialized cells, a trait typical of earth's earliest plant forms.

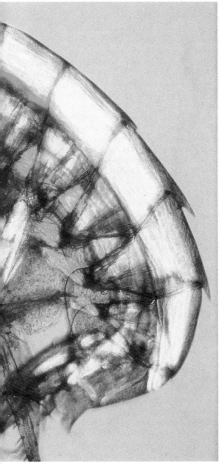

separately, and the light winds of summer can't mix the layers, which remain as distinct as oil and vinegar. Diving through the epilimnion into the metalimnion always shocks my body. The temperature suddenly drops 10°F to 15°F along an invisible boundary less than ten feet below the surface.

Of the three layers in Lake Fairlee, the epilimnion—always in contact with air—is richest in oxygen and lowest in organic nutrients, which settle at the bottom of the lake. The hypolimnion gains all the nutrients that rain down during the summer, but has lost most of its oxygen to the enormous biomass of decomposers that live in the sediments.

With the passing of summer, Lake Fairlee sheds its accumulated warmth. Tendrils of mist curl high into the morning sky and drift up the valley. As nights grow colder and frost bites into the soil, the surface water cools and sinks, cools and sinks, and the warm surface layer shrinks. Days of cooling yield to weeks, then to November, when the lake is a nearly uniform 39.2°F.

As I paddle offshore, Lake Fairlee completes its fall overturn. Having lost its summer stratification, lake water freely circulates, dispersing both nutrients and oxygen. Toxic gases that accumulated in the hypolimnion are released at the surface; plankton floats at all levels; cold-water bottom fish rise to the surface; and warm-water surface fish move to the bottom, taking advantage of the rich supply of oxygen and nutrients.

Below 39.2°F, water becomes less dense—and this cooler water floats. The lake stops circulating, and overturn ends. When ice finally forms—generally by mid-December—it is lighter than the water and rides it.

I cannot see the overturn, of course, but I imagine that the flock of buffleheads, which arrived the other night from central Canada en route to some mid-Atlantic estuary for a winter respite, find plenty of food as aquatic insects and small fish are equally dispersed at all depths. The ducks idle at mid-lake. I paddle toward them. They see me and dive, powered by their large feet. Not far from where they dived, they surface: three males, mostly white, and four dull-colored birds, either females or young of the year.

A beaver lodge—a huge mound of branches and trunks from sugar maples and yellow birches, packed with mud—reaches out from the shoreline like a half-submerged boulder. Last night's harvest floats in front, alders from the banks of Blood Brook, red oak from more than a mile away. Beyond the lodge, two blackcapped chickadees fill their bills with Lake Fairlee, tip their heads back, and swallow. A nervous blue jay bathes, while crows, everywhere and noisy, pass above the lake. Four herring gulls and an immature black-legged kittiwake—a very rare inland visitor from the Arctic—wheel against a peach-colored November sky. Ahead lie the cattail marshes at the mouth of Middle Brook, the largest of the lake's seven tributaries, and beyond, the fork of the Ompompanoosuc's East Branch. With twilight closing in, I turn back north, and home.

Closed-basin bog

Mature closed-basin bog

Gradual encroachment of vegetation on ponds creates the wetland world of the bog. Bogs arise out of unique conditions—poor drainage and deposits of organic material that turn into acid-releasing peat. Most occur in the cooler reaches of the Northern Hemisphere, with climate and terrain defining the specific bog type. Closed-basin bogs, familiar to New Englanders as kettleholes, form within glacier-scoured depressions that later became ponds. Dead plants simultaneously carpet both floor and surface, eventually filling the entire basin with rich organic peat. Farther north, continuing accumulations of peat raise water tables and create the moundlike domes of the raised bog. Heavy rains falling on relatively level terrain underlain by impermeable rock create the blanket bog of northern coastal highlands.

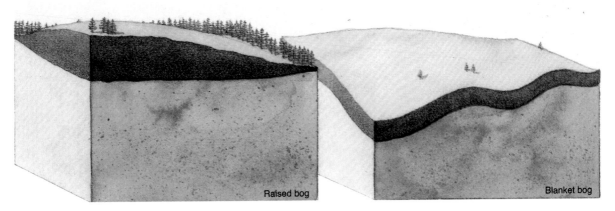

Raised bog

Blanket bog

On the sphagnum cushion of a Maine bog (opposite), burgundy-colored pitcher plants cup small pools where insects drown. Insectivorous plants—which may have evolved in bogs—thrive as few plants can in an acidic, mineral-poor, and oxygen-depleted environment, deriving nitrogen and phosphorus from their prey. Sticky droplets on slender leaf tentacles give the sundew (above) its name, and a strong adhesive for catching prey.

Compared with Blood Brook, the East Branch is a torrent. Between Lake Fairlee and its union with the West Branch, it drains corrugated land—hills, plains, and swamps—dissected by brooks and spotted with lakes. It runs rapidly, tumbles down cascades, leaps over falls, backs up into deep, blue pools surrounded by water-polished granite. Below the junction of the two branches, a flood-control dam forever changes the fortunes of the river. Wide and lazy, its contours softened, the Ompompanoosuc at its mouth looks more like Alabama than Vermont. It is brown with dissolved matter.

Largemouth bass spawn here, and chain pickerel and yellow perch. Mallards nest in the marsh, kingfishers and bank swallows in the flank of the sandy esker above the river. On migration great blue herons and ospreys stop by. Sometimes bald eagles.

To study river otters, I visit the mouth of the Ompompanoosuc. The otters travel up and down the Connecticut River and stop here in the shallow backwaters to feed. I find their toilets—sites along the edge of the water chosen for reasons known only to otters—littered with scat. Each pile supports evidence of a feast: splintered crayfish exoskeletons and snail shells, fish scales and bones, mostly.

Since a fish can be identified by scales alone, I take scat samples home to examine. Slow, abundant suckers, both available and vulnerable to otter attack, account for the bulk of the Ompompanoosuc otter diet, followed by golden shiners and pumpkinseed sunfish. Fish, like trees, grow rapidly in summer and slowly in winter, thus laying down annual growth rings on their scales that mirror the year's growth history. One large, transparent sucker scale I picked had six rings, little raised ridges. Another had five.

Several years ago, a large otter, probably a male, gamboled for six weeks on a small patch of Ompompanoosuc ice, hemmed in by a popular state highway and the Connecticut River. It was cramped quarters for an itinerant species of mammal known to course 50 miles of watershed in a week. It was the best otter-watching I've had.

There is nothing quite like an otter: No other predator I've watched is as adept at catching food. No other animal I know—

except the humans who manage to retain a little childishness—makes such a game of life.

The otter's long, stout whiskers—the vibrissae—sense the slightest vibration and work in concert with its sensitive forepaws to catch food. Whenever my otter dived, he surfaced with food: yellow perch, bullheads, suckers, pumpkinseeds, dace, a fat smallmouth that would have pleased the most fastidious fisherman, bullfrog tadpoles, crayfish, snails, freshwater clams, and even a muskrat, whose fur purged the otter's intestines like bran flakes.

One morning I found the otter gliding through a black lead of water, his head barely above the surface. His dark, sinuous body was curving through the river, powered by large, webbed hind feet and a long, sculling tail. He dived without a ripple, then surfaced rippleless, a bright pumpkinseed sunfish clamped in his mouth.

Tossing the fish up on the ice, he followed in a motion so smooth it was like seeing water run uphill. An improvised ice hockey game quickly took shape. First running, then tobogganing, the otter used his broad nose as the stick, and sent the puck-shaped sunfish spinning past invisible defenders. When the pumpkinseed shot over the edge into the water, the otter hunched up, then slithered and jackknifed into the river. In a moment the hapless sunfish spun down the ice again, the game renewed.

Several weeks later, I watched an odd threesome cavorting on the brittle April ice—two golden retrievers and the otter. When the ice finally gave way, the dogs' owner whistled them out of the river. A bewildered bystander, who had been watching the shenanigans from a safe distance, turned to me.

"Isn't anyone going to help that poor black one, the one that looks like a seal?"

Soaked up to their knees, or aerial roots, cypresses rise from swamp water in North Carolina. Spanish moss, epiphytes, and climbing vines cling to branches beyond reach of water. Aquatic vegetation forms part of the swamp's complex food web, nourishing a nutria (above) and other herbivorous mammals and waterfowl, which, in turn, are prey for the American alligator (left).

By Ann H. Zwinger

Sandy Shores & Coastal Wetlands

Hunkered on the beach at Cape Lookout, the southernmost point of North Carolina's Outer Banks, I steady elbows on knees, focus binoculars, and watch a dozen sanderlings chase the skim of water of each fading wave as it slithers down the beach. They weave back and forth, beaks stabbing rapidly into the wet sand, twinkling across the swash in unison. Six pokes and they scatter back up the beach as the wave breaks and foams, keeping just ahead of the uprush until it loses its thrust, then reversing, black legs reflecting in the sheen.

Trying to see what they're eating frustrates me. I've dug into every nearby bubbling hole, every little dimpled depression, and found nothing. Mole crabs must be in the wet sand, for they are among the few creatures able to exist in such a sloshy, syrupy subsurface continually worked by waves, and furthermore, their half-peanut-size carapaces litter the beach. But no trowelful of sand brings up a live one.

This naturalist's tools in the field are few, and a trowel may be one of the most versatile, a good-for-things-I-haven't-even-thought-of-yet tool. I bring compact binoculars, the prerequisite hand lens, a sturdy, metal-encased thermometer with which to measure sand and water temperatures, and, this trip, a tiny microscope-and-light the size of two breadsticks. My newest toy is the headlamp I wear when moth collecting, brought to observe crabs at night. And a lot of plastic bags—not for collecting, but for corralling small, wiggling things for closer observation.

Annoyed, I take one last scoop of sand and meticulously separate the sand grains. This time out pops a sand-colored, half-inch mole crab. So! I excavate several more holes with equal care, and nearly every cut gives up a frenetic mole crab, a carapace arched over five pairs of wide, paddlelike legs, and a sword-shaped telson, half as long as its body, snugged up against its abdomen. Under my hand lens the minute ridges of a paper-thin shell cast no shadow but still create enough contour to expedite the animal's burrowing, which must be swift after it is sucked out of the sand by an inrushing wave.

Now I look with bird eyes, keyed to what to look for—and where. I see how, uprooted by the wave, the mole crabs burble the thin water film, little nubbins tumbled at the mercy of the wave until they dig in again. No wonder the sanderlings are so diligent.

I dump a scoop of sand into a plastic bag and pop my charge in on top. The mole crab rows out of sight in a nanosecond—the sand

A pair of sanderlings skirts the edge of the sea in North Carolina, searching for tiny crustaceans exposed by the surf's retreat. Sanderlings migrate between South America and the Arctic, stopping to rest and feed in the salt haze of ocean beaches. Such sandy margins harbor crustaceans, mollusks, and worms, whose lives are shaped by salt water and the restless forces of the sea.

touching the base of the telson may instigate its digging reflexes. In the next trowelful of sand is a coquina, a tiny clam shuttered between delicate shells a mere half inch across, porcelain-white rayed with lavender. Two translucent white siphons extend from one side of the shell, a translucent foot from the other. The coquina pushes its foot out like a root, fills it with blood to form a bulb-shaped anchor, then retracts it, pulsating its shell down into the sand. Now not a creature is to be seen. I upend the bag into the retreating swash. The sand quivers, then flattens with the next wave.

Waves angle in from the northeast, roiled with sand, tumbling over one another, a beach on the move. I sense the unseen larger movements: the seasonal pulse of longshore currents, the offshore bars that store sand in the winter and give it up to the beach in the summer, the westward march of the island itself.

In the direct path of hurricanes and northeasterly storms, the Outer Banks bear the brunt of gigantic waves and massive surges of water from the sea. More than twenty hurricanes have beset the banks this century, but it is the more numerous winter northeasters, three or four a year, that smash inlets open, overwash the beaches, and advance the islands shoreward.

In Colorado, before I came, I built three-dimensional mental images from United States Geological Survey maps, traced the big crochet hook that is Cape Lookout, envisioned the sand beach and the salt marsh, read whatever I could get my hands on. But nothing prepared me for this infinity of beach, this pulse of change. Even this warm October afternoon seems transitory: Already summer's southwesterlies have shifted once to winter's northeasterlies, and I luxuriate on the cusp of the season before they shift again.

Wind sculpts tiny triangles like cuneiform writing behind thousands of shell bits. Incessant wind, salt spray, and intense heat, as well as sterile, shifting, well-drained sand, all combine to limit plant growth. Seaside spurge splays flat on the sand, its diminutive leaves able to withstand the heavy heat load of hot beach and the airborne salt. Skeletons of sea-rocket stand gray and indurated. Annuals, they sprout from seeds lodged in beach debris. The seed capsule splits in two. The lower half drops close by; the upper half becomes corky before detachment, able to float or tumble farther away. Silver-leaved croton, a perennial, bears fat tripartite seed heads; stellate hairs frost the whole plant silver. The ubiquitous pennywort leaves,

On a barrier island in North Carolina, low tide reveals only wave-carved ridges of sand. But hidden beneath are myriad creatures seeking refuge from the harsh conditions of low tide—drying sun and the sharp bills of shorebirds. In an underground world of burrows and tubes live crabs and clams, as well as lugworms, tube worms, and plumed worms that will emerge to feed at high tide.

shiny, round, and thick, rise singly from a well-buried connecting stem, and are arrayed vertically like radar dishes in a row.

By far the most prevalent and handsome plants are the sea oats that fringe every dune. The leaves appear dewed, so shiny are they from a protective outer layer of cells. The blades roll inward, protecting the stomata from drying sun and wind. Some leaves bend near the base and some near the tip, pliantly green, each with its own graceful curve. As the wind nudges them, the blades dip and scribe herringbones or repeated arcs in the sand, drawing a cartouche around each dune, wind made visible.

The first row of sea oats is but a foot high; two feet back stands another row of same-age plants, all attached by underground rhizomes by which they reproduce more readily than from seed. A four- to five-inch collar of sand extends downwind from each plant, dropped where stems interrupt the wind. Over time, being buried stimulates sea oats to sprout new rhizomes from which new stems arise and catch new sand. Eventually haystack dunes form, webbed with sand-holding roots, each dune capped with a toupee of sea oats. Storm seas run between these scattered dunes where sand absorbs and dissipates wave energy quickly. Sand gets shifted, sea oats beaten, but such is the elasticity of a natural barrier island that there is seldom devastation, only rearrangement. The berm remains open and wide.

Naturalists are born wanderers, and it takes an hour to traverse the berm and wend between the dunes to the hollow where my tent is pitched. A ghost crab hole is there that wasn't there this morning. A hole so far from the beach suggests a mature crab; young ones burrow closer to high-tide line. I settle a few feet away and wait. At dusk the crab appears. The tips of its starboard legs grope for purchase outside before its carapace appears, port legs still anchored in the hole. It evaporates at my first movement.

A sinking sun incandesces white behind a milky sky. Lavender clouds filter a brightness of peach and leave one slash of opalescent rose along the darkening horizon. I focus the headlamp beam on the crab's hole. The crab reemerges and poises there an eternal six minutes with only stalked eyes moving, then scuttles off to modulate the populations of mole crabs and coquinas.

The lighthouse beam sweeps the dunes. The white, ruffled surf line throws starlight on the beach. In the morning, sand plasters the window netting of the tent on the north side, which suggests that I

Well equipped for fishing, a black skimmer off Florida's Sanibel Island shears the glassy salt water with the lower mandible of its thin black-and-coral bill. When the bird strikes a crustacean or fish, it clamps its upper mandible shut and tips its head down and then up to swallow its prey, never skipping a wingbeat.

Skimmers breed in loose colonies on sandy shores, often in company with terns and other beach nesters. The pale buff down of a newly hatched Caspian tern (lower, far left) camouflages the chick in its primitive nest—just a shallow scrape in the sand. Parent Caspians (lower, middle) feed their young small minnows of different species. Most tern chicks gain powers of locomotion soon after hatching, as shown by a least tern (lower, near left), three days old.

should reorient it—but then I couldn't awaken at night and see the ocean. I covet being here alone: It allows creatures within my purview to acclimate to the new movement on their horizon and allows me to tune in to their patterns of living.

Today my movements do not concern the tentside crabs as I putter about. On this cloudy morning many crabs are out, stippled and mottled like the sand, so well camouflaged I can't see them until they move. One ghost crab backs up against a grass clump and stands on tiptoe, its body nearly vertical, raising startling white claws in a gesture both protective and pugnacious. When I bend over to examine it, I catch a soft burring sound that spells "rattlesnake" to me—knowing there are none here doesn't keep me from checking. Happily it's the crab: The unmistakable burring issues from its mouth in a froth of bubbles.

To climb one of the higher inland dunes, I walk through a pocket salt marsh, batting through clouds of white moths. From the top of the dune, I see the hook of the cape projecting below, fading into the shifting underground shoals that prompted 16th-century mapmakers to label it "Promontorium tremendum."

Cape Lookout anchors the end of the Outer Banks, which formed some 5,000 to 7,000 years ago. During Pleistocene periods of glacial buildup, sea level was some 400 feet lower than now. During the last glacial melt, rising seas inundated the gentle coastal plain of the southeastern United States (the coastline once lay 30 to 50 miles to the east), eventually isolating dune ridges along the shoreline to form a string of barrier islands. Rising sea level has made the islands march landward a little more than four miles in the last 7,000 years through two processes: overwash and inlet formation. The hook of the cape evolved about 4,000 years ago, when littoral currents dropped sand in the slow-water eddies along this southernmost island. Within the last hundred years the cape has shortened and widened, moved east and then west again, and detached from Shackleford Banks to the west.

Rolling dunes hide the curving sandy spit three miles westward that is my destination. When I reach it, I bear inland to walk on firmer beach. A layer of pulverized shells paves the sand in many colors: tan, rose, lavender, rust, yellow, cream, white, charcoal, stabilizing the sand like a desert pavement. What lies on the beach tells of the out-of-sight underwater habitats and the fecundity of animals that prowl and dig, drill and pry, sting and bite.

Here lies the exquisite carapace of a blue crab, a swimming crab distinguished by the lateral flaring points and toothed border of its shell, now faded mauve, speckled with white, flushed with pink and cream. Tiny ivory barnacles encrust it. In life the hindmost pair of legs, now missing, are modified into paddles.

Thick, fist-size cockles hold a glimmer of water from the last high tide. Lacy bryozoans encrust the inside of many; a thin tube worm shell further decorates one. Alive, the cockles inhabit the subtidal sands, clustered in dense colonies below the surface. The two strong,

With its two large compound eyes and several light-sensitive spots, the horseshoe crab navigates from ocean to shore in spring to lay its eggs at extreme high tide. The larger female tows the male ashore, then digs as many as seven shallow nests, depositing up to 28,000 pearly green eggs. Migrating shorebirds descend from night skies to gorge on this rich food supply. Several weeks later, roiling waves and sand break open the remaining eggs, releasing tiny, pale, tailless young. The California grunion (far right), another beach spawner, also synchronizes its egg laying with cycles of moon and tide.

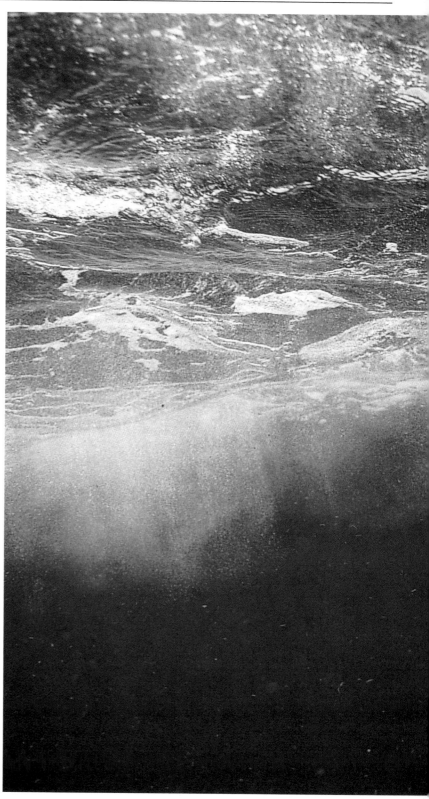

The mucus-coated eggs of an Atlantic loggerhead sea turtle drop gently into a pear-shaped chamber in the sand (above). Every two or three summers, mature female loggerheads abandon the safety of the ocean to deposit more than a hundred eggs in nests dug above the high-tide line on their natal beaches. Females nest an average of four times a season. Raccoons feast on the eggs; storms and invading plant roots also take a toll. Eggs left intact hatch about two months later. The hatchlings swarm toward the surf for a nonstop swim of 20 hours or more to the deeper waters of the Gulf Stream. This current carries the turtles out to open ocean, where they spend their first years.

Like all sea turtles, the loggerhead cannot retract its head and flippers, relying on a thick shell for protection. The massive skull that earned the species its name anchors heavy jaw muscles used for crushing mollusks, the turtle's chief prey. At home in waters from Newfoundland to Argentina, the giant reptile is bound to sandy shores by its ancient egg-laying ritual.

The bill of a sanderling, flexible and sensitive, probes the wet sand for hidden prey: small, delicately colored coquina clams (left) and that proficient burrower, the mole crab. Chief prey of sanderlings during migration, mole crabs gather in great colonies, moving up and down the slope of the beach with the tide, always settling in the churning sand of the swash zone. They feed by extending feathery antennae to capture microscopic plants and animals adrift in the water of spent waves. Coquinas feed in a similar way, thrusting up long tubes, or siphons, through which they draw water rich in oxygen and organic debris. Sought by crabs, fish, and other large predators, both coquinas and mole crabs serve as crucial links in the sandy-shore food web.

radially ribbed shells grow almost all year long except during winter, when the brumal slowdown leaves darker, annual growth rings.

The grace and perfection of a scallop shell—the shell of St. James, the platform upon which Botticelli's Venus rises from the sea—always beguiles me. I nestle the shells together in sets; only one of them is still hinged, the upper valve off-white, the lower, dark gray. Gregarious and mobile, scallops live just offshore, where they swim by rapidly opening and closing their shells. When the single, strong adductor muscle that closes the shell relaxes, it allows water to flow into the mantle cavity; when the muscle contracts sharply, it snaps the shell shut, forcing water backward out of gaps on either side of the hinge, jet-propelling the scallop in haphazard fashion. A change in light intensity or nearby movement may trigger swimming. The stimulus registers on the many sensitive blue eyes studding the edge of the scallop's mantle—eyes with retinas, optic nerves, and lenses.

Most of the clamshells have small, neatly beveled holes, the work of moon snails, which drill with the minute teeth of their rasping, tonguelike radulae and enhance the mechanical action with acid secretions. Moon snails are voracious predators, sometimes imbibing three or four clams a day. A single, pristine lettered olive snail lies nearby. Its huge foot and mantle nearly envelop the shell and protect the gleaming enameled exterior from sand abrasion.

Hundreds of slipper shells of all sizes litter the beach. When alive, they grow in stacks with older, larger females at the base and younger

Wings flared, a young herring gull in mottled plumage vies with a mature great black-backed gull for the carcass of a fish. The older bird will likely win. Largest gull in North America, the great black-backed gull feeds mostly on fish, but sometimes gorges on dead whales or other mammal carrion. The opportunistic herring gull also eats dead animals, along with live fish, snails, worms, and clams, whose thick shells it cracks open by dropping them on hard surfaces. Many gulls have a taste for the eggs and young of other birds and are threats to beach-nesting terns and shorebirds.

males on top. The slipper shells are hermaphroditic, changing sex with age and the amount of hormones given off by the females; when older females die, the stack shifts sex to maintain reproducing females at the base.

It must have taken heavy seas to toss up the huge whelk shells, some of which easily weigh a pound. These gourmands have traveled concealed in the sands of these southeastern beaches for more than 25 million years. The whelk dotes on clams and oysters, wedging open the bivalves, forcing its heavy shell into the gape, and inserting its proboscis into the soft parts.

From this shell-laden, protected southerly beach, I walk around the hook to compare notes on the outer beach, scoured clean by wind and ocean. Here the waves buffet a speckled crab caught in the surf, dark rosy-brown circles laid on the cream background of its beautiful carapace. Thinking it dead, I lean down to grab it, and it thrusts up its claws, belligerence personified.

A speckled crab is well adapted to life in the turbulent swash zone, where it scurries across the sand and digs in backward as quickly as a mole crab. A heavy coat of hairlike setae on either side of its mouth keeps sand out of the mouthparts. By holding its pincers close to its body, the crab insures a free channel for currents to reach gills that have a relatively large oxygen-exchange capacity; this allows strenuous activity in strong surf. Half inundated with sand, the crab disappears with the next flouncing wave.

At Cape Romain, in South Carolina, skeletal trees emerge from the sands of Boneyard Beach (upper left). The fringes of the sea are strewn with flotsam cast up by the surf or carved by its biting spray—from the tough heartwood of old forests to a grass blade in an ephemeral film of bubbles (lower, far left). Driftwood and foam mingle with the fragments of sea creatures: the skull of a loggerhead turtle (above), a worm-eaten whelk shell encrusted with barnacles (lower, near left). Beaches also abound in signs of birth, such as the egg case of the moon snail (lower, middle), a delicate transparent collar built of sand and mucus to hold the snail's thousands of tiny eggs. "One may stand at the breakers' edge," wrote naturalist Henry Beston, "and study a whole world in one's hand."

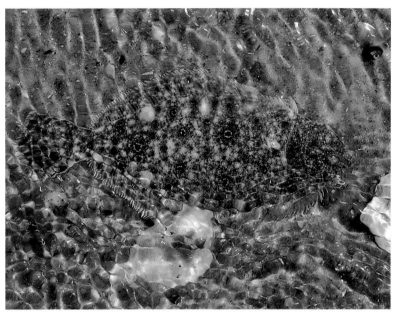

An effective adaptation to shore life, camouflage lends a protective edge to some resident species, on land and in water. A swift-footed ghost crab (opposite) scuttles lightly over the sand. Like apparitions, these nocturnal, sand-colored crabs appear from nowhere, only to vanish as abruptly into their burrows (above), where they retreat from danger and midday heat. At rest in the shallows, the flounder (above, right) also melds perfectly with its environment, changing its color pattern to match its seafloor habitat.

FOLLOWING PAGES: A sinking sun paints a southeastern barrier dune crested by grasses. Such plants stabilize these ridges of fine, blown sand, which, in turn, buffer the mainland against storm waves.

I am peaceably fixing supper that evening when *they* arrive. No breeze blows tonight, so the infamous salt-marsh mosquitoes are out in multitudes. I eat inside by lantern light and listen to them vibrate outside the tent. When I open the fly for a breath of air, they sweep in, whining about starvation and the sanctity of pregnancy. Except for me, who can provide a blood meal to help develop their eggs?

I examine a female Dracula under the microscope: diagnostic dark gray legs banded with white, little ball-like head, bulbous black eyes paved with lenses, all packed into less than a quarter inch, plus an eighth-of-an-inch proboscis at the ready. Out of the proboscis extends the pale stylet that lately pierced my arm.

The next morning is dour. Windy, dank, dark. Quarter-inch water boatmen speckle the tent, caught in the water drops of last night's rain.

Today I drive north to Drum Inlet, 22 miles away. Halfway up the beach I spot a first-year herring gull that has a good-size crab clamped in its bill. It takes off with the crab dangling, lands, holds it by a claw, drops it, flips it over, drops it in a retreating wave, nudges it out of the swash, a study in indecision. Again it totes the crab down to the water, nearly loses it in the backwash, snatches it up, and tosses it onto drier sand. A mature herring gull joins the first gull, sidestepping closer only to be chased off. Then, suddenly, the first gull departs, and the second rushes in and shakes the crab like a dog shakes a bone until pieces of crab fly off. The first gull sidles back, and both, in ungull-like harmony, disassemble the pieces.

Farther north, the jeep starts up a ribbon of feeding great black-backed and herring gulls that wavers and reforms, riding the air like an undulating feather boa. It dismays me that the vehicle of this well-intentioned naturalist upsets birds and compresses the sand for

at least six inches, sometimes with fatal consequences for small creatures buried beneath.

Turtle researchers at Cape Lookout National Seashore have fenced off loggerhead turtle nests to protect newly hatched turtles, which cannot negotiate tire track ridges on their way to the sea. At Mile 17 is a nest where, on August 1, a female found a suitable site—perhaps using cues of temperature or sand-grain size—then dug a nest into which she dropped her eggs. September 30 was hatch date, with hatching influenced by average sand temperature during incubation, which also determines the sex of the hatchlings.

Digging out—signaled by hollows in the sand as the hatchlings literally pull the ceiling of the nest in on themselves—usually doesn't begin until all viable eggs are hatched. Jostling by one hatchling engenders movement in the others. They push up through the sand en masse; if one slows, the one behind butts it, stimulating it to keep moving upward. Young most often emerge from the sand at night, avoiding their most watchful daytime enemies: at Cape Lookout, gulls and hawks. Each baby must make its own way from nest to sea, facing nocturnal predators such as raccoons and ghost crabs. The hatchlings that make it to maturity are imprinted with the information necessary to return to this beach as adults.

At Drum Inlet wind gusts out of the northwest. Sometimes the waves zip together in a seam of white foam; other times they clash, pile up, rear with spray that flies up in the air in a fist-shaking roar. Plumes of spray blow back off the brows of the waves as sea becomes airborne. Clouds drag virga as sky becomes earthborne.

In January 1971, a northeaster closed Old Drum Inlet; the following December, the U. S. Army Corps of Engineers opened New Drum Inlet with a blast of dynamite. Natural inlet formation is one of the two primary processes by which barrier islands move landward; it quickly doubles or triples a barrier island's width. Generally an inlet opens from the sound side. Storm wave action carries sand and water across the island into the sound; when the wind changes direction as the storm passes, water piles up on the inner side of the

The birth of a coastal dune begins on the high drift line, where seeds of American beach grass—the hardy pioneer plant of northeastern shores—germinate and grow. An important dune-stabilizing plant, beach grass thrives on sand burial and depends on ocean spray as its main source of nutrients.

Reading from left to right, the painting below shows how a dune is formed. Wind deposits sand around a young beach grass plant. The plant sends out rhizomes, horizontal underground stems, from which grow vertical anchoring roots. When the plant is buried by sand, it responds by sending up buds at intervals along the submerged stem. Each bud produces roots and a new plant, which accretes its own sandpile. The piles join, forming a dune bound by an underground mat of rhizomes and roots. A high foredune protects the back dunes from sandblast and salt spray, enabling colonization by less resistant plants, such as common bermuda grass (opposite, top) and beach morning glory (opposite, bottom).

island. At narrow points in the island, this superelevated water bursts through, establishing channels by which the ocean's tidal currents carry nutrients and sediments into the sound. Salt-marsh cordgrass quickly colonizes the new flats, which become exceedingly productive areas, serving as nurseries for the myriad young of tidal and pelagic species.

On the overwash flat behind the beach, several hundred feet from the high-tide line, patches of red blanket flower bloom beside brilliant yellow camphor weed. Between plants, whitened shell fragments pave the sand. They have been here long enough that each adheres to a little pedestal of sand bronzed with green-black moss.

Powerful storm waves that crash over the berm and run far inland are the other prime force for building barrier islands landward, and the frequency and severity of major overwashes help determine the width of the island. Overwash builds up the island's surface, keeping it above a sea that is rising an average of one foot per century. After the storm, a layer of bare, fresh sand dries, full of debris that contains, besides shells, the seeds and rhizome fragments of herbs and grasses, which sprout and quickly recolonize the beach. (Like sea oats, salt-meadow cordgrass requires periodic sand cover to flourish.)

Thickening plant growth marks the edge of this most recent overwash. Now the moss that pads the ground is fresh green. Pennywort leaves double, then triple in size. Whitetop sedges look more like small lilies with their uppermost spreading bracts streaked with white. Seaside goldenrod flourishes in these saline sands among silverling, a shrub almost impervious to salt spray or flooding, its female bushes full of silky white seed heads bright against the olive-green wax myrtle. Although myrtle is not a legume, its roots have nitrogen-bearing nodules that enrich the otherwise sterile sands.

I had as my goal a copse of low trees beyond the middle of the island, but now I despair of penetrating the intervening thicket. The problem is not the thickset shrubs and trees barring the way but the vines knotting everything together like a huge fishnet that gives but doesn't break: poison ivy with pink galls, morning glory, Virginia

creeper, beach pea, and catbrier that snags with tiny hooked spines. Equally annoying are the shoulder-high black needlerushes, sharp as their name implies and impossible to avoid because they grow in such solid swaths. Even the newly green ones are indurated to stilettos. I can no longer see where I put my foot.

Beach pea drapes itself up to the top of myrtles or sets unavoidable snares. Three-inch pods hang from one plant. I slip a fingernail into the suture of a ripe pod, and the two valves quickly twist open. When the pod splits naturally, the violence of the torque shoots seeds away from the parent plant. Sand-colored fuzz coats the dark, quarter-inch cylindrical seeds, valuable camouflage, since quail and other sharp-eyed birds and rabbits relish them.

From the sound side of Cape Lookout, I can see the furred horizons of other islands, among them Shackleford Banks. But it is not until a blustery day in November that I get taken there in a national seashore skiff—the only access—and left in splendid solitude.

After anchoring my tent with enough stakes to secure a circus canopy against the wind, I hike to the top of a 30-foot dune, a dunce-cap-shaped single-seater from which I have a 360-degree view of Shackleford Banks. Because the island runs east-west, facing the prevailing southwesterly winds, the dunes rise higher than those of Cape Lookout, whose orientation parallels prevailing winds.

To the east, Cape Lookout Lighthouse pulses a welcome; to the north lies Back Sound. Between this dune and the sound, a dark-green blowing fringe marks the unique maritime forest I have come to see. Although it covers less than 4 percent of the island, its visual presence is strong. Its darkness late on this windy day is foreboding. Stumps of cedar, gaunt and spare, bark silvered by sandblasting, sunlight, and salt spray, stand between the dunes. Once Shackleford Banks was nearly covered by trees, but livestock grazing and the hurricane of 1899 wiped out most of them. In the last half century, migrating sand covered and uncovered the ghost trees, and added half a mile to the western end of the bank.

By five o'clock I expect to see steam erupt where the sun, a molten ball, quenches in the ocean. The eastern sky turns lavender. The landscape grays. The ocean booms a muffled cannonade. I am in my tent and asleep by 6:45.

I awake when it's light, 38°F, and very still within the dunes. The wind stopped at sunset and hasn't arrived with its unwelcome

Feral horses graze on the Outer Banks of North Carolina. Reputedly descended from Spanish horses that swam ashore from 16th-century shipwrecks, these small, heavy-coated ponies are the hardy products of natural selection. Adapted to survive on meager rations of fresh water, they can drink brackish water if necessary.

Life in a Tidal Marsh

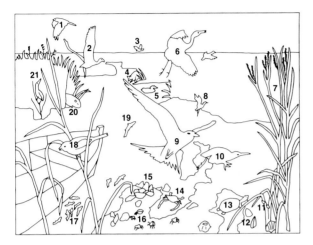

1 Osprey (*Pandion haliaetus*)
2 White ibis (*Eudocimus albus*)
3 Northern harrier (*Circus cyaneus*)
4 Raccoon (*Procyon lotor*)
5 Mallard (*Anas platyrhynchos*)
6 Great egret (*Casmerodius albus*)
7 Salt-marsh cordgrass (*Spartina alterniflora*)

8 Lesser yellowlegs (*Tringa flavipes*)
9 Forster's tern (*Sterna forsteri*)
10 Clapper rail (*Rallus longirostris*)
11 Marsh periwinkle (*Littorina irrorata*)
12 Atlantic ribbed mussel (*Geukensia demissa*)
13 Diamondback terrapin (*Malaclemys terrapin*)
14 Blue crab (*Callinectes sapidus*)
15 Eastern American oyster (*Crassostrea virginica*)

16 Mud fiddler crab (*Uca pugnax*)
17 Mummichog (*Fundulus heteroclitus*)
18 Swamp sparrow (*Melospiza georgiana*)
19 Striped mullet (*Mugil cephalus*)
20 Nutria (*Myocastor coypus*)
21 Least bittern (*Ixobrychus exilis*)

It takes a stealthy naturalist to approach a tidal marsh without disturbing its creatures. Low tide presents the best opportunity for glimpsing a wealth of resident and migratory birds. Great egrets, Forster's terns, and white ibises frequent the meandering channels and muddy banks to feed on mollusks and crustaceans exposed by receding waters. The elusive clapper rail feasts on hordes of fiddler crabs, but darts into the dense cordgrass when alarmed. As incoming tides flood the marsh, they bring replenishing nutrients. Outgoing tides sweep organic detritus to sea.

Cordgrass, or *Spartina* (opposite), crowds a southern tidal creek. Signature of the Atlantic salt marsh, cordgrass is also the key to its productivity. The grass feeds insects, which, in turn, attract birds, such as the seaside sparrow (left). Dead cordgrass generates the nutrient-rich detritus vital to a variety of plants and animals, including fiddler crabs (above)—pictured with eyestalks raised warily above the water. At one with this changing habitat, fiddlers turn dark at low tide during the day. As night falls, their color fades and they are camouflaged in moonlight.

Salt marshes harbor an array of birds, but their populations ebb and flow with the seasons. While some species are permanent residents, most—like the snowy egret (above) and the green-backed heron (opposite)—are transient, using the marsh for nesting, hunting, wintering, or as a way station during migration. Distinctive in their habits, social egrets pursue prey by hovering and diving, running, or stirring up the mud. The solitary heron freezes on its perch and waits patiently, then strikes.

baggage yet. Beyond the dunes, waves chortle in. A flotilla of pelicans beats by, riding the air cushion above the water. As sunlight paces across the dunes, a fragment of opal rainbow crosses a thin blur of clouds in the east and sparkles a patch of white frost on the tent. I would feel deprived if I had to miss the insistence of night and early morning, miss the chance to build a world out of observed details, to understand how sea oats grow and how fast a whelk moves, what the ocean brings in and takes away, and what a sand dollar will buy.

On the sandy path to the maritime forest, I start up many buckeyes, dark brown butterflies with eyespots on their wings, using the path for warmth. I crest a dune and suddenly face a dark wall of woods 30 feet high, the foliage enlivened by sunlight—yaupon with shiny, dark green leaves, cedar loaded with blue, berrylike cones, live oak leafed with vines. From the dune crest, I sight across the

treetops, as high as the dunes and no higher, protected by them from saltwater flooding and spray. Sea oats grow right to the forest edge, where catbrier stitches trees and grass together.

The arched entryway into the forest beckons like the woods in a fairy-tale illustration. I enter the woods and stillness blankets even the all-pervasive sound of the surf. In the sudden, shuttered silence I watch a snail hitching across the damp leaf litter and swear I can hear its rasping. An inch-thick layer of summer's leaves mats a floor patched with lozenges of sunlight. Cones pack the low branches of cedar, and fallen ones pile thick in little hollows like blue shadows. Clusters of small red berries grow from the stems of yaupon. All the trees are slanted, crooked, and quirked, most shrouded with wild grapevines from which a breeze wafts a single yellow grapevine leaf that floats down like a butterfly. The odor is cool, delicate, musty.

An archipelago of mangroves on prop roots fringes a far-southern Florida shore, blurring the line between land and sea. Where temperate climate gives way to tropical, *Spartina* and other grasses are sometimes replaced by mangroves—a diverse group of amphibious shrubs and trees variously adapted to withstand periodic immersion or exposure to seawater. Natural barriers against storm waves, mangroves thrive on sheltered shores with rich silty or muddy floors. Pioneer mangroves actually change the coastline by advancing the forest toward the water: The arching root structures trap sediment and organic debris, enriched by the detritus the trees themselves create. Eventually the soil builds so high that the sea no longer covers it, transforming the aquatic environment into a terrestrial one.

In minutes I walk through and out into a sunlit clearing stuffed with salt-marsh bulrush and broomsedge, and face the sound.

I amble west along the beach, ducking in and out of the woods, relishing the contrasts. The sea has eaten out a scarp at the edge of the forest so that bare roots loop and drape, and trees lean outward, trunks nearly horizontal. The soil, darkened with humus, is damper and more acidic than the well-drained pale sandy soil of the dunes. Strings of Spanish moss drip from the branches of a small live oak. Blue-gray lichens scab the cedars, and lichens coat the deadfall. Foliose lichens ice one small log, one lichen ruffled blue-gray, the other gray-green; between, gray crustose lichens, filled with minute black fruiting bodies, leave not a glimpse of wood.

A continuous one-inch gouge in the sand flanked by five-inch, almost round tracks wavers down the beach, like some lizard with giant webbed feet, dragging its tail. The track is that of a nutria, a South American rodent introduced into the United States in the 1930s and the Outer Banks in 1941. Multiplying on these barrier islands without competition or major predator, nutrias have shifted their eating habits: Elsewhere marsh grasses are their preferred food; here they have taken to eating the natural dune stabilizers, sea oats.

On the surly afternoon I am to leave, I climb a dune overlooking Whale Creek salt marsh. These ebullient salt marshes have been here as long as the islands have, since the retreat of the last glaciers, welcoming the tides and growing ever upward.

The tidal marsh looks like a Japanese dish garden, art nouveau curves of mirror-water set among a mosaic of different communities distinguishable by color and texture. While sea oats form a ragged profile, copper-colored salt-meadow cordgrass looks as neatly trimmed as a scrub brush. Black needlerush, taller and grayer, rims them on higher ground; silverling, still higher, shimmers in the breeze. Tree hummocks flank the dish. The illusion is completed by a blue heron and a white egret that stand doubled in reflection.

I don my wading boots and strike down into the marsh, brushing by lavender-flowered, waist-high salt-marsh asters. Every time I stand still to take notes, my boots sink slowly in the black muck. Somewhere I lose my pencil. Looking for it I discover dozens of periwinkles, so crusted with muck that I had missed them. They parade the grass stems, where they take refuge from incoming tides and graze the microscopic algae that cling there. I pick one off and watch the disklike operculum close slowly over its foot.

Raccoon tracks interlace the mud flat, little handprints of a hurrying and scurrying existence. As I follow one filigree of tracks, to my astonishment the mud flat ahead of me picks up and moves. It is paved with dark fiddler crabs that would be invisible but for their waving claws. The white claw of the male is so large it may be well over half the weight of the whole crab. The whole population on the flat moves at once, windup toys all set in motion by a single impetus, choreographed to wave their claws in unison. Their half-inch holes riddle the mud, all within a handspan of one another, surrounded by

Multifaceted world of water, mud, and trees, a mangrove swamp supports a diverse array of life. Each part of the tree is a distinct ecological niche. The dense tangle of prop roots and breathing roots near the mangrove floor (above) is frequented by the omnivorous raccoon. The dark, damp habitat teems with life, from the spiny orb weaver (opposite, left) to the tree-climbing yellow rat snake (opposite, right). Water birds, such as the great egret (right, top), find the leafy canopy of the mangrove an ideal nesting site. In the shallows below (right, bottom), fish seek shelter and prey among the arched roots.

neat heaps of mud pellets. The crabs survive inundation by taking a bubble of air into their burrows before sealing them.

When I reach the strand, I find a low rim of sand separating the salt marsh from the beach. Here true halophytes grow, runners of salt grass intermixed with the curious jointed glasswort, now tinged ruddy rose. Along the sound's edge, salt-marsh cordgrass grows so thickly that it hides everything; it is one of the few plants able to withstand and even flourish in a twice-daily flooding. Each year the dead plants fall, partially decompose, and become peat, layer upon layer. (Peat deposits carbon-dated on Shackleford indicate that the island has migrated northward hundreds of yards in 200 years.)

All the while I've been on this protected side of the island, the ocean, almost half a mile away, has broadcast its heavy traffic of waves. I walk back across the island to see the ruckus. Huge waves break far out and plow in from the east, and rain begins to pelt the beach. I stand in a windrow of loose shells, watching. A monstrous wave rushes the beach, covers my boots, the pushing water upending all the shell bits and pieces that jingle as melodically as castanets. As the wave glissades downward, it pulls an inch of sand out from under my feet, winter nibbling away at the berm.

Motion fills the air. Rain plummets, waves tumble, shells chatter, wind buffets, sea oats tremble, the island moves. Wind blows time, blows change, hastens the goings, harrows the stayings. Encapsulated in a rain suit, I wait to leave, ready to go but not ready to go.

Water hyacinths clog a channel near the mouth of the Mississippi River. Bane of southern waterways—fresh and brackish—the beautiful but noxious weed slows the flow of water and blocks sunlight crucial to submerged plants. The hyacinth is a favorite food of the endangered manatee (above), which summers in coastal waters and often migrates upstream to winter in warm freshwater springs.

By Douglas H. Chadwick

Rocky Shores

Not long after nightfall, I came to the edge of the world, and the ground dropped away into an endless expanse of dark. I started down. At the bottom lay a different realm of creation, where nature imagines animals shaped like tree branches and stars. Crabs that adorn themselves with other animals and plants. Types of slugs and worms that I had never seen before; parts of them seemed to have put forth flowers. Rainbow seaweed that shimmered like an aurora in my flashlight beam and shrimps whose stalked eyes shone with reflected light. Sometimes the water itself glowed where I touched it, stirring the single-celled bioluminescent creatures known as dinoflagellates.

Here lay monsters, too. Something big barged by a point of rocks, so big that I could hear its breath spew above the beating wind and surf. It was probably a killer whale. Or it could have been one of the gray whales that migrate between Alaska and Mexico's Baja California. Great monsters that sing to one another in a language all their own. The killer whales even use dialects that vary subtly from one pod, or family group, to the next.

I hope I may one day learn to speak whale. But for a start, I wanted to learn about the more common life-forms found along rocky shores. So I had loaded up on wading boots, rain gear, field guides, field notebooks, and other equipment, then headed for Puget Sound and the Olympic Peninsula of Washington.

The ocean shore is the border of borders in the biosphere—the place where the patchwork of terrestrial habitats meets the salt water that rolls across almost three-quarters of the planet. With its tides and gales and bursting waves, this boundary would appear to be a risky place for an organism to make a living. In many respects, it is. Water is about 800 times as dense as air and can pile into the rocks with a force of more than two tons per square foot, transforming a solid wall of bedrock into a grand ruin of archways, caverns, and freestanding pillars, or sea stacks. Powerful surging waves pack air into crevices under so much pressure that fragments of the stone are blown loose.

The rocky shore exposed at low tide can be divided into four horizontal levels: Topmost is the spray zone; below it are the upper, mid-, and lower intertidal zones. Virtually all the life-forms of the intertidal area are shaped by the surf's action. In one intriguing fashion or another, they are able to hide from the breakers or else anchor

In a surf-cut cave, a tide pool mirrors a sea stack, all that remains of a headland whittled away by pounding waves on the rugged shores of Olympic National Park in Washington State. On rocky coasts from the Pacific Northwest to Canada and New England, the dynamic confrontation of ocean and land has shaped rich habitats that support a remarkable diversity of species.

Sculptured by wind and sea spray, a gnarled cypress survives nature's onslaughts at Point Lobos State Reserve in California. Such exposed, rugged coastlines have no barrier islands to blunt the crushing force of the sea. Still, rocky shores provide footholds and food for teeming plant and animal communities.

themselves firmly enough to endure the pounding waves straight on.

Yet for all its restless energy, the ocean remains over time and over distance a far more constant environment than the land. For instance, while Washington's central prairies endure 100°F summer days and sub-zero winter ones, its coastal waters, swept by the Kuroshio (Japan Current), vary only 10 degrees or so annually—from about 54°F to 44°F. Stability through the ages has made possible the tremendous richness of marine ecosystems.

Before the open coast comes into view, you can scent pulverized seawater. And you can see the power of coastal winds in the Sitka spruce and shore pine, which are reduced to a lopsided few with limbs like trimmed sails. The waves of fresh air carry cries of gulls, crows, and ravens. Remains of their shellfish harvest lie scattered about. Sometimes a larger beach scavenger—the bald eagle—calls through the fog from a nest near the forest edge. In the understory, salal and salmonberry shrubs yield to smooth balconies of lupine, Indian paintbrush, and other wildflowers. They in turn grow progressively more stunted until they are replaced by patches of salt-tolerant plants such as seaside plantain, whose spiky green blooms grow out of crevices in the wave-cut slopes.

Marine life begins where only mist and storm lash reach. Much as lichens colonize the high limit of life on mountaintops, maritime lichens encrust the uppermost level of the rocky shore domain, the spray zone. Whether the coast is in northern California or southern Alaska or New England, one genus in particular, *Verrucaria*, stands out in a distinct black line. It is as if nature for once decided to match the neat diagrams found in biology texts.

The whitewash on prominent rocks in the spray zone simply shows where cormorants and other seabirds like to rest and eat, leaving phosphate-rich droppings. Some sea stacks and offshore nesting islands become nearly buried under this guano. But the whitish band beneath the line of black lichen marks the appearance of barnacles. They are crustaceans, distantly related to shrimps and crabs. In their larval phase, barnacles swim about freely—part of the great drifting legions of plankton, the minute aquatic organisms near the base of oceanic food chains. But then one day nature spurs each larva into cementing its head to a rock—or dock piling, boat hull, clam shell, or whale's skin—with one of the strongest natural adhesives known. Next, the larva secretes hard protective plates of calcium carbonate around its body, and its legs become feathery cirri that strain the water for a share of plankton to eat.

Our most complete early classification of barnacles came from Charles Darwin. The task kept him busy from 1846 until 1854 and revealed just the sort of minute variation within groups of species that he spent the rest of his life working to explain. The author of evolutionary theory knew the small acorn barnacle now called *Chthamalus dalli* that pimples rocks of the upper spray zone. Compact and able to seal itself tightly against the outside air, the species is adapted to withstand long periods without water. Among the barnacles, little snails known as periwinkles graze on lichens and algae, retreating into crevices under harsh conditions. During especially hot, dry spells, the checkered periwinkle temporarily glues its coiled shell to the stone to prevent evaporation. Deeper within the crevices wait rock lice. These isopods—the maritime version of the pill bugs found beneath leaf litter on forest floors—emerge at night to feed on rotting plant debris tossed their way by the waves.

A key inhabitant farther down in the spray zone is the limpet, a snail with a low, conical shell. Its flattened design deflects the waves' grasp. It grips the rock so tightly with its fleshy foot that you need a penknife to pry even a tiny one loose. When the limpet first feels a touch, it clamps down harder yet, causing some of the liquid it has stored to ooze out past the shell's edge. Yet if you're there when seawater is splattering on all sides, you'll find the creature lifting

The rocky shore is divided into four intertidal zones—determined, in part, by how long organisms must endure exposure to air. In zone 1, lichens, periwinkles, limpets, and other creatures receive only erratic drenching sprays. Barnacles and periwinkles close their shells to hold in moisture. In zone 2, immersed only at high tides, some animals find shelter beneath the damp masses of sea palms, red algae, and rockweed. Goose barnacles and dense beds of California mussels mark the transition to the next zone, covered and uncovered twice each day. The nooks and crevices of the mussel beds harbor worms and isopods. Farther down lives the ochre sea star (right), which preys on the mussels, limiting their spread. Species more vulnerable to exposure reside in zone 4, uncovered only at extreme low tides.

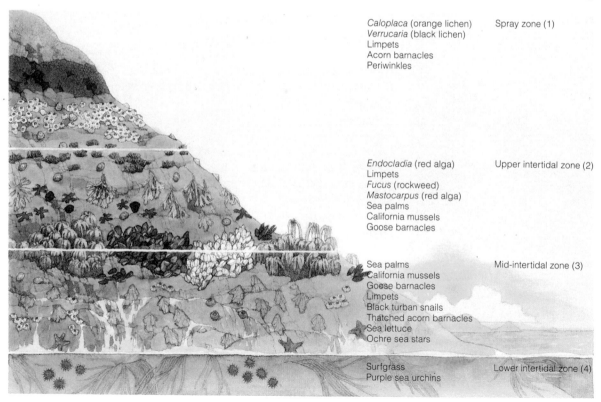

Caloplaca (orange lichen)   Spray zone (1)
Verrucaria (black lichen)
Limpets
Acorn barnacles
Periwinkles

Endocladia (red alga)   Upper intertidal zone (2)
Limpets
Fucus (rockweed)
Mastocarpus (red alga)
Sea palms
California mussels
Goose barnacles

Sea palms   Mid-intertidal zone (3)
California mussels
Goose barnacles
Limpets
Black turban snails
Thatched acorn barnacles
Sea lettuce
Ochre sea stars

Surfgrass   Lower intertidal zone (4)
Purple sea urchins

its hard canopy to roam as far as six feet away over algal pastures.

Curiosity is the only real talent a naturalist needs, but it works best blended with a lot of patience. Then observations have time to link up. Patterns form. The *Aha! That's why* begins. Like most people, I'm tempted to hustle over the shore hunting for the spectacular and unusual—the big find. What I really want to comb those rocky beaches for, though, is a deeper understanding of how living communities operate. So I try to take my own advice: Stick around in one spot a while. Keep your eyes open. Linger, loiter, and look.

You may notice the appearance of a larger acorn barnacle, *Balanus glandula,* amid the smaller barnacles—and realize that these two animals, which can seem so inanimate, are actually engaged in a race for more living space. The lower and wetter the rock surface, the better the larger species thrives. Laying down more and more

Long strands of the seaweed *Enteromorpha* drape rocks on the shores of Maine's Appledore Island (above). The dense, sodden mats provide refuge for some creatures that otherwise might not survive exposure at low tide. An extreme ebb tide reveals a rich mosaic of life encrusting a rock face (above, right) on Washington's Tatoosh Island. Spiny purple sea urchins find their niche at the lowest water levels. Pink coralline algae also mark these levels. A solitary green sea anemone will unfurl its feeding tentacles when the sea returns.

calcareous layers, these larger barnacles undercut and loosen the smaller acorns, crunch them between two large acorns, or eventually plaster right over them.

As you move from the spray zone closer to the ocean, things get steadily thicker and more slithery. The next zone, the upper intertidal, is submerged only during high tides. That's long enough to support a fairly lush growth of seaweed, tied to the rocks with tough, rootlike holdfasts. More often than not, this zone starts with a brown alga known as rockweed. The plant's tips are swollen with male and female gametes for reproduction and little bubblelike air sacs for flotation. They pop softly underfoot—or between your teeth. After all, *Fucus*, harvested through history for cattle fodder and fertilizer, is edible by humans. Other algae in this zone have common names that describe them nicely: sea lettuce, bright green and "leafy"; sea

Life in a Tide Pool

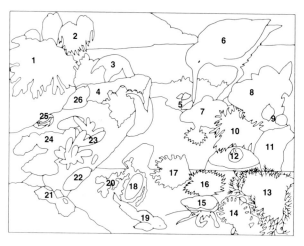

1 Rockweed (*Fucus distichus*)
2 Sea palm (*Postelsia palmaeformis*)
3 Ochre sea star (*Pisaster ochraceus*)
4 Green alga (*Cladophora*)
5 Limpet (*Lottia pelta*)
6 Black oystercatcher (*Haematopus bachmani*)
7 Aggregating anemone (*Anthopleura elegantissima*)
8 California mussel (*Mytilus californianus*)
9 Emarginate dogwinkle

(*Nucella emarginata*)
10 Red alga (*Mastocarpus papillatus*)
11 Sea lettuce (*Ulva fenestrata*)
12 Black turban snail (*Tegula funebralis*)
13 Red alga (*Odonthalia floccosa*)
14 Calcareous tube worm (*Serpula vermicularis*)
15 Hairy hermit crab (*Pagurus hirsutiusculus*)
16 Red coralline alga (*Corallina*)
17 Red alga (*Rhodomela larix*)
18 Lined chiton (*Tonicella lineata*)

19 Tide-pool sculpin (*Oligocottus maculosus*)
20 Encrusting coralline alga (*Lithothamnium*)
21 Thatched acorn barnacle (*Semibalanus cariosus*)
22 Black chiton (*Katharina tunicata*)
23 Red alga (*Halosaccion glandiforme*)
24 Brown alga (*Leathesia difformis*)
25 Purple shore crab (*Hemigrapsus nudus*)
26 Goose barnacle (*Pollicipes polymerus*)

"Tide pools contain mysterious worlds," wrote naturalist Rachel Carson, "where all the beauty of the sea is subtly suggested and portrayed in miniature." In the calm waters of these basins live brightly colored chitons, crabs, snails, sculpins, and tube worms with feathery sprays of tentacles. On the more exposed rock surfaces outside the pool are colonies of barnacles and mussels, verdant sea palms, rockweed, and other algae. Ochre sea stars cling to the rocks, along with clusters of anemones and limpets—easy targets for the probing bill of the black oystercatcher.

moss, in brownish cushions; and sea tar, in scattered black blobs. Considered a separate species until a few years ago, sea tar turns out to be the spore-producing phase in the life cycle of the larger red alga, *Mastocarpus papillatus,* that flourishes at about the same level.

Robust black turban snails forage on algae in the upper intertidal zone. Carnivorous snails called whelks, whose spiral shells are sharply pointed and ridged, prey on a wide range of other shelled creatures. They feed with a long tonguelike radula, the rasping organ found in most gastropods. Studded with hard cusps, it enables the limpet to scrape off algae and the whelk to lick-drill its way into a soft meal of, say, a barnacle or mussel. Whelks flood their drill site with shell-dissolving chemicals plus a tranquilizer that relaxes whatever muscles the victim may be using to keep its armor in place. Because whelks usually feed only while submerged, their presence helps

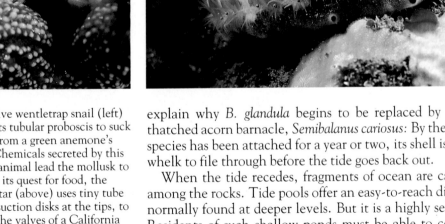

A diminutive wentletrap snail (left) elongates its tubular proboscis to suck the juices from a green anemone's tentacle. Chemicals secreted by this flowerlike animal lead the mollusk to its prey. In its quest for food, the ochre sea star (above) uses tiny tube feet, with suction disks at the tips, to pull apart the valves of a California mussel. The sea star can evert its stomach and insert it into the gap to digest the mussel's soft insides. A pink scallop (above, right) draws water through its gills and filters plankton for food.

explain why *B. glandula* begins to be replaced by the still larger thatched acorn barnacle, *Semibalanus cariosus:* By the time the larger species has been attached for a year or two, its shell is too thick for a whelk to file through before the tide goes back out.

When the tide recedes, fragments of ocean are caught and held among the rocks. Tide pools offer an easy-to-reach display of sea life normally found at deeper levels. But it is a highly selective display. Residents of such shallow ponds must be able to cope with frosty winter temperatures, intense summer sun, and oxygen shortages, since warming water loses its capacity to hold the vital gas.

Looking tools generally accompany me to these natural aquariums. The most important one is a hand lens; mine is part of the pocketknife I carry. Surely this simple bulge of glass is one of man's grand inventions, an instrument of revelation. Through it expand

Preparing to reproduce, two blood stars (left) hunch up on their rays in a spawning posture. The release of sperm or eggs by one of these sea stars triggers a synchronous spawning by other males and females of the species—a response that ensures the maximum number of fertilized eggs. Mating red rock crabs (far left, top) rub their belly plates together. The eggs are not fertilized until the female molts, a process that takes seven days or more. During this time the male carries his mate around and then remains with her while the new shell hardens. After spawning, a top shell snail (far left, middle) releases a double strand of eggs into the sea, where fertilization takes place. Offspring encircle a brooding anemone (far left, bottom). The larvae, developed from eggs fertilized within the parent's body, swim out through its mouth and attach themselves to its base, where they grow into juveniles. After a few months they glide away.

Adapted to withstand heavy surf, sea palms (above) thrive in the rough waters of the open coast. A tough, flexible, stemlike stipe enables the brown alga to bend without breaking when a powerful wave strikes. A strong holdfast with many branches anchors the plant firmly to rock or to a tight colony of California mussels and goose barnacles (opposite). The two-foot-high sea palm inhabits the most exposed places, where other algae would be ripped away.

the structures that enable smaller life-forms—the overwhelming majority of life-forms—to move, feed, and mate. For them, success or failure in the struggle for existence doesn't take place on the scale of a frond or antenna so much as on the still more intricate scale of the bristles and grooves and pits and pigments along those organs.

Ease one of the slender ribbon worms, classified as nemerteans, from its travels between the seaweed and barnacles. Named after Nemertes, a sea nymph who attended the Greek god Poseidon, the ribbon worm has unerring aim. It shoots out a proboscis to grasp worms, small mollusks, and other animals. The proboscis of some nemerteans exudes a venom to paralyze prey. Now, focus on the cirri protruding from the hard white coils of a calcareous tube worm on the tide-pool wall. They are a red or orange blossom of about 40 pairs of featherlike tentacles that act both as gills and as traps for micro-

scopic food. It's wishful thinking, I know, but if all of us were to peer though a hand lens for only a few moments each day at the supremely functional architecture of natural beauty under our noses, I wonder if the conservation movement would have any opponents left.

Another looking tool is less profound: a mat or foam pad. If you're going to stick your nose into a tide pool for a spell, the rest of your body need not stick to wet seaweeds and sharp barnacles. A skin diver's face mask helps to get past reflections and ripple distortions.

The snail shells that drop into hiding from the sides of a tide pool when you approach are inhabited by hermit crabs, which have little body armor of their own. These creatures are hard to sneak up on. Just recently, they were found to possess a previously unknown type of eye structure, and it appears to be one of the most elaborate light-gathering devices in the animal kingdom.

Two kinds of algae live within another prominent tide-pool beast—the aggregating anemone. They are the source of its color: pure emerald when zoochlorellae dominate; olive-green when zooxanthellae are more numerous. Both kinds of algae use their host's waste products to make food for themselves; the zooxanthellae share some of this food with the anemone. Probing a sea cave, I found a related anemone species, a green anemone, hanging like a strange fruit from the sunless reaches. Like its relatives, the green anemone is usually colored by symbiotic algae. This one, however, was pale and algaless but apparently getting by fine. Green anemones are basically hunters—aggressive ones, attacking prey with the microscopic stinging capsules on their tentacles.

Coralline algae make the dazzling pink veneer on tide-pool rocks. Some send up pink, crusty growths. Like corals, they are stiffened by concentrations of calcium carbonate that discourage grazers. Along the pond bottom flit little tide-pool sculpins with big heads and spiny fins. The northern clingfish, whose head is even bigger in proportion to its body, uses its pectoral fins to suction-grip surfaces. The best place to find one is in a habitat somewhat similar to a tide pool—the moist areas beneath loose rocks along the shore. Wriggling in the same puddle are likely to be eel-like blennies called cockscombs, and any number of shore crabs and porcelain crabs.

Turning over rocks is a great way to surprise yourself with scuttling outbursts of critters. And it can be the best way to locate some of the least familiar marine organisms: hydroids, tentacled cousins of sea anemones and corals, here in minuscule branching colonies; colonial bryozoans; colonial tunicates; sponges—Puget Sound has more than 50 species, many of them small rock-coating varieties.

On the other hand, turning over stones is also a way to expose a great many creatures to the harsh sunlight, winds, and predators they were trying to avoid, so I replace each chunk carefully right side up. Black oystercatchers also poke around in the rocky intertidal zones. It is their chief feeding area, where they pluck not oysters, but limpets, mussels, and crabs. Instead of migrating, they stay year-round within 30 miles or so of the center of their range, nesting in

the spray zone when spring comes. They are especially sensitive to human disturbance then, and will chide you for coming too close. Pay attention to that shrill whistle-cry piercing the noise of wind and surf. Give ground. Their presence is considered an indicator of a rich, unspoiled—and uncrowded—rocky shore environment. It says: Here is the sort of place where mink, raccoons, river otters, and possibly a black bear or two are likely to patrol the beaches.

While you can almost always reach the upper two zones during a trip to the shore, the mid-intertidal and lower intertidal zones require a much closer look at tide tables. You may want to bring hip waders—keeping in mind that too high a wave could suddenly fill them, and the weight can drag you under. Consider a wet suit if you would like more freedom to explore.

The mid-intertidal level gets covered and uncovered by the sea twice each day. At its upper end, the acorn barnacles start to compete for space with beds of blue mussels—yet another species that lives as a free-swimming larva before settling down to a sessile, or stationary, existence, attached by strong threads and filter feeding on microscopic organisms. California mussels, with even stronger attachment threads, take over on exposed outer shores. On one 4.5-inch specimen's ribbed shell, I counted 17 large acorn barnacles, dozens of small ones, 8 limpets, 13 snails, 4 hermit crabs, several types of algae, and 1 anemone. But the California mussel's struggle for space is primarily with the goose barnacle, which forms hummocks of tightly packed individuals. Rising from a rubbery stalk, each is able to slowly—somewhat eerily—bend and twist to position itself for feeding at high tide. Whereas an acorn barnacle constantly extends and contracts its cirri in a grabbing motion, the goose barnacle waits until sensory receptors announce the passing of a wave above. Then it simply holds its cirri out like a basket to strain the water washing back down off the rocks. In other words, the goose barnacle lets the sea do much of the work, which is why it favors open coasts or at least areas with strong tidal surges.

Algae typical of the mid-intertidal zone once again have common names that define them handily: sea cabbage, sea lettuce, sea sac, and sea palm, which forms little groves where the waves hit hardest. Part the algae. You'll soon meet kelp crabs and scores of the isopod *Idotea*, present since the upper intertidal level. Both the crabs and the isopods may be green, brown, or red, depending upon the color

Fronds of rockweed dangle across a rock at low tide on the coast of Maine. Anchored by a holdfast at its base and buoyed by air-filled bladders, the rockweed rises and sways with the ocean's surge at high water. Periwinkles creep along the fronds. In feeding, they graze on the algae that blacken the rock.

FOLLOWING PAGES: Three cormorants skim storm-tossed waves off California's Point Lobos State Reserve. Such battering surf may uproot seaweed gardens and sweep away mussels, providing opportunities for new colonizers to move into the gaps.

of the seaweed they've been eating. A sharp-nosed crab is tougher to pick out. Its rough carapace encourages a masking growth of colonial creatures. With luck, you'll go on to uncover a decorator crab, which uses glue from its mouth to stick seaweed cuttings onto its back and legs for camouflage.

The chiton, one of the chief herbivores at this level, has eight overlapping plates on its back instead of a solid shell. Look for a dead, dried-out specimen, analyze its radula, and you will discover it to be as much as 65 percent magnetite, an iron compound stronger than some grades of steel. Sawing through the thicker seaweeds with its radula, the black chiton creates open habitat essential to limpets, which prefer their algae in thin rinds underfoot. Remove the chitons, as a group of scientists did in one study area, and the limpet population virtually disappears.

For that matter, as many as 25 different species depend on the ochre sea star to clear living space for them through its hungry forays. Constellations of this predator converge to pillage crowded mussel beds. En route, they devour barnacles and limpets. One of every four black turban snails also succumbs to an ochre star. It was largely through studies of the ochre star's wide-ranging role in rocky shore habitats that marine ecologist Robert T. Paine of the University of Washington developed the concept of keystone species during the 1970s. Such species exert a controlling influence on the makeup of an entire ecological community. Today, we apply such thinking to the wolf's dominant role in Arctic regions and the elephant's giant effects on African forests.

At this mid-intertidal level, aggregating anemones are common. They spread in colonies, or, to be more accurate, as clones. The animals are able to reproduce asexually by splitting into identical twins—like a dividing cell. A densely packed existence helps prevent drying when the tide is out. It also helps exclude competitors. But when one expanding clone group bumps into a genetically different one, these beasts do battle, firing toxic threads at one another from stinging capsules at the base of their tentacles. Afterward, an uninhabited line, like a demilitarized zone, is left between the two groups. The anemones' feeding style, surprisingly, is quite passive. They rely mainly on barnacles that drop onto them, having been knocked loose by storms, lashing kelp fronds, or rolling logs. As a result, the anemones do well below areas populated by barnacles.

We have worked our way down to the lower intertidal zone, uncovered only during the lowest tides (which occur a few times each month). Here I take back those encouragements to linger long and look. If you become engrossed in the private lives of this zone, you need to keep an equally careful watch over your shoulder at the sea. All too quickly, you might find yourself stranded by the incoming tide or ground against the rocks by a rogue wave. Yet I notice the ocean's relentless power sharpening my senses as I draw closer.

The very turbulence of this level improves its ability to support life. Those same forces that bring prey to aggregating anemones—

A towering submarine forest of giant kelp near Santa Barbara, California, provides a lush habitat for hundreds of species of fish and invertebrates that creep, climb, and swim among the swaying plants. Moored by extensively branched holdfasts, giant kelp grows all along the Pacific coast in depths of 35 to 50 feet and at rates that can exceed a foot a day. At the surface the fronds spread into a dense canopy that creates a shadowy world below. A shorter species of brown alga, azure at its edges (above), gains a foothold in places where sunlight filters through.

Lolling on its back in California waters, a sea otter holds a sea star in its forepaws. Usually these diving mammals find sea urchins, mussels, abalones, and crabs more appetizing. The empty abalone shell near the otter's head suggests the voracious eater has just devoured a treat.

When eating urchins, an otter lies on its back and beats the shell against a flat stone on its chest to break the spines, then bites through the creature and licks up its sweet flesh. By feasting on the urchins, which eat kelp, the otter helps to preserve the kelp-forest habitat. Because an entire community depends on the sea otter for survival, scientists refer to the mammal as a keystone species.

storms and pummeling by masses of kelp and log flotsam—continually encourage new growth and diversity. A static climax community seldom has a chance to develop. The effect is most pronounced on exposed shores. Strong wave action protects kelp from predators such as urchins, which can't tolerate the rough conditions. It also carries oxygen, nutrients, and plankton past sessile organisms more frequently than quieter waters can. Whatever wastes envelop densely populated areas are swept away sooner. Tide pools are freshened. Finally, crashing surf keeps plants in constant motion, exposing more of their fronds to the sun's rays. In short, the greater kinetic energy embodied by the waves translates into greater biomass.

Eelgrass—or, on open coasts, surfgrass—often appears in the lower intertidal zone. These are both distantly related to true grasses and develop tiny flowers that are fertilized underwater, with their pollen borne by ocean currents rather than winds. Large algae drape against the rocks and one another: split kelp, giant kelp, feather boa, *Alaria*, sugar kelp, and bull kelp, with its long bullwhip stipe and bulbous air bladder. Many smaller plants grow from their sides as epiphytes. Brown and red algae predominate among the algae at lower levels, in part because their pigments absorb light in the blue end of the spectrum more efficiently than green chlorophyll does. And blue light penetrates farthest beneath the surface of water.

As quickly as storms uproot huge masses of kelp and pile them on the beach, more flourish in their place. Bull kelp is one of the fastest-growing plants on earth, sometimes adding about a foot in length a day until it totals roughly 80 feet. Among the chitons rasping away at this bounty is the world's largest—the gum boot of the northern Pacific. It often has both a commensal scale worm and a pea crab boarding on its underside. The chitons are joined by three sea urchin species: red, green, and purple. These gnaw kelp with a unique kind of circular, clamping chisel called Aristotle's lantern. Like the many-rayed sunflower stars, brittle stars, and sea cucumbers found here, sea urchins are echinoderms—Greek for "prickly skin." Most share a characteristic five-part symmetry and rows of mobile little tube feet, used for locomotion, attachment, and feeding.

Many other phyla also increase their showing at this level. A six-rayed star, known as the brooding star, spends much of the winter humped over its developing offspring to protect them. An orange-red species called the blood star takes its pigment from the sponges it preys upon here. An equally livid sea slug also gets its pigment from eating these orange-red sponges. One graceful hydroid suits its name, ostrich plume. The red rock crabs grow big enough to look fit for a dinner plate. Limpets, considered a delicacy in the Orient, graze alongside their much sought-after larger relative, the abalone. Mussels disappear, but rock scallops thrive—where they haven't been overharvested by people.

Certain species dwell less on the shore than *in* it. Long, tapered piddock clams burrow through sandstone and other soft rock, twisting back and forth to grind away with the sharp cuff near the front of

On long, black-tipped wings, a northern gannet (opposite) flies toward a cliff swarming with nesting black-legged kittiwakes at Cape St. Mary's in Newfoundland. Though marine birds may range far out to sea for food, they must return to these rocky coasts to lay their eggs. An Atlantic puffin (above, top) carries a beakful of fish ashore to feed its young. Attentive parents, thick-billed murres guard their egg (above), taking turns incubating it with their belly feathers. The stocky birds lay their eggs on bare cliff ledges. If the eggs are pushed, their unusual pear shape keeps them rolling in a circle, rather than straight off the ledge.

Raucous, throaty barks, blunt noses, and very small ears characterize Steller's sea lions (right) floating in nearshore waters of the Aleutian Islands. Like all pinnipeds—aquatic mammals with flippers—these eared seals congregate in rookeries where they mate, pup, and raise their young. To defend their territories, males rarely leave the rookery during the two-month breeding season.

A massive, all-male congregation of walruses (opposite) throngs a narrow beach on Round Island in Alaska's Bristol Bay. While bulls gather to feed and store energy on communal beaches, cows and calves swim north to distant ice floes in the Arctic waters of the Chukchi Sea. The herds reunite to mate in the early months of the year.

When a walrus dives for food in frigid waters, the blood vessels in its skin constrict, giving it a whitish cast. But after a rest in the sun, the vessels dilate, restoring the mammal to its rich reddish brown color.

their shell. In a sense, they are only doing what most clams do; it's just that piddocks bury themselves in sand and gravel that have hardened into sedimentary rock. Fossil holes far up on the sea cliffs prove that other piddocks were doing the same millions of years ago. You would think that these mollusks would gain a safe haven in return for their efforts. But a whelk known as the leafy hornmouth sends its proboscis right in after them. The boring by piddocks contributes heavily to erosion by weakening the soft, sea-hammered stone where they live.

Beyond the lower intertidal zone lies the ocean domain of octopus, rockfish, lingcod, and surf smelt. Kelp forests shelter eggs and hatchlings from all manner of free-ranging animals. They used to shelter plentiful sea otters, which feed chiefly on urchins and wrap themselves in the kelp fronds to keep from drifting while they snooze. When the otters nearly became extinct in California, urchin populations boomed and grazed out the kelp in places.

It is nearly impossible now for us to envision what our rocky coasts were like before market hunting destroyed the tribes of sea otters, seals, sea lions, and whales—barking, singing, and splashing at the

Mouth agape, a feeding humpback whale rises to the surface in the food-rich waters of Frederick Sound in southeastern Alaska. To make its fishing easier, the 40-ton creature sometimes blows a "net" of bubbles that herds together small schooling fish and crustaceans. The whale surges up through this concentration, gulping dinner in its great maw. Gulls, ever ready for a meal, flock to the seafood feast gathered within the bubble net.

ocean's rim. Many have come partway back from their brush with oblivion. I watched dozens of seals and a few sea lions fishing in company with the surf scoters, merganser ducks, loons, and grebes.

I carried binoculars, of course, and a cloth to wipe them clean of damaging salt spray. From the top of cliffs that fell sharply into the sea, I spent many hours swinging those lenses from auklets to guille-mots, and from murres to diminutive murrelets, as they flew deep down through the chill water on short, finlike wings. These are the alcids, plump and sleek—our northern counterparts of penguins.

Before you take leave of the ocean, scoop a jar full of tidal water and watch it closely in a slanting light. You may see some minuscule plants and animals, tumbling and pulsing, as well as the shadows that transparent ones cast on the glass. The first thing you realize is why so many creatures of the rocky shore have taken up the sessile

life of a filter feeder. The second thing to think about is how little we have learned yet about the larval stage—or stages—of even our most common coastal neighbors. Most sea stars and sea urchins, for instance, have free-swimming larval stages that differ from the adult. Where do they travel? How do they recognize suitable places to settle? No one knows for sure. Nor, in many species, are the adults' habits anywhere close to fully explained.

The rocky shore is a naturalist's frontier. It waits out there as wide and deep with mystery as the sea itself, the womb of life. Study it as a scientist. Study it also as a poet. While infusions of mist sweep the dark forests at your back. While quicksilver currents of light play across the endless horizon before you. While at the edge of the world, where the contemplation of great questions seems as natural as the flight of gulls.

By Diane Ackerman

Sky

I am sitting at the western edge of the continent, at Point Reyes National Seashore, where the land gives way to the thrall of the Pacific and the arching blue conundrum of the sky. When cricket-whine, loud as a buzz saw, abruptly quits, only birdcalls map the quiet codes of daylight. A hawk leans into nothingness, peeling a layer of flight from thin air. At first it flaps hard to gain a little altitude, then it finds a warm updraft and cups the air with its wings, spiraling up in tight circles, while it eyes the ground below for rodents or rabbits. Banking a little wider, it turns slowly like a parasol. The hawk knows instinctively that it will not fall.

Though we move through air's glassy fathoms, we rarely think of it as the mixture of gases it is: a substance, not an absence. We rarely wonder about the blue phantasm we call the sky. *"Skeu,"* I say out loud, the word that ancients used; I try to utter it as they might have, with fear and wonder: *"Skeu."* Actually, it was their word for a covering of any sort. To them, the sky was a roof of changing colors. Small wonder they billeted their gods there, like so many quarrelsome neighbors who, in fits of temper, hurled lightning bolts instead of crockery.

Look at your feet. You are standing in the sky. When we think of the sky, we tend to look up, but the sky actually begins at the earth. We walk through it, yell into it, rake leaves, wash the dog, and drive cars in it. We breathe it deep within us. With every breath, we inhale millions of molecules of sky, heat them briefly, and then exhale them back into the world. At this moment, you may be breathing the same molecules once breathed by Leonardo da Vinci, William Shakespeare, Hector Berlioz, or Colette. Inhale deeply. Think of *The Tempest,* of spirits melting "into thin air." Air fills the bellows of our lungs, and it powers our cells. How often we say "light as air," but there is nothing lightweight about our atmosphere, which weighs 5,000 trillion tons. Only a clench as stubborn as gravity's could hold it to the earth; otherwise it would simply float away and seep into the cornerless expanse of space.

Without thinking, we often speak of an "empty" sky, but the sky is never empty. In a mere ounce of air, there are a thousand billion trillion gyrating molecules of such stuffs as oxygen and nitrogen, made of electrons, quarks, and ghostly neutrinos. Sometimes we marvel at how "calm" the day is, or how "still" the night. Yet there is no stillness in the sky, or anywhere else where life and matter meet.

Lightning splits the night sky above Tucson, Arizona. The powerful electrical discharge between thundercloud and ground sometimes takes life. But it sustains life, too, by "fixing" atmospheric nitrogen, converting the element into a form that can nourish living things. Always changing, the sky is a dynamic habitat of molecules, plants, and animals in perpetual motion.

A summer rain drenches wild lilies on a northern Illinois prairie (above). Rain has its beginnings in water that evaporates from the surface of lakes, rivers, and oceans. As the warm air, moist with water vapor, rises, it begins to lose heat and the ability to hold water. Soon the water vapor condenses into tiny droplets that form around particles in the air, creating clouds. The droplets coalesce and grow heavier, then fall to earth as rain.

As rains end, rainbows often begin. Sunlight strikes water droplets, which act as prisms and mirrors, bending, separating, and reflecting the component colors of light into bands visible as arcs. In the Rocky Mountains (right), the spectacle doubles with both a bright primary arc and a duller secondary arc, in which the color order reverses.

The air is always vibrant and aglow, full of staggering spores, dust, viruses, fungi, and animals, all stirred by a skirling and relentless wind. There are active fliers such as birds, bats, butterflies, and other insects; and there are passive fliers such as autumn leaves, pollen, and flying squirrels, which just float or glide.

Storms have been fretting the coast here for days, and now thick, gray clouds stagger across the sky: mashed-potato heaps of cumulus (a word that means "heap") and broad bands of stratus (which means "spread out"). Clouds in stable air tend to form sheets, long smears across the sky, which tell you that a warm, moist mass of air has crawled over the top of a cold air mass. On the other hand, clouds in unstable air tend to build towers. When you see fluffy clouds scattered like tufts of wool across the blue, you're looking at the result of rising air currents. Pilots know that fair-weather cumulus clouds may be bumpy to fly under, since the air is surging up and down on invisible elevators inside the clouds. Huge, marauding thunderstorms, with cloud tops that stretch up many thousands of feet, are full of savage updrafts and downdrafts. A cloud is a sort of floating reservoir. Although the atmosphere always has water vapor in it, when the air becomes saturated, some of the water vapor condenses into droplets, which we see as clouds or fog (a cloud that touches the ground). When the water droplets grow heavy enough, they fall. If the air is cold enough, they fall as snow or sleet.

I run from the beach to take shelter on a porch, as a real toad-strangler starts, a full-blooded, hell-for-leather thunderstorm, rare in these parts. The sky crackles and throbs. In thunderstorms, the cloud tops become positively charged and the bottoms, negatively charged, with zones of positive charges. The earth normally carries a negative charge, but the friction of rain can change that, and when it does, lightning appears to plunge out of the sky with a pitchfork it stabs into the ground. But the sky really sends down a short electrical scout, or leader, first, and the earth replies by arcing a long bolt up through the sky, heating the air so fast that it explodes into a shock wave, or thunder. Counting the seconds between a lightning flash and its thunder—25—I then divide by five and get a rough idea of how far away it is: five miles. In one second, sound travels 1,100 feet. So it takes less than five seconds for it to travel a mile.

In a little while the storm quiets, as the thunder bumpers roll farther up the coast. But some clouds still stalk the sky. A cloud rhinoceros metamorphoses into a profile of Eleanor Roosevelt, then a bowl of pumpkins, then a tongue-wagging dragon. How many vacant afternoons people have passed watching the clouds drift by. The ancient Chinese amused themselves by finding shapes in the clouds, just as Inuit, Bantus, and Pittsburghers do now. Sailors, generals, farmers, ranchers, and others have always consulted the crystal ball of the sky to foretell the weather (a dappled or mackerel sky—rain is near; low, thick, dark, blanketlike stratus clouds—a stormy cold front may be coming; puffy, white cumulus—fair weather; high, feathery cirrus, which are made of ice crystals—a change in the

The Troposphere

We live at the bottom of the troposphere, the lowest layer of earth's atmosphere. Reaching an average of six miles into the sky, the troposphere produces most of our weather.

Clouds play an important role in weather and in the hydrologic cycle, the continuous process that circulates the planet's water. The cycle starts with the evaporation of surface water and its transformation into invisible water vapor (yellow arrow pointing upward), which rises, cools, and condenses into water droplets that form clouds.

Ten types of clouds are shown here together for comparison. The terms "stratus" (spread out), "cumulus" (heaped), and "cirrus" (wispy) describe the basic shapes. The prefix "alto-" describes clouds 6,500 to 20,000 feet high and "cirro-," clouds above 20,000 feet. "Nimbo-" and "-nimbus" refer to clouds that produce precipitation.

Stratus clouds occur in stable air and blanket the sky with gray, becoming more translucent with altitude. Nimbostrati usually signal long, steady precipitation. Fluffy cumulus clouds develop from updrafts of warm air. Delicate, icy cirri often portend a change in the weather.

The clouds to watch out for are the cumulonimbi, the thunderheads, bearing lightning and heavy rains that replenish surface water and groundwater (yellow arrow pointing downward). Hail forms in the clouds' freezing upper reaches. As updrafts lift the hailstones repeatedly, they receive layer after layer of ice until they finally fall to earth.

Fog, a cloud at ground level, forms in various ways. Advection fog occurs on coasts when warm, moist air moves over cool water. Radiation fog develops when radiant heat escapes the ground and cools the air above, causing condensation.

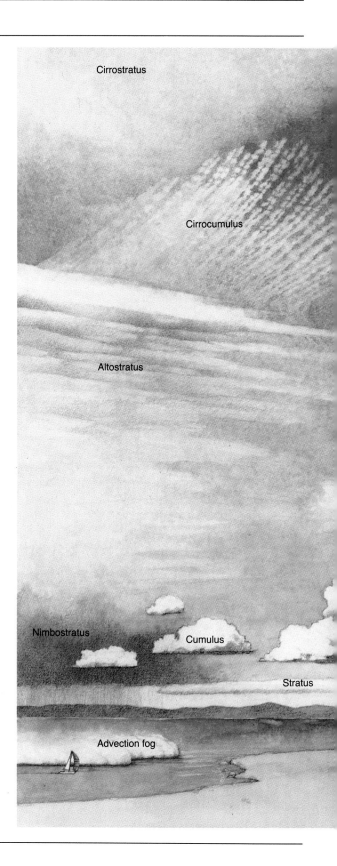

Cirrus

Cumulonimbus

Hail formation

Altocumulus

Freezing line

Stratocumulus

Radiation fog

Fog consists of drops of water less than $\frac{1}{200}$ of an inch in diameter suspended in air. At right, radiation fog blankets a valley in the Colorado Rockies. This type of fog usually forms at night, then burns off as air heats up during the day. A foggy sunrise (far right) greets San Francisco. The city experiences advection fog when warm air moving inland from the Pacific cools as it blows over the water. Water vapor and dust particles in the atmosphere enhance the color of sunsets—such as the one below in Florida's Everglades—by scattering blue light and reflecting and intensifying red, orange, and yellow light.

weather), devising jingles, maxims, and elaborate cloud charts and atlases, which are as beautiful as they are useful.

Throughout time, people have been obsessed with the many moods of the sky. Not just because crops and journeys depend on the weather, but also because the sky is such a powerful symbol. The sky that gods inhabit, the sky whose permanence we depend on and take for granted, as if it really were a hard, vaulted ceiling on which stars were painted, as some of our ancestors thought. The sky that can fall in nursery rhymes. In the nuclear-disarmament marches of the sixties, some people wore signs that read: "Chicken Little Was Right." The sky we picture as the final resting place of those we love, as if their souls were perfumed aerosol. We bury them among pine needles and worms, but in our imaginations we give them a lighter-than-air journey into some recess of the sky, from which they will watch over us.

Driving south from Point Reyes, along spectacular cliffs and a wild and dramatic ocean, where sea otters bob in the kelp beds, sea lions bark, harbor seals clump together like small mountain ranges, and pelagic cormorants, sanderlings, murres, and other birds busily nest, I pause on a wind-ripped slope of Big Sur. A Monterey pine leans out over the Pacific, making a ledge for the sunset. The pummeling wind has strangled its twigs and branches on the upwind side, and now it looks like a long division sign or a shaggy black finger pointing out to sea. People pull up in cars, get out, stand and stare. Nothing need be said. They nod to one another. The cottony blue sky and dark blue sea meet at a line sharp as a razor's edge. The prevailing winds here are from the west, as I can see from the weird and wonderful shapes of the vegetation along the beach. A light, steady breeze blowing off the Pacific has swept back the wild grasses into a sort of pompadour. A little farther back, in a more protected glade, I find a small clump of them, around which a circle runs in the dirt. It looks like someone laid down a cookie cutter, but the wind alone has done it, blowing around the grass and turning it into a natural compass.

Wind is really just warm air and cool air trading places. When the

sunbaked earth warms the air above it, the warm air expands, grows lighter, and rises, as cold air flows underneath to replace it. Eventually, the rising warm air gets high enough to cool and fall as heavy, cold air, to be heated again and rise again in a continuous cycle.

The winds we're familiar with mainly swirl through the lowest level of the atmosphere, the troposphere, which stretches from the ground up about 6 miles and contains most clouds and weather. Above that, up to about 30 miles, lies the stratosphere, with its strong, horizontal winds; and above that, up to 50 miles, the cold mesosphere, with erratic, high-speed winds and thin, wispy clouds; then the thin-aired ionosphere, 50 to 310 miles up, where the solar wind bumping into the earth's magnetic field leaves a gorgeous shimmer behind—thick veils of light we call auroras; and then finally the exosphere, a mysterious region of extreme temperatures and dangerous levels of cosmic rays. Jet streams, ribbons of strong winds (as high as 200 knots), roam the tropopause, the boundary between the troposphere and the stratosphere.

We often hear of the wind as a destructive force—a sudden funnel that rips the roof off a schoolhouse in Oklahoma—but the wind is

The ominous funnel of a tornado looms on the North Dakota plains. This terrifying by-product of a thunderstorm builds when an updraft of warm air rises into a storm cloud. There, winds of varying speed and direction make the updraft rotate, usually in a counterclockwise motion. Then the winds descend to the ground as a roaring funnel. Winds can reach 300 miles per hour, causing massive destruction of houses and trees. Pressure drops so low inside the funnel that buildings nearby sometimes explode from within.

Making a Barometer

Air surrounds us, but we are seldom aware of its weight. This weight, called atmospheric or barometric pressure, varies from time to time and place to place. Shifts in barometric pressure often portend changes in the weather.

A simple jar barometer will help you keep track of these changes. To make one, cut a square of plastic wrap large enough to cover the opening of a widemouthed jar and extend several inches down the sides. Apply a line of glue to the jar's rim and stretch the plastic tautly over the opening, holding it in place with a rubber band. Then rest a coffee stirrer or other lightweight stick on top of the plastic.

Put the barometer indoors or out, but keep it out of the sun and in a spot with constant temperature. Check the position of the stick each day. Low pressure will make the plastic dome rise, pushing the stick up (A), while high pressure will force the plastic down, and the stick with it (B).

most often a powerful mason that gradually sculpts the landscape, carving cliffs, eroding hillsides, re-creating beaches. Wind carves the sensuously rippling dunes of Death Valley and the sand waves along the changing shorelines. Wind hauls away topsoil as if it were nothing more than a dingy tablecloth on checkerboard fields in the Midwest. It can power generators, windmills, sailboats, move gliders and kites. It sows seeds and pollen. Along rugged coasts and at high elevations in the mountains, one often sees trees dramatically carved by the relentless wind.

Today the ocean pours dark blue with a white surf pounding over and over. Close to shore, the thick, white wave-spume looks applied by palette knife. The grass rustles like stiff petticoats in the damp, salty wind. One gull finds a shellfish and begins picking it apart—while the others fly after it and try to snatch the food away, all of them squeaking like badly oiled machinery—then finally flies toward a nearby stand of eucalyptus trees. The talcky-leaved eucalyptuses, nonnative trees that are so hardy and fast growing they've taken over whole forests in California, look like bedraggled heads of freshly shampooed hair. In the fall and winter, you can find among their branches long garlands of monarch butterflies, which have migrated as far as 2,000 miles from the northern United States and Canada to overwinter on the California coast or in central Mexico. Each year, tens of millions of monarchs migrate in a great journey of the sort we tend to associate with animals on the plains of Africa. When they arrive, they clump together in thick orange ropes, hanging on by their feet, which have claws like grappling hooks.

The butterflies may gather in the groves to improve their odds of surviving an attack against predators. Birds occasionally attack the monarchs when they leave their cluster to drink nectar or sit in the

Dewdrops sag the web of an orb weaver spider (opposite). When air near the ground cools to a temperature at which it can no longer retain all of its water vapor, some of the moisture condenses, causing beads of water to collect on vegetation and other objects. Dew formation requires stillness of both air and object, conditions met in the case of a dew-shrouded damselfly (left).

FOLLOWING PAGES: A balloon sails over frosted treetops along a North Dakota river. Frost, like dew, forms from water vapor—but at temperatures below freezing.

open and spread their wings wide as solar collectors. (If the temperature drops below 55°F, butterflies have difficulty using their muscles to fly. To warm them, they shiver or bask in the sunlight.)

Monarchs eat milkweed, a plant that produces a poison like digitalis, to which they are insensitive, but which makes *them* poisonous; and birds quickly learn that eating monarchs will make them sick. If you see a monarch flying around with a wedge-shaped piece of wing missing, you may be looking at a veteran of a bird attack. Once, when I was helping to tag monarchs at an overwintering site in Pacific Grove, California, I saw just such a female monarch trembling on the porch floor outside my motel room window. A huge jay perched on the porch rail in a nasty temper, screeching and flapping, and getting ready to dive at the monarch again. Though I usually know better than to intrude in nature's doings, I'm afraid my instincts took over and I rushed outside, lunged at the jay, and punched it in the chest, just as it leapt up with a great squawk and mad flap, truly terrified by my sudden attack. The jay flew away, but the butterfly stood her ground and shook. I picked her up carefully and checked to see if she had successfully mated by pressing her abdomen gently between my thumb and forefinger (feeling for the hard pellet, or spermatophore, deposited by a male). She hadn't, and the missing wedge of wing didn't look too bad, so I carried her to the base of a tree, at the top of which swayed a long orange string of monarchs. Then I held her above my open mouth and breathed warm air over her body to help heat her flying muscles, since it was a chilly morning, and tossed her into the air. She fluttered right up to the cluster, and I saluted her as I walked back to my room.

Scientists have found magnetic particles in monarchs, which may navigate by using the earth's magnetic field. But it's still a wonderful puzzle how new generations of butterflies find their way to the same trees visited by their ancestors. Monarchs don't live long enough to teach a route to their offspring. Birds, on the other hand, do, but young birds tend to migrate on a different schedule than their parents; like the butterflies, they have to find their own way.

Most birds migrate at night, spending their days looking for food and taking pains to avoid hawks and other predators. It's a little hard to see them en route except when they are backlit by the moon, which is as lovely a vision as one could wish. Most night-traveling songbirds fly invisible airways at about 1,000 feet and keep to their usual flight speed of 20 to 30 miles per hour. Hawks and shorebirds, which travel by day, fly a little faster, about 45 miles per hour; and geese, swans, falcons, and other avian hot rods reach speeds of 50 to 55 miles per hour.

Since different bird species migrate at different times in spring and fall, crisscrossing the country in various directions, some mob of migrating birds is bound to pass over your yard, regardless of where you live. Listen for their clamor. Watch the sky for their signatures, which may be **V**-shaped or wedge-shaped or look like a shake of black pepper. On a bright September day full of northerly breezes, head for

Frost's many patterns include feathery plumes on a windowpane (above) and delicate tipping on strawberry leaves (opposite, far left). In frigid, drier air, slow-growing crystals develop fragile clusters attached to supporting structures such as the points and stem of a black oak leaf (opposite, middle). After a sleet storm, ice molds a leaky spigot over a plant stem (left).

Heavy snow bows, but does not break, evergreen trees (opposite). The trees' supple trunks and drooping branches are adapted to such winter burdens. Snow is precipitation that falls as masses of tiny ice crystals. It originates in the subfreezing temperatures of clouds' upper reaches. There, either water vapor or supercooled water forms crystals on tiny particles in the cloud called ice nuclei. The crystals combine as they fall through the freezing air, forming snowflakes. Snow and cold challenge animals. Some migrate to warmer climates. Others, such as the young raccoons huddled in a tree (above, right), may become dormant during the coldest part of winter. Raccoons accumulate extra body fat in anticipation of winter and will periodically hole up in their dens for a long, but not deep, sleep. A northern cardinal (above), which remains active in winter, fluffs its feathers to trap warm air near its body.

a tall lookout—say, a hill known for having updrafts—and you may see hawks hitching a ride on the thermals. If you're lucky, migrant birds will pause in your backyard, which, empty one minute, the next becomes a sideshow of raucously flocking red-winged blackbirds or warblers. As with monarch migration, there are many mysteries about bird migration. Each day brings new evidence that birds navigate by the sun and other stars, by landmarks, and by the earth's magnetic field. It may be a combination of all of these skills that ultimately guides them.

At Big Sur, the hawks are working the thermals like barnstormers, swooping and banking as they ride invisible towers of warm, rising air above the sun-heated ground. Birds are such active fliers, so nimble and adroit. Each species has its own architecture, flight habits, and talents to make the most of the sky. Owls, for instance, have soft, fringed feathers that muffle the sound of their approach to prey. Goldfinches flap hard for a few beats, then close their wings to rest a little. Doves flap continuously when they're on the wing. Peregrine falcons fold in their wings when they dive. Storks and pelicans flap their long wings slowly as they hunt their prey. Many fast-flying birds (such as the swift, which averages about 25 miles per hour, but can reach speeds of 80 miles per hour) have very pointy wings that make them sleeker by cutting down on drag. Swifts dart and glide with startling ease. In the Grand Canyon, you can see them working the canyon walls with masterful aerobatics. If you could look closely at a bird's wing in flight, you would see that the flight feathers tighten when the bird pushes its wings down, so that it can cup the air; then they separate slightly to let the air rush through, so the bird can lift its wings easily for another flap.

The sky also fills with passive fliers. Female ash trees loose their

Riders on the wind, animals and plants exploit air's free transport. Just-hatched spiderlings disperse by ballooning (top, left). From a height, the spider releases threads from its spinnerets. Wind catches the threads and launches the spiderling on a journey that may cover 200 miles or more. The fruits of clematis, a flowering vine (top, right), have long filaments that catch the wind and carry the fruits to new sites for seed germination. By producing millions of pollen grains, timothy grass (above) stands a better chance to complete airborne pollination. The round heads of dandelions (opposite) contain tiny seeds, each with a parachute of fine hairs that helps it float in the air or attach to pedestrian carriers such as bears.

winged keys, and aspens and other trees produce long catkins that blizzard across the ground. Maples launch tadpole-shaped seeds that fall whirligig down, all blade, all propeller, like small helicopters. Thanks to the wind, the sex lives of many plants have evolved. Dandelions, milkweed, thistles, cottonwoods, and others have developed wind-riding seeds in the shapes of parachutes or sails. Pine, spruce, hemlock, maple, and ragweed don't have flamboyant flowers, but they don't need them to attract a bird or bee. The wind is go-between enough. Plants can't court, so they've devised ingenious ways to exploit the animals and their environment.

How tiny pollen grains are—only $\frac{1}{5000}$ to $\frac{1}{125}$ of an inch in diameter—and yet they must travel uncertain winds and strike home. Using a wind tunnel, Karl Niklas, a Cornell University scientist, recently discovered that plants aren't just hobos, hoping their pollen will catch a passing breeze and get off at the right stop. He found that the pinecone has evolved a shape perfect for capturing wind from any direction, a turbine shape with petal-like blades that set the air spinning all around it. The pinecone swaddles itself in an atmosphere of rapidly moving air. Just below the swirling layer of air, there is a still, vacant layer; the pollen entering it cascades right down into the cone. Niklas also tested the airflow dynamics of the jojoba plant, which uses two leaves shaped like rabbit ears to direct air with similar finesse.

Some pollen grains look like balls covered in spikes, tiny Sputniks. Others are football-shaped, like the pupils of alligators. Pine pollen is winged, with what looks like a pair of ears attached to each side. The different shapes of wind-borne pollen grains make them move, or fly, at different speeds and in different patterns, so that there's little danger of the wrong pollen swamping the wrong plant.

Wings give some animals mastery of the sky. Insects were the first to fly, more than 300 million years ago. A green lacewing fly (opposite) "claps" its wings on takeoff to obtain maximum lift. Air moving faster over curved wing tops allows higher pressure beneath the wings to raise a bald eagle (above) to majestic flight. The only true fliers among mammals, bats (top) scan the night sky for insects.

It's odd to think of the sky as having niches, but it does; even the wind has niches.

As night falls at Big Sur, all the soot of the world seems to pour down into the sunset. A swollen yellow doubloon drops slowly into the ocean, shimmer by shimmer, as if it were being swallowed whole. Then a tiny green ingot hovers for a second, and vanishes. The "green flash," people call it with mystical solemnity. It is the briefest flash of green, and this is the first time in all my sunset watchings I've seen it. Green, azure, purple, red: How lucky we are to live on a planet of colored skies.

Why is the sky usually blue? The sun's white light is really a bouquet of six colors, a spectrum. And our atmosphere is made up of atoms of oxygen and nitrogen. These atoms tend to scatter the short wavelengths of blue light coming from the sun more readily than the longer wavelengths of red light. So the sky seems to be full of blue. At sunrise or sunset, the light has to travel farther, through the thick, humid region of the lower atmosphere, packed with dust particles and water droplets. These reflect the red light, which bounces off the base of clouds or reaches the eye directly. The setting sun may

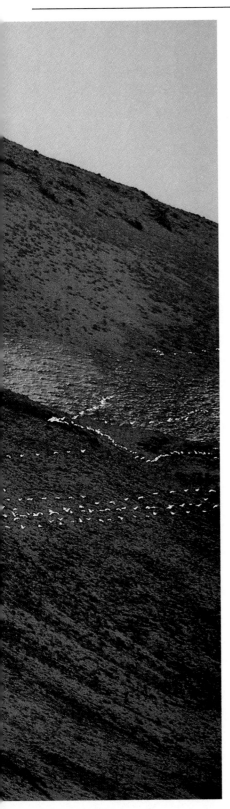

appear magnified or slightly elliptical or even above the horizon when it's really below it, thanks to refraction, the bending of light waves. What we see is a huge red sunset. The last color to plow through the atmosphere before being scattered is green, hence the green flash we sometimes see right after the sun disappears.

At the Big Sur lighthouse, perched on a distant promontory, a beacon flashes to warn ships of the rocks and shoals, its light zooming out to them at 186,000 miles per second. The light of the sun takes about eight minutes to reach earth. And the light we see from the North Star set sail in the days of Chaucer. I'm always amazed to think how straight the path of light is, that it doesn't turn corners. Pass sunlight through a prism, though, and the light does bend. Because each ray bends a different amount, the colors separate into a band. Many things catch the light—fish scales, the mother-of-pearl inside an oyster shell, oil on a slippery road, a dragonfly's wings, opals, soap bubbles—but perhaps the best known is water. When it's raining but the sun is shining, or at a misty waterfall, the sunlight hitting the drops of water casts a prism across the sky—what we call a rainbow. On such a day, rainbows are always about, hidden somewhere behind the skirts of the rain, but you have to be positioned at just the right angle vis-à-vis the sun and the raindrops to see one. Rainbows aren't really arcs, they're circles; but since we're watching them from the ground, we see them halved by the horizon.

It is nighttime on planet Earth, but that's only a whim of nature, a result of our planet rolling in space at 1,000 miles per hour. What we call night is the time we spend facing the secret reaches of space, where other solar systems dwell. Don't think of night as the absence of day; think of it as a kind of freedom. Turned away from our sun, we see the dawning of far-flung galaxies. We are no longer sun blinded to the star-coated universe we inhabit. The endless black, which seems to stretch forever between the stars and even backward in time to the Big Bang, we call "infinity," from the French *infini,* which means "unfinished" or "incomplete." Night is a shadow world. The only shadows we see at night are cast by the moonlight, or by artificial light, but the night itself is a shadow.

In the country you can see more stars, and the night looks like an upside-down well that deepens forever. If you're patient and wait until your eyes adjust to darkness, you can see the Milky Way as a creamy path across the sky. The "backbone of night," the Bushmen

Snow geese head for California after a summer of breeding along the Arctic Ocean. Twice a year, many bird species around the world take to the sky for epic migrations, some following standard routes that cover up to 25,000 miles round-trip. Research demonstrates that some birds rely on the sun and natural landmarks to guide them by day and can navigate unerringly by the stars at night.

One of the few butterfly species to migrate long distances, the monarch undertakes seasonal flights that rival those of many birds. Monarchs mate on the ground, then the male carries his partner aloft (top). Metamorphosis from egg to butterfly takes about a month (see page 99). The last generation of butterflies born each summer become fall migrants to coastal California or Mexico. With no older generations to guide them, monarchs migrate by a genetically inherited navigation system, traveling in fronts of hundreds of thousands of insects. They can cover up to 180 miles a day, flying, gliding, and soaring on updrafts of air (above, right). Reaching their destination, the butterflies spend the winter clustered in groves of trees (opposite). Tattered wings (above) testify to the rigors of monarch migration.

of the Kalahari call it. But in the city you can pick out some of the major constellations more easily because there are fewer stars visible to distract you. Wherever you are, the best way to watch stars is lying on your back. Tonight the half-moon has a Maya profile. It looks luminous and shimmery, a real beacon in the night, and yet I know its brilliance is all borrowed light. By day, if I held a mirror and bounced a spot of sunlight around the trees, I would be mimicking how the moon reflects light, having none of its own to give.

Above me, between Sagittarius and Aquarius, the constellation Capricornus ambles across the sky. To the Aztecs it was a whale *(cipactli)*, to the Tamil an antelope *(makaram)*, to the Greeks who followed Plato "the gate of the gods," to the Assyrians a goat-fish *(munaxa)*. When I was little, I used to take an empty can with both ends removed, stretch a piece of tinfoil over one end, pierce holes in it with a pin in the outline of a constellation, and then hold a flashlight in the other end to make my own private planetarium. Apart from the sun, perhaps the best known star is the North Star, or Polaris, though of course it has many other names, such as the Navajo's "Igniter" or the Chinese's "Great Imperial Ruler of Heaven." How many wanderers, hideously lost on land or sea, have waited till night to figure out their whereabouts with help from the North Star. Locating it as they did connects us across time and country to those early nomads. First you find the Big Dipper and extend a line through the outer two stars of its cup. Then you'll see that the North Star looks like a dollop of cream fallen from the upside-down Dipper. If the Big Dipper isn't visible, you can find the North Star by looking for Cassiopeia, a constellation just below Polaris that's shaped like a **W** or an **M**, depending on the time of night you see it. To me, it usually looks like a butterfly. Because the earth spins on its axis from

An aurora glows eerily in the night sky above Alaska (opposite). Like many natural phenomena, the ethereal beauty of the aurora belies a complex structure and process. Auroras begin when the sun's gaseous elements split into electrically charged particles. The sun's surface continuously sheds these particles, some of which flow toward earth as solar wind. Those particles that penetrate the earth's magnetic field enter the upper atmosphere and bombard its gases. The collisions produce energy visible as arcs, streaks, or curtains of colored light. Auroras visible in the north are called borealis and those in the south, australis.

Long before science began to parse auroras, humans marveled at their existence and created myths to explain their origin. Our growing scientific understanding does not diminish the wonder of natural phenomena; if anything, it enhances and enlarges our awe.

west to east, the stars seem to drift from east to west across the sky. So, another way to tell direction is to keep your eye on one bright star; if it appears to rise up higher in the sky, then you're looking eastward. If it seems to be falling, then you're looking westward.

When I was a Girl Scout, we told direction during the day by putting a straight stick in the ground. Then we would go about our business and return when there was a shadow about six inches long. The sun would have moved westward, and the shadow would be pointing east. Sometimes we used a wristwatch as a compass: Lay the watch face up with the hour hand pointing toward the sun. Pick up a pine needle or twig and hold it upright at the edge of the dial so that it casts a shadow along the hour hand. South will be halfway between the hour hand and twelve o'clock. There are many other ways to tell direction, of course. Roaming is one of the things human beings love to do best—but only if they can count on getting home safely. If you see a tree standing out in the open, with heavy moss on one side, that side is probably north, since moss grows heaviest on the shadiest side of a tree. If you see a tree stump, its rings will probably be thicker on the sunny, or south, side. You can also look up at the treetops of pines, which mainly point east. Or, if you happen to know where the prevailing winds are coming from, you can read direction from the wind-bent grasses.

Sunrise. The darkness begins to wash out of the sky. A thick layer of fog sits in the valley like the chrysalis of a butterfly. Venus, Jupiter, and Saturn burn bright silver holes in the slowly bluing sky. Two black shapes in the fog reel into focus as cows. A calf appears. Learning about the world is like this—watching and waiting for small shapes to reveal themselves in the fog of our experience. A wan sky curdles with gauzy streaks of clouds. The land is veiled in mist. The highest hill looks like a train's smokestack: Clouds trail behind it. Now the cloud world that was horizontal becomes vertical, and cumuli begin to rise over the mountain. Venus throbs like a broken lighthouse in the western sky. A nation of cloud teepees rises along the top of the ridge. The first hawk of the day glides on warm air, wings arched. On the clover-rich grass, the dew sits in round, bluish drops. Because last night was clear with no wind, the grass cooled to the dew point (the temperature at which the air becomes saturated with water vapor), and moisture condensed on the leaves of grass as "sweat" does on a pitcher of ice water in a warm room. If the temperature had been colder than freezing, I would find frost instead of dew. A squadron of 18 pelicans flies in a long checkmark overhead, turns on edge and vanishes, turns again and reels back into sight. A huge river of fog rolls through the valley. The cows disappear, but the sky grows bluer, even Venus fades, and white clouds begin to form, the fog lifts like a fever, a house and more cows appear, a lone, lightning-struck tree stands like a totem pole on a hillside, the light quickens, and birds begin their earnest songs, as the first yellow floats up like egg yolk over the ledge of the world, and then the sun is a canary singing light.

About the Authors, Photographers & Illustrators

Authors

Poet and naturalist DIANE ACKERMAN is the author of nine books of poetry and prose, among them, *The Moon by Whale Light*, a collection of nature essays; *Jaguar of Sweet Laughter: New and Selected Poems; A Natural History of the Senses;* and *On Extended Wings*, a memoir about learning to fly. A staff writer for *The New Yorker*, she has covered topics ranging from bats to whales, from crocodiles to penguins and tamarins. She lives in Ithaca, New York.

Trained as a wildlife biologist, DOUGLAS H. CHADWICK has written about grizzly bears, Namibia's wildlife, sagebrush country, and other subjects for NATIONAL GEOGRAPHIC and about black-footed ferrets for *Defenders of Wildlife*. His books include *A Beast the Color of Winter: The Mountain Goat Observed* and *The Kingdom: Wildlife in North America*, published in 1990. Chadwick lives near Glacier National Park in Montana and travels often to the Pacific Northwest.

Writer and naturalist JOHN HAY is the author of *The Bird of Light, The Immortal Wilderness*, and *The Undiscovered Country*, among other works. A resident of Massachusetts, he was the president of the board of directors at the Cape Cod Museum of Natural History for 23 years. His book *The Great Beach* won the 1964 John Burroughs Medal for Nature Writing.

TED LEVIN leads natural history tours throughout the U. S., from the deserts of the Southwest to New Hampshire's White Mountains and Florida's Everglades. A writer and photographer, he is the author of *Backtracking: The Way of a Naturalist* and the forthcoming *Bloodbrook*, about the Vermont valley in which he lives. His articles have appeared in NATIONAL GEOGRAPHIC TRAVELER and in *Sports Illustrated, Yankee, Harrowsmith Country Life*, and *Living Bird Quarterly*. His photographs, widely published, are on exhibit at the American Museum of Natural History in New York.

MICHAEL PARFIT's latest book, *Chasing the Glory*, is a view of the American cultural landscape from the air. Parfit's articles on science and the outdoors have appeared in National Geographic Society books and magazines and in *Smithsonian, The New York Times Magazine*, and *Field and Stream*. A resident of Montana, Parfit traveled extensively in the treeless reaches of Antarctica for his award-winning book *South Light: A Journey to the Last Continent*.

DAVID RAINS WALLACE won the 1984 John Burroughs medal for *The Klamath Knot: Explorations in Myth and Evolution*. A resident of Berkeley, California, he is the author of *Bulow Hammock: Mind in a Forest; The Untamed Garden and Other Personal Essays; The Dark Range: A Naturalist's Night Notebook;* and other books. He has also written two "nature" novels, *The Vermilion Parrot* and *The Turquoise Dragon*. In 1991, he completed a history of Costa Rica's national parks.

Naturalist, writer, and artist ANN H. ZWINGER has written about her wanderings in *Aspen: Blazon of the West; Utah; The Mysterious Lands: The Four Deserts of the United States; A Desert Country Near the Sea; Wind in the Rock;* and other books. Her *Run, River, Run* won the 1976 John Burroughs medal. Most of her books are illustrated with her own pencil sketches and line drawings. She is currently working on a natural history of the Colorado River in the Grand Canyon.

Photographers

Since ANNIE GRIFFITHS BELT began taking pictures for National Geographic in 1978, she has covered Baja California, North Dakota, and Britain's Pennine Way. Recent book projects include *A Day in the Life of Italy, Baseball in America,* and *Heartland of a Continent*, a forthcoming National Geographic book about North America's plains and prairies.

Natural history photographer JIM BRANDENBURG has worked as a free lance for the National Geographic Society since 1978, traveling widely to photograph such subjects as bamboo, rhinoceroses, red deer, and South Dakota's Badlands. Brandenburg's pictures of Arctic wolves, collected in his book *White Wolf: Living With an Arctic Legend*, have won him national and international awards. His work has also appeared in *Audubon, Smithsonian, Natural History,* and *National Wildlife*. Brandenburg makes his home in northern Minnesota.

DAVID CAVAGNARO is a photographer, writer, biologist, and teacher who lives on a farm in Iowa. His books include *Feathers*, a collection of nature essays, and *This Living Earth*, about meadow ecology in California. A member of Seed-Savers Exchange, a grassroots network of gardeners devoted to preserving rare and endangered vegetable varieties, Cavagnaro is currently focusing on horticultural photography.

FARRELL GREHAN's photographs have appeared in NATIONAL GEOGRAPHIC, *Smithso-nian, Life,* and other publications. Assignments for National Geographic have taken him to the Okeefenokee Swamp, the Olympic Mountains, Henry David Thoreau's New England, and the Sierra of John Muir.

A full-time natural history photographer since 1971, C. C. LOCKWOOD has published several books, among them *Atchafalaya, America's Largest River Basin Swamp* and *The Gulf Coast: Where Land Meets Sea*. He has contributed photographs to NATIONAL GEOGRAPHIC articles on Atchafalaya and the Mississippi Delta. Lockwood's current projects include a book on the natural history of the United States and a nature guide to Louisiana for children.

Illustrators

A world traveler and an amateur archaeologist, MICHAEL A. HAMPSHIRE has been illustrating National Geographic books since 1978. His paintings have appeared in National Geographic's *Peoples and Places of the Past; Lost Empires, Living Tribes;* and *Realms of the Sea*. Born in Yorkshire, England, he now lives on a mountain in Arizona.

For BIRUTA AKERBERGS HANSEN, science and art have always gone hand-in-hand. While earning a degree in biology at the City University of New York during the day, she took art classes in the evenings. Since then, her illustrations have been published in books and in magazines such as *Smithsonian, Discover,* and *Scientific American*. Hansen lives and works on 21 wooded acres in Pennsylvania, close to the nature she often depicts.

The work of illustrator GREG HARLIN has appeared in a NATIONAL GEOGRAPHIC article about jumping spiders, a planetarium exhibit at the Smithsonian Institution in Washington, D. C., and National Park Service brochures. Weekends find him hiking with his daughter near the Chesapeake Bay.

Free-lance artist ROBERT HYNES has been illustrating National Geographic Society books, magazines, filmstrips, and game packages for close to 15 years. Thirteen murals painted by Hynes appear at the Smithsonian Institution's National Museum of Natural History. His work has won awards from the Children's Book Council and the National Science Teachers Foundation.

MICHAEL WOODS was born in Downe, Kent, in England, once the home of Charles Darwin. A free-lance illustrator since 1972, he specializes in wildlife and biology. His paintings and drawings have appeared in *Hedgerow, Longman Illustrated Animal Encyclopedia, The Animal Family, The Country Companion,* and other books.

Acknowledgments & Bibliography

Acknowledgments

The Book Division is grateful to the many individuals and organizations that helped in the preparation of this book. The following institutions and their staffs were generous with their time and resources: the American Forestry Association, the American Museum of Natural History, the Arizona-Sonora Desert Museum, the National Park Service, the National Museum of Natural History, the U. S. Fish and Wildlife Service, and the U. S. Forest Service.

For their help, we wish to thank Arthur Bogan and Daniel Otte, Academy of Natural Sciences, Philadelphia; at the Arizona-Sonora Desert Museum, Lauray Yule, Mark Dimmit, Howard Lawler, and Peter Siminski; Eirik A. T. Blom; David A. Brennan, Yosemite National Park; Lincoln P. Brower, University of Florida; at Cape Hatteras National Seashore, Kent Turner and Warren Wrenn; at Cape Lookout National Seashore, Susan Chambers, William Harris, Pat Lineback, Julie Parrish, and Felix Rebello; Norman L. Christensen, Duke University; Richard Coles, Washington University; Michele Dionne, Wells National Estuarine Research Reserve, Wells, Maine; John Douglas; Tim Duval; Elmer J. Finck, Emporia State University; Richard B. Fischer, Cornell University; Carol Folt, Dartmouth College; Deborah Gangloff, American Forestry Association; Hugh Genoways, University of Nebraska State Museum; Klaus J. Geyer, Hernando County Cooperative Extension, Florida; Arthur Gibson, UCLA; Neil Greenberg, University of Tennessee; Lynn Allan Hetlet, Mammoth Site, South Dakota; Charles W. Johnson, Vermont Department of Forests, Parks, and Recreation; Clyde Jones; Eugene N. Kozloff, University of Washington; Richard W. Klukas, Yellowstone National Park; Joseph Lescinski, Jones Beach State Park, New York; Elbert L. Little, Jr.; Mark Lowery, New York State Department of Environmental Conservation; W. Patrick McCafferty, Purdue University; Robert McGraf; Richard Miller; Curtis D. Mobley, U. S. Navy's Office of Naval Research; at the Montshire Museum of Science, Norwich, Vermont, Linny Levin, Sandra Miller, and Joan Waltermire; James G. Moore, U. S. Geological Survey; at the National Weather Service, James D. Belville and Tom Dietrich; at North Carolina State University, Steve Broome and Roger A. Powell; Ronald M. Nowak; Robert O.

Petty; Miles Roberts, National Zoological Park; Frank Schwarz, University of North Carolina; at Sequoia and Kings Canyon National Parks, David M. Graber and William Tweed; Alex L. Shigo; Michael Smithson, Olympic National Park; David M. Sutherland, University of Nebraska at Omaha; Philip Sze, Georgetown University; Gordon Thayer, National Marine Fisheries Service; at the Smithsonian Institution's National Museum of Natural History, Phillip J. Angle, Frederick M. Bayer, Jonathan A. Coddington, Mason E. Hale, Robert Hershler, Gary Hevel, Horton Hobbs, Ronald Hodges, Richard Houbrick, Brian Kensley, Byrdina Miller, Paul Peterson, Robert K. Robbins, Raymond T. Rye II, Thomas Waller, Austin Williams, and George R. Zug; at the U. S. Department of Agriculture, James Plaskowitz and Robert L. Smiley; at the U. S. Fish and Wildlife Service, Richard C. Banks, John E. Byrne, John G. Nickum, Earl E. Possardt, and Jay Sheppard; at the U. S. Forest Service's Northeastern Forest Experiment Station, Raymond E. Graber, William B. Leak, and Mariko Yamasaki; at the University of Maryland, Stephen P. Leatherman, Charles McClurg, and James Reveal; at White Mountain National Forest, William Eley, John Lanier, and Ned Therrien.

We are grateful to Anna Botsford Comstock, Vinson Brown, and Gerald Durrell, whose nature study guides were an inspiration for this one.

We are also indebted to the National Geographic Library and its News Collection, Administrative Services, Illustrations Library, Messenger Center, Photographic Laboratory, Pre-Press/Typographic Division, Records Library, and Travel Office.

Bibliography

The staff consulted many references in preparing this book. The reader may wish to consult those cited below.

A classic how-to book for amateur naturalists is Anna Botsford Comstock's *Handbook of Nature Study*, originally published in 1911 as an aid to teachers. Other nature study guides include *The Nature Observer's Handbook* by John Brainerd; *The Amateur Naturalist's Handbook* by Vinson Brown; *Tom Brown's Field Guide to Nature Observation and Tracking* by Tom Brown, Jr.; *The Naturalist's Year* by Scott Camazine; and *The Amateur Naturalist* by Gerald Durrell.

Among the many field guides useful for the identification of plants and animals are the Audubon Society Nature Guides; the Peterson Field Guides; the Sierra Club Naturalist's Guides; Stokes Nature Guides; *Fieldbook of Natural History* by E. Laurence Palmer; and National Geographic's *Field Guide to the Birds of North America.*

The following books are designed to encourage children to learn about and enjoy the world of nature: *The Sierra Club Summer Book* by Linda Allison; *The Family Water Naturalist* by Heather Angel; *Sharing Nature with Children* by Joseph Bharat Cornell; Eyewitness Books; *Teaching Kids to Love the Earth* by Marina Lachecki Herman; *Hands-On Nature* edited by Jenepher Lingelbach; and the National Geographic Society's *Exploring Your World.*

To further explore subjects in specific chapters of THE CURIOUS NATURALIST, readers may refer to the following works: For the **Introduction:** *Women in the Field* by Marcia Myers Bonta; *Speaking for Nature* by Paul Brooks; *Natural History in America* by Wayne Hanley; *This Incomperable Lande* edited by Thomas J. Lyon; and the writings of William Bartram, John Muir, Aldo Leopold, Joseph Wood Krutch, and Rachel Carson. For **Local Wilderness:** *The Wildlife Gardener* by John V. Dennis; *The Urban Naturalist* by Steven D. Garber; *Suburban Wildlife* by Richard Headstrom; *The Local Wilderness* by Cathy Johnson; and *Garden Life* by Jennifer Owen. For **Woodlands:** *Northwoods Wildlife* by Janine M. Benyus; *Forest Ecology* by J. P. Kimmins; and *North Woods* by Peter J. Marchand. For **Grasslands:** *The Prairie World* by David Costello; *Where the Sky Began* by John Madson; *Konza Prairie: A Tallgrass Natural History* by O. J. Reichman; *The True Prairie Ecosystem* by P. G. Risser; and *Grasslands of the Great Plains* by J. E. Weaver. For **Deserts:** *Sonoran Desert Spring* by John Alcock; *Drylands* by Philip Hyde; *Desert, The American Southwest* by Ruth Kirk; *The Desert* by A. Starker Leopold; and *The Life of the Desert* by Ann and Myron Sutton. For **Mountains:** *The High Sierra* by Ezra Bowen; *The Mountains of California* by John Muir; *Sierra Nevada Natural History* by Tracy I. Storer; and *Sequoia-Kings Canyon* by William C. Tweed. For **Streams, Lakes, Ponds & Bogs:** *Downstream* by John Bardach; *Pond and Brook* by Michael J. Caduto; *Aquatic Entomology* by W. Patrick McCafferty; and *The Pond* by Gerald Thompson. For **Sandy Shores & Coastal Wetlands:** *Treasures of the Tide* by Tom Allen; *The Outer Banks* by Patrick D. Crosland; *Barrier Island Handbook* by Stephen P. Leatherman; *The Beachwalker's Guide* by Edward R. Ricciuti; and *Islands, Capes, and Sounds* by Thomas J. Schoenbaum. For **Rocky Shores:** *Seashore Life of the Northern Pacific Coast* by Eugene N. Kozloff; *Natural History of Marine Animals* by G. E. and Nettie MacGinitie; and *Between Pacific Tides* by Edward F. Ricketts. For **Sky:** *The Sky Observer's Guidebook* by Charles E. Roth; *The Constellations* by Lloyd Motz; *Meditations at Sunset* by James Trefil; and *The Life of Birds* by Joel Carl Welty.

Illustrations Credits

Abbreviations for terms appearing below:
(t) top; (b) bottom; (l) left; (r) right; (c) center; BCI-BRUCE COLEMAN INC.; DPA-DEMBINSKY PHOTO ASSOC.; DRK-DRK PHOTO; SRW-SRW, INC.; NGP-National Geographic Photographer; WH-WILD HORIZONS

2-3, Art Wolfe. 7, Richard Hamilton Smith. 8, (t) Helen Muir, Bancroft Library, U. Calif., Berkeley; (b) Robert McCabe, U. Wisc.-Madison Archives. 9, (t) New-York Historical Society; (b) from *The Natural History of Carolina, Florida, and the Bahama Islands*, Library of Congress, Rare Book and Special Collections Division. 10-11, Tom Bean/DRK. 12-13, Carl R. Sams II. 14-15, Breton Littlehales. **Local Wilderness:** 17, George H. Harrison. 18, Daniel J. Cox. 19, (t) Richard Hamilton Smith; (b) Robert McCaw. 20-21, 22-23, Annie Griffiths Belt. 24, David Cavagnaro. 25, Michael A. Hampshire. 26 & 27, (t) Charles Krebs. 27, (b) Dwight R. Kuhn. 28, Michael A. Hampshire. 29, (t) Len Rue Jr.; (bl) (br) Steven C. Wilson/ENTHEOS; (bc) Bianca Lavies. 30, Kasandra Wood/SRW. 30-31, Biruta Akerbergs Hansen. 32, (t) Jean F. Stoick/DPA; (l) (c) (r) & (b) Mark W. Moffett. 33, Mark W. Moffett. 34, Michael A. Hampshire. 35, Andreas Sterzing. 36-37, Annie Griffiths Belt. 37, Tom A. Schneider/DRK. 38, Breck P. Kent. 39, (t) Jane Burton/BCI; (b) David Scharf. 40, Stephen Dalton/NHPA. 41, (t) Laura Riley; (b) E. R. Degginger. **Woodlands:** 43, Larry West. 44-45, Biruta Akerbergs Hansen. 46, Kasandra Wood/SRW. 46-47, Michael Woods. 48, (l) (r) Farrell Grehan; (c) Judy Brandenburg. 49, Michael A. Hampshire. 50, (t) Farrell Grehan; (bl) (bc) & (br) Carter Harmon. 51, (l) Farrell Grehan; (r) David Cavagnaro/DRK. 52, Farrell Grehan. 53, Michael A. Hampshire. 54, Tom Nebbia. 55, (l) Robert McCaw; (c) Wayne Lankinen; (r) Farrell Grehan. 56, Farrell Grehan. 57, Pat O'Hara. 58, Gregory K. Scott. 58-59, Wayne Lankinen. 60-61, Biruta Akerbergs Hansen. 62, Robert McCaw. 63, (tl) Robert McCaw. 63, (tr) (c) & (b), Farrell Grehan. 64, David Cavagnaro/DRK. 65, E. R. Degginger. 66-67, Farrell Grehan. 68, Barbara Miller. 69, (l) Jim Brandenburg; (r) Wayne Lankinen. 70, Jim Brandenburg. 71, Mitch Kezar. 72, (l) John Serrao; (r) Jeff Henry. 73, Michael A. Hampshire. 74, David Muench. 75, (l) Carl R. Sams II; (r) Breck P. Kent. **Grasslands:** 77, David Cavagnaro. 78-79, Gary Withey. 79, Annie Griffiths Belt. 80 & 80-81, Jim Branden-

burg. 81, Jerry L. Ferrara. 82, Kasandra Wood/SRW. 82-83, Michael Woods. 84, (t) Jim Brandenburg; (b) Ted Levin. 85, (t) Stephen J. Krasemann/DRK; (b) David Cavagnaro. 86, (l) Larry Ditto; (r) Gary Withey/BCI. 87, Steven C. Wilson/ENTHEOS. 88, Jim Brandenburg. 88-89, Michael Sample. 90 & 91, (c) (b) David Cavagnaro; 91, (t) Nick & Gidge Drahos. 92-95, David Cavagnaro. 96, Biruta Akerbergs Hansen. 98-99, David Cavagnaro. 100, Greg Harlin/SRW. 101 & 102, David Cavagnaro. 103, Daniel J. Cox. **Deserts:** 105, Art Wolfe. 106-107, Jack W. Dykinga. 108, Kasandra Wood/SRW. 108-109, Greg Harlin/SRW. 110, Kasandra Wood/SRW. 110-111, Greg Harlin/SRW. 112, (l) Stephen J. Krasemann/DRK; (r) George Wuerthner. 113, C. Allan Morgan. 114, Farrell Grehan. 115, George H. H. Huey. 116, (l) Jeff Foott; (r) Thomas Ives. 117, G. C. Kelley. 118, Greg Harlin/SRW. 119, George H. H. Huey. 120-121, Thomas Wiewandt/WH. 121, William E. Ferguson. 122, Thomas Wiewandt/WH. 123, William Helsel. 124-125, Peter L. Kresan. 126-127, Fred Hirschmann. 127, Thomas Wiewandt/WH. 128-129, C. Allan Morgan. 130, Dan Suzio. 131, (t) William E. Ferguson; (bl) Dan Suzio; (br) Wolfgang Bayer/BCI. 132, Bruce Dale, NGP. 133, Bill Ratcliffe. **Mountains:** 135, Becky & Gary Vestal. 136, (t) William E. Ferguson; (b) Farrell Grehan. 137, Greg Harlin/SRW. 138-139, Michael & Patricia Fogden. 139, Nicholas DeVore III/PHOTOGRAPHERS ASPEN. 140, Art Wolfe. 141, W. Wayne Lockwood, M.D. 142, (t) James L. Amos; (b) William E. Ferguson. 143, Michael A. Hampshire. 144-145, Pat O'Hara. 146, (t) David Cavagnaro; (b) Art Wolfe. 146-147, Jim Brandenburg. 147, Wayne Lankinen. 148, Art Wolfe. 148-149, David Cavagnaro. 150, (l) Douglas T. Gruenau; (r) Thomas Kitchin. 151, Michael S. Quinton. 152-153, Jeff Henry. 154, (l) Cindy Ederegger; (b) Joel W. Rogers/EARTH IMAGES. 154-155, George Wuerthner. **Streams, Lakes, Ponds & Bogs:** 157, Richard Hamilton Smith. 158, Greg Harlin/SRW. 159, Farrell Grehan. 160, Thomas Kitchin. 161, Michael H. Francis. 162, (t) Joseph H. Bailey, NGP; (b) Tom McHugh/PHOTO RESEARCHERS, INC. 163, Robert Hynes. 164, Rollie Ostermick. 164-165, Michel Roggo. 165, (l) Steven C. Wilson/ENTHEOS; (c) (r) Bianca Lavies. 166-167, Jim Brandenburg. 167, Ron Sanford. 168-169, Jim Brandenburg. 170-171, Michael Woods. 172, Art Wolfe. 172-173, Keith Szafranski. 174, Kasandra Wood/SRW. 174-175, Robert Hynes. 176, (l) Gwen Fidler/COMSTOCK; (tr, br) Dwight R. Kuhn. 177, Robert Hynes. 178, (t) (b) Carl R. Sams II. 178-179, James Brant. 180, Jeff Simon/BCI. 181, Bianca Lavies. 182, (t) William H. Amos;

(b) Dwight R. Kuhn. 183, Michael A. Hampshire. 184, (tl) Dwight R. Kuhn; 184, (tr), 184-185 & 185, A. Rakosy. 186, David Muench. 186-187, Greg Harlin/SRW. 187, Jim Brandenburg. 188-189, David Muench. 189, (l) Jeff Foott; (r) John Eastcott & Yva Momatiuk/DRK. **Sandy Shores & Coastal Wetlands:** 191-193, C. C. Lockwood. 194, (l) David S. Soliday; (r) Carl R. Sams II. 194-195, Farrell Grehan. 195, Steven C. Wilson/ENTHEOS. 196-197, Robert F. Sisson. 197, (l) C. C. Lockwood; (r) Jeff Foott. 198, Lynn M. & Lynda Stone. 198-199, Doug Perrine/DRK. 200, Robert Hynes. 201, C. C. Lockwood. 202, (l) (r) David Cavagnaro. 202-203, David S. Soliday. 203, (r) (b) C. C. Lockwood. 204, Stephen J. Krasemann/DRK. 205-207, C. C. Lockwood. 208-209, Robert Hynes. 209, (t) C. C. Lockwood; (b) David Molchos. 210-211, C. C. Lockwood. 212, Kasandra Wood/SRW. 212-213, Michael Woods. 214-215, David Muench. 215, (t) C. C. Lockwood; (b) Philip Moylan. 216-217, David S. Soliday. 217, Ronny Paille. 219, Michael Freeman. 220, (l) Charles Krebs; (r) Bianca Lavies. 220-221, Charles Krebs. 221, (t) David Smart/DRK; 221 (b) & 222-223, C. C. Lockwood. **Rocky Shores:** 225, Glenn Van Nimwegen. 226-227, Art Wolfe. 228, Greg Harlin/SRW. 229, Jeff Foott. 230-231, Thomas Wiewandt/WH. 231, Anne Wertheim. 232, Kasandra Wood/SRW. 232-233, Michael Woods. 234, Robert F. Sisson. 235, (l) Patricia M. Sisson; (r) David Doubilet. 236, (t) David Doubilet; (c) (b) Anne Wertheim. 236-237, Howard Hall/HHP. 238-239, Steven C. Wilson/ENTHEOS. 239, Anne Wertheim. 240-241, Ted Levin. 242-243, Ernest Braun. 244, Chuck Davis. 245, OCEAN IMAGES, INC./Al Giddings. 246-247, Kennan Ward. 248, Tim Fitzharris. 249, (t) Robert McCaw; (b) Wayne Lynch/DRK PHOTO. 250, Steven C. Wilson/ENTHEOS. 251, Erwin & Peggy Bauer. 252-253, OCEAN IMAGES, INC./Rosemary Chastney. **Sky:** 255, Thomas Ives. 256, Lynn M. & Lynda Stone. 256-257, Jim Brandenburg. 258-259, Greg Harlin/SRW. 260-261, (t) Tom Bean; (b) Stan Osolinski/DPA. 261, Chuck Place. 262, Edi Ann Otto. 263, Michael A. Hampshire. 264-265, John Shaw/BCI. 265, Skip Moody/DPA. 266-267, Annie Griffiths Belt. 268, (l) Joanne Pavia; (c) Carl R. Sams II; (r) Robert McCaw. 268-269, Christian Autotte/EARTH IMAGES. 270, Jackie Gilmore. 271, (l) Carl R. Sams II; (r) Joseph R. Pearce/DRK. 272, (tl) Kenneth Lorenzen; (tr) David Cavagnaro; (b) Mitch Kezar. 273, Tom & Pat Leeson. 274, (t) Robert & Linda Mitchell; (b) Glenn W. Elison. 275, Stephen Dalton/NHPA. 276-277, David Madison/BCI. 278, Frans Lanting/MINDEN PICTURES. 279, Bianca Lavies. 281, Ron Sanford.

Index

Illustrations appear in **boldface**.

Type composition by the Typographic section of National Geographic Production Services, Pre-Press Division. Color separations by Graphic Art Service, Inc., Nashville, Tenn.; Lincoln Graphics, Inc., Cherry Hill, N.J.; Phototype Color Graphics, Pennsauken, N.J. Printed and bound by Arcata Graphics-Hawkins, New Canton, Tenn. Paper by Mead Paper Co., New York, N.Y.

Library of Congress CIP Data

The Curious naturalist.
     p.   cm.
   Includes bibliographical references and index.
   ISBN 0-87044-861-7 (reg. ed.)
   ISBN 0-87044-862-5 (deluxe ed.)
   1. Natural history—United States. 2. Habitat (Ecology)—United States. 3. Nature study—United States. 4. Natural history—Study and teaching—United States—Activity program. 5. Natural history—United States—Pictorial works. 6. Habitat (Ecology)—United States—Pictorial works. I. National Geographic Society (U. S.)
QH104.C87   1991
508.73—dc20   91-27559
                                 CIP
                                 r91